HISTORY OF INTERNATIONAL RELATIONS

History of International Relations

A Non-European Perspective

Erik Ringmar

https://www.openbookpublishers.com

© 2019 Erik Ringmar

This work is licensed under a Creative Commons Attribution 4.0 International license (CC BY 4.0). This license allows you to share, copy, distribute and transmit the work; to adapt the work and to make commercial use of the work providing attribution is made to the author (but not in any way that suggests that they endorse you or your use of the work). Attribution should include the following information:

Erik Ringmar, *History of International Relations: A Non-European Perspective*. Cambridge, UK: Open Book Publishers, 2019. https://doi.org/10.11647/OBP.0074

Copyright and permissions for the reuse of many of the images included in this publication differ from the above. Copyright and permissions information for images is provided separately in the List of Illustrations. Every effort has been made to identify and contact copyright holders and any omission or error will be corrected if notification is made to the publisher.

In order to access detailed and updated information on the license, please visit https://doi.org/10.11647/OBP.0074#copyright

Further details about CC BY licenses are available at http://creativecommons.org/licenses/by/4.0/

All external links were active at the time of publication unless otherwise stated and have been archived via the Internet Archive Wayback Machine at https://archive.org/web

Digital material and resources associated with this volume are available at https://doi.org/10.11647/OBP.0074#resources

Every effort has been made to identify and contact copyright holders and any omission or error will be corrected if notification is made to the publisher.

ISBN Paperback: 978-1-78374-022-2
ISBN Hardback: 978-1-78374-023-9
ISBN Digital (PDF): 978-1-78374-024-6
ISBN Digital ebook (epub): 978-1-78374-025-3
ISBN Digital ebook (mobi): 978-1-78374-026-0
ISBN Digital (XML): 978-1-78374-778-8
DOI: 10.11647/OBP.0074

Cover image: Al-Idrisi, *Tabula Rogeriana* (1154), Bibliotheque nationale de France (MSO Arabe 2221). Wikimedia, http://commons.wikimedia.org/wiki/File:TabulaRogeriana.jpg

Cover design by Anna Gatti.

All paper used by Open Book Publishers is sourced from SFI (Sustainable Forestry Initiative) accredited mills and the waste is disposed of in an environmentally friendly way.

Contents

The Author vii
Acknowledgments viii
This book ix

1. Introduction

Comparative international systems 2
Institutions, rules, and norms 3
Non-state societies 5
Walls and bridges 6
Further reading 10
Think about 11

2. China and East Asia

The Warring States period 14
The development of the Chinese state 19
The overland system 30
The tribute system 33
A Japanese international system? 36
Further reading 40
Timeline 41
Short dictionary 42
Think about 43

3. India and Indianization

Vedic India 46
Classical India 52
Indianization 58
The Mughal Empire 64
India as an international system 67
Timeline 69
Short dictionary 70
Think about 70

4. The Muslim Caliphates

The Arab expansion 74
The Umayyads and the Abbasids 78
The Arabs in Spain 81
A caliphal international system 86
The Ottoman Empire 91
Further reading 96
Timeline 97
Short dictionary 98
Think about 99

5. The Mongol Khanates

From Temüjin to Genghis Khan	102
A nomadic state	103
How to conquer the world	106
Dividing it all up	112
An international system of khanates	116
Further reading	122
Timeline	123
Short dictionary	124
Think about	125

6. Africa

The Nile River Valley	129
North Africa	131
The kingdoms of West Africa	133
East Africa and the Indian Ocean	139
An African international system?	144
Further reading	146
Timeline	147
Short dictionary	148
Think about	149

7. The Americas

The Maya	152
The Aztecs	160
The Incas	163
North America	170
Further reading	174
Timeline	175
Short dictionary	176
Think about	177

8. European Expansion

A sea route to India	180
Europeans in the "New World"	182
A commercial world economy	186
An industrial world economy	189
The apotheosis of colonialism	194
Decolonization	197
Further reading	200
Timeline	201
Short dictionary	202
Think about	203

Afterthoughts: Walls and Bridges — 205

The Author

Erik Ringmar is professor in the Department of Political Science and International Relations at Ibn Haldun University, Istanbul, Turkey. He graduated from Yale University in 1993 with a PhD in political science and has subsequently worked at the London School of Economics and as professor of international politics at Shanghai Jiaotong Daxue in Shanghai, China.

Acknowledgments

I am grateful to the students who have taken my course on comparative international systems over the past years. They were the first ones to be exposed to the chapters that follow. It is more than anything their questions and objections that have forced me to think harder and explain better. Thanks also to Jorg Kustermans and Victor Friedman who tried out the material in their respective courses and provided feedback. Downloaders and commentators at Academia.edu helped improve the argument as did suggestions from Klara Andrée, Magnus Fiskesjö, Jonas Gjersø, Ville Harle, Markus Lyckman, John Pella, Frank Ejby Poulsen, Diane Pranzo, James C. Scott, Farhan Hanif Siddiqi and Max de Vietri. Thanks also to Alex Astrov, Gunther Hellmann and Iver B. Neumann. The indefatigable librarians at the Internet Archive and Library Genesis provided all the books I needed. Thanks to Julie Linden for proof-reading, to Luca Baffa and Anna Gatti for layout and design, and to Alessandra Tosi for believing in the project and for guiding the text into print. As always, I am indebted to Ko Jenq-Yuh and Hong Ruey-Long.

This book

Names of people and places are generally given in the original language but other versions are included for ease of identification. Hence "Kongzi," but also "Confucius," "Palashi," but also "Plassey." All years given refer to the Common Era, "CE" or *Anno Domini*, "AD," except when indicated. All years associated with names of rulers refer to the length of their reign.

In addition to the main chapters there are a large number of boxes in which more specific topics are introduced. Many of these topics expand on the story told in the main chapters, but some introduce new themes. The purpose is to show the contemporary relevance of the historical material, but also to provide a sense of the culture and traditions of each respective part of the world.

The book is accompanied by a dedicated website: http://ringmar.net/irhistorynew/. Here you will find links to more material, primary sources and a complete bibliography, as well as podcasts to listen to and video clips to watch. Look out for the *Read More* call-outs, which link to specific resources in the irhistory website (direct links and QR codes for each webpage are provided for ease of access).

1. Introduction

International relations as a university-level topic is usually taught with little historical depth. In an introductory class, your instructor might tell you that the basic rules of international politics were established in the aftermath of the Thirty Years War in the seventeenth century, or you might hear something about European colonialism in the nineteenth century, and perhaps a word or two about the First World War. Once the class gets going, however, historical references are unlikely to stretch further back than to 1945. It will be as though the world was created less than a hundred years ago.

In addition, international politics, as it is usually taught, is hopelessly Eurocentric. The discipline takes Europe as the standard by which every other part of the world is measured — although "Europe" here also includes the United States and other places where the Europeans settled. The European model is obviously the most important one, your teacher will imply, since this is the model that came to organize international politics everywhere else. The world in which we live today is the world which the Europeans made in their own image.

One of the most important things you learn at university is to question authority, and this includes the authority of your teachers. No matter how smart or well read, your teacher's perspective will always be only one view among many. There is always another story to tell. In this book, we will tell other stories. Our historical perspective goes back to the first millennium of the Common Era (CE) and our perspective is explicitly non-European. This is a textbook on international politics which takes history seriously and which puts Europe firmly in its place. Europe matters as well of course, but, as it turns out, not all that much — not once we take a historical look at the world as a whole. It is simply not the case that the history of other parts of the world began the day the first European colonizers arrived. The Europeans did not, as a previous generation of scholars used to argue, "awaken" the natives, or "invite them into world history." Non-Europeans were always plenty awake, thank you very much, and the idea that the history of Europe is equal to the history of the world is just ridiculous. In this book, it is these non-European histories we are going to tell, and we will try to tell them on their own terms, not as they were impacted by, or had an impact on, Europe.

Furthermore, just to be clear, this alternative perspective is not motivated by an attempt to be "politically correct." The aim is not to set the record straight out of a

© 2019 Erik Ringmar, CC BY 4.0 https://doi.org/10.11647/OBP.0074.01

concern for balance or respect for people who are marginalized and silenced. These are worthwhile concerns to be sure, but our task is rather more straightforwardly to provide a better account of the kind of knowledge we need in order to understand today's world. History is constantly making itself present and today people and countries outside of Europe are asserting themselves. The world is once again changing and changes, once underway, can be quick and dramatic. Today, Europe and North America play a far less important role in world politics than in the past century, and in the future this role is likely to become less important still. The world is about to flip and our perspective on the past must be revised. The traditional European version of world history is no longer valid.

As you soon will discover, this book is very much an introductory textbook and anyone with a proper background in world history is bound to find the text far too basic. Yet chances are you do *not* have a proper background in world history, and if that indeed is the case, there is a lot here for you to learn. Think about the text that follows as a form of remedial education. It provides a chance for you to make up for the gaps that exist in your knowledge of things that all educated people should know.

Comparative international systems

A textbook on world history might appear to be a somewhat mad undertaking. A book that discusses "everything that ever happened" would surely have to be just as long as history itself. Yet this is not that book. We are not all that interested in the events, wars, names, and dates of the past. Instead, the aim is to introduce you to a subject that we could call the "comparative study of international systems." Let's think a bit about what such a comparative study might be. A system, first of all — any kind of system — is made up of units that act independently of each other. At the same time, the behavior of one unit in the system always depends on the behavior of all the others. They are part of the same environment and this influences what they do. There is a systemic effect, we could perhaps say, which is exercised not by the units themselves, but by the terms of their interaction.

So what is an international system? Well, it is a system which is made up of political entities — we usually call them "states" — which act independently of each other at the same time as they are forced to consider the actions of all other entities in the system. They act on their own, but also always together with, and in relation to, all the others. The international system provides an environment which determines, in broad outline, what political entities do and what they cannot do. The reason the international system has this effect is that it has a certain logic, and it is this logic, more than anything, that students of international relations study. The logic of the international system is expressed in institutions, rules, and norms. When studying an international system, we study the institutions that have been created, the rules by which the interaction takes place, and the norms that political entities follow.

Yet, there are many international systems, and not all of them are organized in the same fashion. That is, different international systems have different institutions, rules, and norms. These differences are the subject matter of a comparative study of international systems. And yet, it is no longer possible to make such comparisons using contemporary data. The reason is that, today, there is only one international system. This is the system that originated in Europe around the sixteenth century and spread to the rest of the world as a result of European colonialism in the nineteenth century. As a result, we find that the different international systems that previously existed were destroyed. Today, the rules of international politics are European rules, and the norms and institutions are European norms and institutions. The entire world has been recreated in Europe's image, and there is consequently nothing with which this system can be compared.

This is why a comparative study of international systems must be a historical study. There have been many international systems in the past, we will discover, some of them existed simultaneously and more or less independently of each other. Going back no further than to the middle of the nineteenth century, we find distinctly non-European ways of organizing international politics, and the non-European examples multiply the further back we go in time. These systems had other kinds of institutions, and they often followed other rules and norms. As a result, we find that these political entities and their members acted differently and for different reasons. Reading about them allows us to take leave of our present world and visit some very distant, different, and sometimes quite strange places. The kind of international politics that your teachers have taught you thus far, it turns out, is only one possible kind of international politics. In this book, we will introduce you to others.

More concretely, we will discuss six different regions of the world: China and East Asia, India, the Muslim caliphates, the Mongol khanates, Africa, and the Americas. There is no separate chapter on Persia, although the Persian influences on India and on the Muslim world will be discussed; there is nothing on Australia, and apart from a brief discussion of Hawaiʻi, we will not deal with the Pacific islands; Southeast Asia will be mentioned, but mainly in the context of Indian cultural influences. The final chapter deals with European expansion and colonialism, but there is no separate chapter on Europe as such.

Institutions, rules, and norms

Before we proceed to discuss the rest of the world, let's say a few words about the institutions, rules, and norms which characterize the one international system in which we all now live. This is a system that takes the state as its basic unit. The state is the subject of international politics, as it were. It is states that do things — go to war, conclude peace treaties, engage in foreign trade. From around the seventeenth century onward, states have been thought of as "sovereign." A sovereign state is a state which exercises supreme authority within a given territory. A sovereign state determines its own affairs in accordance with its own interests and aspirations, or rather, in the sixteenth century, in accordance with the interests and aspirations of its ruler.

Sovereignty is a basic institution of the European international system, we can conclude, and as such it implies a number of social practices and administrative arrangements. There are borders to be identified and protected, border crossings to be guarded, passports to be issued, flags to be flown and national anthems to be sung. These practices and arrangements are, in turn, associated with various rules and norms. One rule says that all states are equal to each other. All states are the same kinds of entities, doing the same kinds of things, and they all have the same status as members of the same system. They are functionally equal, that is, despite the fact that some obviously are far larger, richer and more powerful than others. As far as the norms of the system are concerned, one example is the norm which says that sovereignty must be respected. States should not interfere in each other's domestic affairs. All states have a right to self-determination.

In an international system of this kind, there is no common authority. And this, it soon becomes clear, is a problem as each state looks after itself, and no one looks after, or takes any responsibility for, the system as a whole. The term which scholars of international relations use for this condition is "anarchy." The European international system is an anarchical international system. In an anarchical international system, states are permanently insecure and war is a constant threat. Since they cannot trust their neighbors to behave peacefully towards them, each state must be prepared to defend itself, with weapons if needs be. Yet this, in turn, makes the neighbors feel more insecure, and they must arm themselves as well. States that fail to respond to this logic — states that trust in the goodwill of their neighbors — are punished for their naivety. In the end, the search for security makes everyone more insecure. And every so often the threat of war is replaced by actual cases of warfare. Not surprisingly, since its inception, the European international system has been extraordinarily violent. In the twentieth century alone, almost 100 million people died in European wars.

This is where a comparative study of international systems can make a contribution. Other, non-European international systems, as mentioned above, have distinct institutions, rules, and norms. They are all different from each other, but also different from the European system. For one thing, non-European international systems have often contained other political actors than states, and in many of them, empires have played a prominent role. Moreover, territory has often been defined quite differently. Where land is endlessly abundant, such as on the steppes of Central Asia or in much of Africa, possessing a particular piece of it has not been a crucial concern. As a result, borders have a different meaning. Where the borders should be drawn between two countries may matter far less than the relationship which both of them have toward a powerful state in the center of the system. The maps of some international systems look like subway maps — they tell you how to get from one place to the other, but they do not tell you much about the features of the land you are passing through.

In such an international system, sovereignty is not going to be a commonly invoked notion. Or rather, sovereignty is not an absolute value as much as a variable. Some political entities are fully independent while others are far less so. Here, different political entities are not functionally equal to each other; moreover, there is no absolute norm of non-interference and self-determination. The system is not anarchical in the same way as the European system. In fact, many non-European international systems have been quite hierarchical and held together by means of a common culture and a shared set of values, often under the auspices of a state with imperial ambitions. As a result, it has often been possible to ensure a measure of prosperity and peace. Yet one should not romanticize. Wars have been common, and horrendously destructive, outside of Europe too.

If we return to Europe with these lessons in mind, we will discover that the European international system suddenly looks quite different. From our new, non-European point of view, we are able to see a number of things that we previously failed to notice. In the European system too, it turns out, there are not only states but many other political entities, and here also empires have often played a prominent role. In general, sovereignty is not the absolute principle which it has been taken to be and the functional equality of states is not always respected. The European international system, when we look at it carefully, is actually quite hierarchical. Indeed, Europe is also united around a common culture and a set of shared values, and despite the wars, there have been times of prosperity and peace. In this way, by looking at it from a non-European point of view — by relativizing it — we can learn more about Europe too.

Non-state societies

Even from an alternative perspective, however, there will be many things that we still cannot see. Every perspective allows us to notice some things while making us blind to others. For example, we still take it for granted that states are the proper subject of history. We assume that world history is equal to the history of the state. Yet there are good reasons to question this assumption. Before we proceed to compare different international systems, let's say a few words about what this book fails to discuss.

Today the world is completely divided up between political entities. All territory belongs to one state or another and no land belongs to more than one state. States are mutually exclusive and together exhaustive of political space. Yet this has not always been the case. It was only as a result of the introduction of farming some 12,000 years ago that the first states appeared. Before that, during some 95 percent of human history, we were hunters and gatherers who moved around in response to the seasonal variations in the availability of food. Since these hunters and gatherers were constantly on the move, it was difficult for political authorities to exercise control over them. As a result, hunters and gatherers lived in "stateless" societies. Moreover, since they constructed only temporary buildings, there are few ruins for archaeologists to investigate. As a result, a history of a society of hunters and gatherers is difficult to write — hunters and gatherers "have no history."

Farmers are far easier to subdue and exploit. They live in a particular place and cultivate a given piece of land. After the harvest, the tax collectors dispatched by the king show up and demand their due. This was how the first states were established in the valleys of great rivers — Euphrates and Tigris, the Nile and a few others — around three thousand years Before Common Era (BCE). The transition to agriculture and the rise of the state, we have often been told, constituted a great improvement on the nomadic condition of statelessness. It was only then that human beings could acquire a culture and that human history, properly speaking, began. However, it is questionable whether the shift to agriculture really constituted an improvement. Hunters and gatherers seem to have enjoyed a more varied diet than farmers, and they were less exposed to contagious diseases. In addition, stateless societies were far more egalitarian than state-dominated societies. There are still hunters and gatherers in the world today, but they are not many. Read more: *People of the forest* at p. 140.

There are other kinds of nomadic people who make a living by moving around. Pastoralists are one example, and they have been just as difficult for states to control. Pastoralists are people who keep animals such as sheep, cows, horses, and reindeer. Their animals graze the land, and when they run out of food in one place, their owners move in order to find new pastures. As a result, pastoralists are difficult to tax and they have little respect for borders. The interior of the Eurasian continent and the savannas of Africa have been good places for pastoralists. Here, farming has been impossible to pursue since there is little rain and not many rivers. What there is, however, is an abundance of grassland. Relying on their fast horses, the pastoralists raid the sedentary communities of farmers and laid their hands on all kinds of things that life on the steppe cannot provide. Such "barbarian invasions" are a theme in both Chinese and Indian history. Indeed, invasions by peoples of the steppes have been important in European history as well. Read more: *The Mongol invasion of Europe* at p. 109.

The point, for our present purposes, is that a study of comparative international systems will misrepresent the past by telling the history of the state, not the history of stateless people. Or rather, when stateless people appear, they will do so only to the extent that they have an impact on states and their sedentary subjects. The incompleteness of this account becomes obvious when we remember that, until recently, much of the world was populated by nomads. It was only in the latter part of the nineteenth century, when the first railways were built, that the interior of the great continents came under the effective control of states. It was only then that the government of the United States finally subdued societies of Native Americans and that the Chinese government was able to properly police its borders with Mongolia. States, until recently, were like little islands in a large stateless sea. A comparative study of international systems is a study of these islands.

Walls and bridges

There is probably no prejudice which is as widely shared as the prejudices which sedentary people express towards people who are on the move. And, one might add, for good reason. The nomadic peoples that periodically swept into China, India and Europe looted, killed, and destroyed. One thing they destroyed were the fences that farmers had built around their plots. Fences, to pastoralists, are offensive since they prevent grazing animals from moving around. The nomads besieged cities too and destroyed city walls. Moreover, they were notorious destroyers of culture. When Genghis Khan entered Bukhara in 1220, he rounded up all the inhabitants in the city's main mosque, informed them that he was a punishment sent by God, and proceeded to kill them all. Read more: *A nomadic state* at p. 103.

Likewise when they sacked Baghdad in 1258, the Mongols destroyed libraries, killed scholars, poets, and artists, and put an end to the era which came to be remembered as "the Arab Golden Age."

Yet to call Mongols and other nomadic tribes "barbarian" might be unfair. Better, perhaps, to say that they have a different outlook on life. Compare the close connection between culture and agriculture. "Culture" refers to cultivation, to the "tilling of the land." To cultivate a plant is to care for it and to make it grow. In order to protect what we grow, we drive stakes into the ground and build fences that separate what is ours from that which belongs to others. Private property requires walls, and good walls make for good neighbors. Walls are also needed if we are to create a home for ourselves. On this side of the wall, we are safe and we are together with people like ourselves; on the other side of the wall, we are away from home and we interact mainly with strangers. Cultures, we believe, must be nurtured and protected in the same fashion. A culture is always *our* culture, it belongs to people like us and to the place where we live. The walls that surround us protect our way of life and allow us to continue to be who we are.

Some international systems have been surrounded by walls, actual as well as metaphorical. As a result, interaction with the rest of the world has been limited; the international system is isolated from external influences, but it is also independent and self-sufficient. Much as a biological species which is confined to a specific ecological niche, the international system evolves in its own fashion. The most striking example is the international systems of the Americas, in which different societies had some contact with each other, but which developed in complete isolation from the rest of the world. Read more: *The Columbian exchange* at p. 156.

Foreign trade was, for extensive periods in its history, limited and the leaders of the Chinese Empire also sought to build walls to isolate themselves from the outside world and to keep foreigners out. Read more: *The Great Wall of China does not exist* at p. 26. Likewise, Japan was officially closed to foreigners from the years 1600 to 1868. Read more: *A Japanese international system?* at p. 36. In fact, before the year 1500, Europe too showed only limited interest in the world beyond its borders.

But there are also international systems that display the opposite logic. These international systems are outward-looking and expansive and seek to connect different parts of the world with each other. The Mongol khanates in the thirteenth century are a striking example, but there are others. In the seventh century, the Arabs expanded rapidly from the Arabian Peninsula, conquering the Middle East, Central Asia, North Africa and the Iberian Peninsula. In 732, a hundred years after the death of Muhammad, the Arab armies had reached as far as central France. However an international system can be outward-looking and expansive without being violent. This describes the international systems that have existed around the Indian Ocean.

A 1763 Chinese map of the world, claiming to be a reproduction of a 1418 map made from Zheng He's voyages. Photo from www.economist.com. Wikimedia, https://commons.wikimedia.org/wiki/File:Zhenghemap.jpg

Here people have interacted with each other from the earliest times. This is why we find shards of Chinese pottery in archaeological sites in southern Africa and why to this day people throughout Southeast Asia are Hindus, Buddhists and Muslims — all three religions brought to Southeast Asia from India. Read more: *Indianization* at p. 58.

This is how civilization spreads. If culture finds its metaphorical basis in agriculture, civilization finds it in exchange. When our society is connected to other societies, we are connected to other people, and we can suddenly compare things and judge them in relation to each other. As a result, we have a choice between better and cheaper options; we can pick the new and the never-before-tried. Such choices broaden our horizons and improve our lives. This is why civilization depends on the unencumbered circulation of goods, people, ideas, faiths, and ways of life. The consequences of such interaction may be unsettling, but they can also be liberating. We no longer have to be confined to, and carry the burden of, our culture, and we no longer have to be who we are. Civilization provides us with a means of escape. Or, differently put, exchange is the enemy of culture. When presented with alternatives, we give up our old ways. We no longer do the things we used to do and we are no longer quite the same people as before. This is how civilization undermines and destroys culture.

Take the example of the Muslims in al-Andalus. Read more: *The Arabs in Spain* at p. 81. The Arabs civilized Spain in the ninth century by connecting its cities to the great centers of learning in the Middle East. As a result, the previous Visigoth culture was destroyed. The people of al-Andalus grew to eat lemons, play the lute and compose far better poetry; they used better ploughs and irrigation techniques too, put on deodorants, and used toothpaste to brush their teeth. Read more: *Deodorants and the origins of flamenco* at p. 82.

The great library in Córdoba was far larger than any library in Christian Europe and it contained the entire canon of classical Greek texts, saved for posterity by the caliphs of Baghdad. Read more: *The translation movement* at p. 80. In the thirteenth century, these books were translated and became available in Latin for the first time. The Europeans were later to refer to this as "the Renaissance." The Renaissance destroyed the culture of the Middle Ages, but it civilized Europe.

Or, and more controversially, compare the impact which the European expansion has had on the rest of the world. For much of their history, the Europeans were not that interested in other continents, but around the year 1500 — at the time of the rise of the sovereign state — this changed. The Europeans began looking for ways to trade, above all with India and China, and little by little they came to acquire colonies overseas. For a while, at the time of the First World War, the Europeans controlled much of the rest of the world. This expansion had a profound, destructive impact on the cultures of the societies with which they came into contact. All parts of the world were suddenly connected to the same global network of trade, and politically dominated by Europe, so it was no longer possible for people in the rest of the world to live as before and to be what they previously had been. And yet, the benefits are undeniable. Today, in the wake of the cultural devastation brought by the European expansion, people around the world are far better educated, in a better state of health, and with more opportunities open to them. Cultural devastation is a tragedy, but civilization is a blessing. It is not obvious how to assess these contradictory effects and this is why the history of European expansion is still a controversial topic.

Further reading

Abu-Lughod, Janet L. *Before European Hegemony*: *The World System A.D. 1250–1350*. New York: Oxford University Press, 1991.

Bentley, Jerry H. *Old World Encounters*: *Cross-Cultural Contacts and Exchanges in Pre-Modern Times*. New York: Oxford University Press, 1993.

Bozeman, Adda B. *Politics and Culture in International History*: *From the Ancient Near East to the Opening of the Modern Age*. Princeton: Princeton University Press, 1960.

Bull, Hedley. *The Anarchical Society*: *A Study of Order in World Politics*. New York: Columbia University Press, 2002.

Buzan, Barry, and Richard Little. *International Systems in World History*: *Remaking the Study of International Relations*. New York: Oxford University Press, 2000.

Hui, Victoria Tin-bor. *War and State Formation in Ancient China and Early Modern Europe*. Cambridge: Cambridge University Press, 2005.

Quirk, Joel, Yongjin Zhang, and Shogo Suzuki, eds. *International Orders in the Early Modern World*: *Before the Rise of the West*. London: Routledge, 2014.

Scott, James C. *Against the Grain*: *A Deep History of the Earliest States*. New Haven: Yale University Press, 2018.

Siddiqi, Farhan Hanif and Muhammad Nadeem Mirza. *Introducing International Relations*: *Concepts, Theories and Practice*. Karachi: Oxford University Press, 2019.

Watson, Adam. *The Evolution of International Society*: *A Comparative Historical Analysis*. London: Routledge, 2009.

Think about

Comparative international systems

- What is a "system"?
- What do you study if you are studying "comparative international systems"?
- Why must a comparative study of international systems become a historical study?

Norms, rules, institutions

- What is a "sovereign state"?
- What do scholars of international relations mean by "anarchy"?
- What can a study of non-European international systems tell us about Europe?

Non-state societies

- What are "non-state societies"?
- Describe the lifestyle of hunters and gatherers.
- Why was pastoralism until recently a successful form of social and economic organization?

Walls and bridges

- What is "culture"?
- What is "civilization"? How do civilizations spread?
- Why have many societies decided to construct walls around themselves?

Map of Asia from Abraham Ortelius, *Theatrum orbis terrarum* (Antverpiae: Apud Aegid. Coppenium Diesth, 1570), p. 31, https://archive.org/details/theatrumorbister00orte

2. China and East Asia

For much of its history, China was the dominant country in East Asia and international relations in this part of the world were, more than anything, organized by the Chinese and on Chinese terms. China itself was an empire but the international system of which China was the center concerned the external relations of the empire — its relations with the rest of East Asia. In order to describe these relations the metaphor of a "solar system" is sometimes used. Here, China is the sun around which other and far smaller political entities, located at increasing distances from the center, are circulating in their respective orbits. Some historians use the term "suzerainty," referring to a relationship in which "a dominant state has control over the international affairs of a subservient state, while the latter retains domestic autonomy."

At the same time, there was a great difference in the way the Chinese dealt with neighbors to the north and the west of the country and neighbors to the south and the east. The former relations were organized according to what we will call the "overland system," and the latter relations according to the "tribute system." The people to the north and the west constituted permanent threats. They were nomads who grazed their animals on the enormous steppes of inner Asia. Despite their economic and technological backwardness, they had access to the most advanced military technology of the day — fast horses — and in addition they were highly skilled archers. Since the terrain was flat and since there were few natural obstacles in their way, it was easy for the nomads to raid Chinese farming communities. Occasionally they made it all the way to the capital itself. The imperial authorities always struggled with how best to respond to these threats, mixing defensive and offensive strategies, without ever finding a satisfactory solution. As a result, China was periodically invaded and two major dynasties were founded by tribes from the steppes — the Yuan, 1271–1368, which was of Mongol origin, and the last imperial dynasty, the Qing, 1644–1911, which was Manchu.

As far as China's relations with countries to the east and the south were concerned, they were far easier to manage. Since the Himalayas effectively blocked any invasion from the south, there were no military threats from this direction and, instead, communications took place across the ocean. From Korea, Japan and states throughout Southeast Asia the Chinese emperors demanded tributes. The foreigners were required to make the journey to the Chinese capital at regular intervals and present gifts to the emperor. In this way the Chinese were confirmed in their view of themselves. They really were the country at the center of the world — the "Middle Kingdom" — to which all human beings paid tribute.

The Warring States period

Chinese people are fond of saying that their land has the longest continuous history of any existing country, yet the subject of this history — "China," "the Middle Kingdom" — has itself varied considerably over time. What we mean by "the Chinese people" is also less than clear. People who historically have lived in what today is the People's Republic of China represent many hundreds of different ethnic groups. Even within the largest of these — the Han people — a number of mutually incomprehensible languages have been spoken. It was only in the latter part of the nineteenth century that it became possible to talk about a Chinese "nation," understood as a community of people which encompassed most of the country.

What made a person Chinese, and what brought a sense of unity to the Chinese people, was not state power but more than anything a shared set of rituals and seasonal celebrations. These rituals go way back in time. The first rulers — the Shang dynasty, 1600–1046 BCE — engaged in human sacrifice and ancestor worship. They were also the first to use characters — divinations inscribed on so-called "oracle bones" — as a means of writing. While human sacrifice soon ceased, ancestor worship and the unique Chinese form of writing have survived to this day. During the following dynasty, the Zhou, 1050–777 BCE, the kings became more powerful and the territory they controlled increased dramatically. The Zhou kings regarded themselves as "Sons of Heaven" who had been given a "Mandate of Heaven" to rule the country. This mandate could be revoked, however, by any rebels who could demonstrate that they were powerful enough to take over the state. A successful uprising was proof that Heaven had withdrawn its favors and instead bestowed them on the rebels.

Towards the end of the Zhou dynasty, political power began to fragment as regional leaders who had been given land by the kings asserted their independence. Eventually, seven separate states emerged, and they were constantly at war with each other. This era has been referred to as the "Warring States period," during 475–221 BCE. During the Warring States period, China was not a country as much as an international system in its own right. The seven independent states engaged in traditional forms of power politics: they forged alliances, made treaties and fought battles, and they took turns in the position as the most powerful state in the system. The armies were enormous, counting up to perhaps one million men, and it was said that some hundreds of thousands of soldiers might die in a single battle. Not surprisingly, the Warring States period is a favorite of twenty-first century costume dramas on Chinese TV. Eventually one of the states, Qin, emerged on top. The question for the smaller states was how to react to Qin's ascendancy. The topic was much discussed by the philosophers and military strategists of the day.

Sunzi and modern management techniques

The Art of War is a manual of military strategy and tactics ascribed to Sunzi, 544–496 BCE, a general active during the Warring States period. Although there indeed was a general by that name, it is not entirely clear that he was the author of the work in question, although in China the book is known as *Sunzi bingfa*, or "Master Sun's Rules for Soldiers." Sunzi emphasized the importance of intelligence gathering, of subterfuge and dissimulation, but he also discussed the role of diplomacy, and how best to deploy troops.

In Japan, *The Art of War* was used as a textbook in military academies at the end of the nineteenth century. Admiral Togo Heihachiro, who destroyed the Russian navy at the Battle of Tsushima in 1905, was reputed to have been an avid Sunzi reader. The Japanese victory in the war with Russia was the first time since the Mongols that an "eastern people" had defeated a "western people." In the wake of this triumph, *The Art of War* came to be read as a manual, embodying a uniquely "eastern" way of making war. This, at any rate, was how the book was understood by students from various East Asian countries who studied in Japan in the first decades of the twentieth century. Taking *The Art of War* home with them, they used it as a manual for how to liberate themselves from European colonialism. Ho Chi Minh, leader of the Vietnamese independence movement, translated portions of the book and it was read by Võ Nguyên Giáp, the general who defeated the French army at the battle of Dien Bien Phu in 1954.

This was when Americans started reading Sunzi. Much as in Japan, the book was used at military academies and it was suggested reading for American officers dispatched to Vietnam. From the American military academies, Sunzi's fame spread to the American business community, thanks to writers who claimed that his nuggets of wisdom had a direct application to matters of business strategy. It was only by learning from Sunzi, these authors claimed, that European and American companies could take back market shares captured by their East Asian competitors. This is how a Chinese military manual from the fifth century BCE became readily available in bookshops the world over.

Read more online: https://hdl.handle.net/20.500.12434/79fbc3b3

This was a bleak time of insecurity and war, but the Warring States period was also a time of great economic progress. Military competition, it seems, helped spur innovation. The imperative for all seven states, as the popular dictum put it, was to "enrich the nation and to strengthen the army." This was first of all the case as far as military hardware was concerned, with new forms of swords, crossbows and chariots being invented. In addition, each state became far better organized and administrated. Taxes were collected more efficiently, the independent power of the nobility was suppressed, and a new class of bureaucrats took over the running of state affairs and organized their work according to formal procedures. A powerful state required a powerful economy, and, to this end, farming techniques were developed, and major irrigation projects undertaken. The amount of cast iron produced by China already in the fifth century BCE would not be rivaled by the rest of the world until the middle of the eighteenth century — over two thousand years later. Economic markets developed as well, with coins being used to pay for goods coming from all over China but also from distant lands far beyond, including Manchuria, Korea, and even India.

The intellectual developments of the period were just as impressive. The Warring States period was known as the age of the "Hundred Schools." This was the time when all major Chinese systems of thought first came to be established. Eventually nine of these schools dominated over the others, a group which included Confucianism, Legalism, Daoism, and Mohism. These teachings were propagated by scholars who wandered from one court to the other, looking for a ruler who would be interested in their ideas. Those who were successful found themselves jobs as advisers and courtiers. Since there were many states, and multiple centers of competing power, even unorthodox ideas could be given a sympathetic hearing somewhere.

Kongzi, 551–479 BCE — better known outside of China as Confucius — is the most famous of these wandering scholars. Born in the state of Lu in what today is the Shandong province — the peninsula which juts out in the direction of Korea — Kongzi rose from lowly jobs as a cow-herder and clerk to become an adviser to the king of Lu himself. Yet, eventually, political intrigues forced him to leave the court; this was when his life as a peripatetic teacher began. Kongzi's philosophy emphasized the importance of personal conduct and he insisted that the virtue of the rulers was more important than the formal rules by which the state was governed. Moral conduct, as Kongzi saw it, is above all a matter of maintaining the obligations implied by our social relationships. Society in the end consists of nothing but hierarchical pairs — relations between father and son, husband and wife, older and younger brother, ruler and subject, and between friends. The inferior party in each pair should submit to the power and will of the superior, but the superior has the duty to care for the inferior, to look after his or her welfare. A well-ordered society is a society in which these duties are faithfully carried out.

Kongzi and his institutes

Kongzi, or Confucius, has experienced a roller-coaster-like career during the past half-century — quite an achievement for a philosopher who has been dead for over 2,500 years. During the Cultural Revolution, 1966–76, he was reviled as an "enemy of the people." Read more: *Chairman Mao and the Legalists* at p. 19. Yet in the 1980s, Lee Kuan Yew, the prime minister of Singapore, turned to Confucianism as an ideology which could help unify his multi-ethnic city-state. Confucianism, Lee decided, was an expression of time-honored "Asian values," a series of moral precepts, which included respect for one's elders, the importance of the family, and deference to political authority.

Since the 1990s, the Communist government has radically changed its view of Kongzi. At a time when philosophers such as Karl Marx and Friedrich Engels no longer find many adherents, the Chinese authorities have begun to worry about the lack of moral direction in Chinese society. The obvious person to turn to for guidance is Kongzi. For the Chinese authorities, his teachings have the added attraction that they, as Lee Kuan Yew argued, can help promote political obedience.

Since 2004, the Chinese government has established over 300 educational institutions around the world, named after the old philosopher. Modeled on the German Goethe Institute, the Confucius Institutes offer courses in Chinese language, organize seminars and cultural events, and sponsor research on China. However, in contrast to the cultural institutes of other countries, the Confucius Institutes have located themselves on university campuses, integrating themselves with the teaching and research conducted there. This tight connection has been questioned by critics, who point out that there are far too many topics the Communist government prefers not to discuss.

There are indications that the Chinese leadership is not entirely united in its Confucian convictions. In early 2011, a ten-meter-tall bronze statue of Kongzi was unveiled with much fanfare near Tiananmen Square in central Beijing. Yet four months later, the statue suddenly vanished overnight. A descendant of the philosopher blamed "leftists" within the government. Meanwhile, a contributor to a Maoist discussion forum insisted: "The witch doctor who has been poisoning people for thousands of years has finally been kicked off Tiananmen Square!"

Read more online: https://hdl.handle.net/20.500.12434/6a067ab6

Daoism is a philosophy associated with Laozi (born 601 BCE), a contemporary of Kongzi's. Laozi is the author of the *Daodejing*, a text of aphorisms and assorted teachings. Yet there is little historical evidence for the actual existence of a person by that name. Hence the teachings are best regarded as a compilation of texts produced by others. Dao, "the way," does not only provide you with religious wisdom but also hands-on advice for how to live a successful life. Daoist monks emphasized the spiritual dimensions of human existence and sought to communicate with the spirits of nature. In addition, Daoism has had an impact on politics. Its spiritualism and disdain for formal rules have been an inspiration for several political movements which have risen up against the political authorities.

However, it was the Legalists who were to have the most direct impact on practical politics. Legalism is the school of political philosophy which the Chinese know as *fajia*. The law was indeed important to them but only as a tool of statecraft. The Legalists assumed that all people act only in their self-interest and that they follow only moral codes which benefit themselves. It is consequently only the law and its enforcement which can keep people in line and guarantee peace and order in society. The law must therefore be clear enough for everyone to understand it, and the punishments which it requires must be harsh enough to ensure that everyone obeys. In the end, it was only the state and its survival that mattered to the Legalists. The ruler was free to act in whichever way he chose as long as it benefited the state. This applied not least to matters of foreign policy. Alliances could be made but also broken; ostensibly friendly countries could be attacked without warning; peace negotiations could serve as a pretext for starting another war, and so on.

Qin Shi Huang, often referred to as "the First Emperor," 220–210 BCE, came to power on the back of advice such as this. He suppressed the rivaling states and united the country. He standardized weights and measures, the Chinese language, and even the width of roads and of the axles of carts. In an attempt to restart Chinese history, and to do it on his own terms, he ordered all classical texts to be burned and had Confucian scholars buried alive.

The necropolis of the First Emperor

In 1974, peasants digging a well on the outskirts of Xi'an, the capital of the Qin dynasty, came across an unexpected find — a life-size statue, made in terracotta, of an ancient Chinese warrior. The warrior, it turned out, was not alone. Digging further, archaeologists soon unearthed another 2,000 soldiers. The excavations have not yet been completed and there are an estimated 8,000 terracotta soldiers buried in the ground. What farmers and archaeologists had come across were the troops guarding the mausoleum of Qin Shi Huang, the First Emperor of China. Or, perhaps, necropolis, "city of the dead," is a more appropriate term for this complex of underground palaces and courtyards which house his remains.

The historian Sima Qian, writing one hundred years after the death of the First Emperor, tells us that 700,000 men helped build this site. "Palaces and scenic towers for a hundred officials were constructed, and the tomb was filled with rare artifacts and wonderful treasure." The necropolis was protected by crossbows and arrows which were set to shoot at anyone who entered, and it was surrounded by rivers of poisonous mercury. The concubines who had not produced male heirs were buried with the emperor. The craftsmen who had constructed the tomb were all trapped inside their creation, in order not to give them an opportunity to divulge any of the secrets it contained.

Emperor Qin Shi Huang's tomb itself has yet to be excavated, and the Chinese authorities have been reluctant to start the work. The reason, it seems, is that archaeologists are still busy unearthing terracotta warriors. In addition, there are concerns regarding how best to protect whatever treasures they will come across. A particularly exciting prospect would be the discovery of a library. As Sima Qian tells us, the First Emperor ordered all books in China to be burned, but it could just possibly be that he preserved a copy of each one of them in his personal library. If this library is buried with the emperor, and if it has not been destroyed by over 2,000 years of natural decay, it is likely to give us an entirely new understanding of ancient Chinese history.

Read more online: https://hdl.handle.net/20.500.12434/f706c02d

Despite the Legalists' ruthless advice, or perhaps because of it, the Qin dynasty only lasted fifteen years. After Qin Shi Huang's death, the country soon descended into another round of wars. Yet the many philosophical schools of the period — Confucianism

and Legalism in particular — would continue to play an important role throughout Chinese history.

> **Chairman Mao and the Legalists**
>
> Qin Shi Huang, the First Emperor of China, relied heavily on advice from the so-called "Legalist" school of political philosophy. Their suggestions emphasized ruthless policies and underhanded tactics. Yet, the Qin dynasty lasted only fifteen years. When it was replaced by the Han dynasty, the new line of emperors decided that Confucians should replace the Legalists as advisers. The teachings of Confucius were very different. He emphasized the role of virtue, both in the rulers and in his subjects, and the importance of fulfilling one's social obligations. Yet, as many Chinese people have been quick to point out, the ruthless power politics of the Legalists did not disappear. In fact, references to Confucianism have often been seen as a pretense, and Legalism as the enduring reality of politics in China.
>
> To reformist Chinese intellectuals at the turn of the twentieth century, Confucianism came to symbolize everything that was wrong with the country. Emphasizing literary studies at the expense of science and technology, Confucianism had allegedly blocked economic development, and it was said to stifle creativity and entrepreneurship. To these conclusions, the Chinese Communist Party added that Confucianism was a feudal doctrine, which gave ideological support to an exploitative landowning class. During the Cultural Revolution, 1966–1976, Mao Zedong, China's leader, relied on gangs of Red Guards, militant militia groups, to intimidate his enemies. During the last stage of these campaigns, 1973–1976, Confucius became an official enemy of the state. In gigantic posters and in constantly repeated speeches, Chinese people were encouraged to "Criticize Lin, Criticize Confucius" — "Lin" referring to Lin Biao, one of Mao's contemporary enemies. Read more: *Kongzi and his institutes* at p. 16.
>
> In contrast to all previous Chinese leaders, Mao was not afraid to declare his admiration for the methods employed by the Legalists. In fact, he quite explicitly modeled himself on Qin Shi Huang. Mao only criticized him for not being ruthless enough. The First Emperor, said Mao, buried 460 scholars alive, but "we have buried forty-six thousand scholars alive … We have surpassed Qin Shi Huang a hundredfold."
>
> *Read more online:* https://hdl.handle.net/20.500.12434/039af23f

The development of the Chinese state

During the subsequent two thousand years, the leaders of the Chinese state would all be referred to as "emperors" and the country itself referred to as an "empire." Yet since one dynasty was constantly replaced by another, there is little continuity in Chinese history, and the struggles for political power resulted in both revolutions and prolonged periods of wars. Moreover, several of the dynasties were not Chinese at all, but established by foreign invaders. Despite this political diversity, there is a striking continuity when it comes to cultural values. Most emperors embraced Confucian ideals and were active participants in the various rituals which Chinese culture prescribed — including ancestor worship and offerings to Heaven at various times of the day, month and year. The emperors saw themselves as "Sons of Heaven" who ruled by virtue of the mandate that Heaven had given them. In addition, a large and rule-bound bureaucracy helped to provide a sense of continuity from one dynasty to the next. For our purposes, there is no reason to discuss every dynasty, but we should briefly mention the most important ones — the Han, Tang, Song, Ming and Qing — with a focus on China's relations to the rest of East Asia.

The rulers of the Han dynasty, 206 BCE–220 CE, were far more successful than the Qin when it came to maintaining their power. The Han dynasty lasted for well over four hundred years. While the First Emperor may have established many of the imperial institutions, it was during Han that those same institutions were consolidated and developed. The Han state organized a proper bureaucracy run by a professional class of administrators whose salaries were paid by taxing key commodities, such as salt. In a sharp break with the cynical doctrines of the Qin, the Han emperors made Confucianism into the official philosophy of the state. All administrators were supposed to read the Confucian classics and to serve the people with virtue and benevolence. The emperor was placed at the head of the administrative system, but in practice his power was constrained by court conferences where his advisers made decisions by consensus. The Han state took charge of society and organized economic activities, including the building of roads and canals. Large state monopolies were established for the production and sale of salt, iron and liquor. The coins minted during the Han dynasty helped expand trade, and they made it possible to pay taxes in cash rather than in kind. Han-era coins, with their distinctive square holes at the center, were to remain the standard means of payment until the Tang dynasty, three hundred years later. Not surprisingly, the Chinese to this day refer to themselves as *hanren*, "Han people."

Speaking of trade, it was during the Han dynasty that the caravan routes first were developed which connected China with Central Asia, India, and the world beyond.

Sogdian letters

Sogdia was a Central Asian kingdom that flourished between the fourth and the ninth centuries CE. The Sogdians are famous above all for their business acumen. They bought paper, copper, and silk in China and traded in Persian grapes and silverware, glass, alfalfa, corals, Buddhist images, Roman wool and amber from the Baltic. They operated as financial intermediaries too, setting up business deals, organizing caravans, arranging for money to be transferred and invested. While most other merchants only traveled short distances, Sogdian communities could be found along the entire network of Asian trade routes. There were Sogdians in Constantinople as well as in Xi'an in China. The Sogdian language was the universal language of commerce across the Eurasian landmass. In this way, they created a commercial empire which was far bigger than their own, rather small, Central Asian kingdom.

In 1907, the British archaeologist Aurel Stein discovered a pouch of papers in the ruins of an old watch-tower in the Chinese city of Dunhuang, on the edge of the Taklamakan Desert. The letters turned out to be far older than anyone could have imagined — dating from early in the fourth century. Unusually, the letters were not written by officials but by ordinary people. One of them, a wealthy Sogdian merchant, writes to his home office to give an account of a recent attack by Xiongnu forces; another merchant complains about the trustworthiness of his business partners Read more: *The Xiongnu confederation* below. The most touching letter, however, is from a woman, Mewnai, to her mother. She complains that her husband has deserted her and her young daughter and that they are not allowed to leave Dunhuang on their own. "I live wretchedly; without clothing, without money; I ask for a loan, but no-one consents to give me one, so I depend on charity from the priest." Perhaps her husband perished somewhere along the perilous trade routes. Yet the letter was never delivered. For one reason or another, it was left in the watch-tower for over fifteen hundred years.

Read more online: https://hdl.handle.net/20.500.12434/9295e291

Although the Roman Empire and Han China had no direct connections with each other, the goods traded along these routes did. It was then that Chinese silk became a fashionable item among Roman elites and Roman glassware ended up in China. This trading network is often referred to as the "Silk Road" (although that term is a nineteenth-century invention by a German scholar). Besides, many more items than silk were traded and there was never just one road. The caravan routes brought foreign people and ideas to China too, such as Buddhism, which has its origin in India. Central Asia was not only a site of trade, but also of military engagements. The Han state was continuously harassed by a confederation of nomadic peoples known as the Xiongnu.

The Xiongnu confederation

The Xiongnu were a pastoral people who formed a state, or rather a loose confederation of tribes, on the steppes to the north and west of China, two thousand years ago. The Xiongnu were the original Chinese example of an unsettled, uncivilized, nomadic people. The name itself means "fierce slave" in Chinese. The very first Chinese rulers made war on the Xiongnu. Qin Shi Huang, the First Emperor, drove them away from the plains of the Yellow River and forced them to retreat to Mongolia. However, the Xiongnu continued to cause trouble. In 200 BCE, Emperor Gaozu, the founder of the Han dynasty, personally led a military campaign against them, but was ambushed and only barely escaped with his life.

Instead, the Han emperors sought to pacify the Xiongnu by means of lavish gifts of silk, liquor, and rice, and they sent princesses to their leaders as brides. Official treaties were brokered too — the first one signed in 195 BCE — and, unusually for the Chinese, they were concluded on a basis of equality. However, each time the treaty was to be renewed, the Xiongnu asked for higher payments and in the end, the Chinese were effectively transformed into tribute bearers to Xiongnu, rather than the other way around. Dealing with people like this was humiliating, ineffective, and expensive. Furthermore, despite the various agreements, Xiongnu raids on Chinese settlements continued. Eventually, however, the power of the Xiongnu declined. The Chinese exploited divisions within the confederacy, whose leaders never found an orderly way to settle matters of succession. In the end, a southern group of Xiongnu tribes defected to the imperial side.

The ethnic background of the Xiongnu is disputed — they may have been Turks, Mongols, Huns, or even Iranians. Recently, several Xiongnu burial sites have been excavated in Mongolia where archaeologists have found works of art, including small statues of tigers carrying dead prey and golden stags with the heads of eagles.

Read more online: https://hdl.handle.net/20.500.12434/d14850b6

Nomadic peoples would continue to make trouble for Chinese farmers and for the Chinese state for much of the subsequent two thousand years.

The Tang dynasty, 618–907 CE, is perhaps best remembered today for its cultural achievements. It was during Tang that arts like calligraphy and landscape painting were first developed, and when writers like Li Bai and Du Fu composed the poems which all subsequent generations of Chinese schoolchildren have been made to recite. Economically the country was thriving. China-wide markets in land, labor, and natural resources were developed, and many technical innovations took place, including paper-making, and woodblock printing. There was extensive mining and manufacturing of cast iron and even steel, and trade was brisk along the caravan routes. Well-fed and prosperous, China's population grew quickly, numbering some fifty million people. It was during Tang that the system of entrance examinations was conclusively established. In order to get a job as a government official, you were required to pass a demanding test on Confucian philosophy and on the classics of Chinese literature. Since the imperial bureaucracy was the main road to social and economic success, the country's elite effectively came to be selected through these examinations. It was no longer enough to come from an aristocratic family or to have money.

Tang dynasty China exercised a strong cultural influence over all countries with which it came into contact. This was, for example, the time when Japan, Korea, and Vietnam adopted a Chinese-style writing system and when Confucian philosophy and Chinese arts spread far and wide. During the Tang period it was very fashionable to be Chinese. At the same time, the Tang dynasty was wide open to the rest of the world, with foreign goods, fashions, and ideas entering China along the caravan routes.

> **Journey to the West**
>
> Xuanzang was a Buddhist monk from Chang'an, today's Xi'an, who, in the year 629 of the Common Era, traveled all the way to India. Buddhism was a relatively recent arrival in China at the time and Chinese Buddhists often had to make do with poor translations of Buddhist scriptures. The purpose of Xuanzang's journey was to look for original texts in the Buddha's homeland from which more faithful translations could be made. He traveled westward into Central Asia and then southward, through Afghanistan. Once Xuanzang reached his destination he spent the next thirteen years visiting various pilgrimage sites, studying with renowned teachers, and looking for manuscripts. When he eventually returned home in 646, he received a warm welcome. Xuanzang obtained the emperor's support in building a pagoda where the manuscripts could be stored and an institute was founded where the arduous task of translation began.
>
> *Journey to the West* is an immensely popular Chinese novel from the sixteenth century which gives an account of Xuanzang's story, told as a comic adventure that mixes fantasy and folktales. In *Journey to the West*, Xuanzang is given four traveling companions — a monkey, a pig, an ogre, and a white steed, who actually turns out to be a dragon prince. The story, which has been filmed several times and exists both in *gongfu* and children's versions, soon becomes the vehicle for a series of amazing events, miraculous transformations, and extended fighting sequences. Much of the book is set in the wildlands which separate China and India, where the deep gorges and tall mountains turn out to be populated with demons and animal spirits. Eventually, the traveling companions return home and are amply rewarded for their troubles. Xuanzang attains Buddhahood and Jubadie, the pig, gets to eat all the excess offerings that worshipers bring to the altars of Buddhist temples. *Journey to the West* is a comic adventure, but also — for those who prefer to read it that way — an allegory of a group of pilgrims who travel together towards enlightenment, where the success of one of them depends on the success of the others.
>
> *Read more online:* https://hdl.handle.net/20.500.12434/afa6eefb

Through renewed contacts with India, Buddhism was further established and indigenous Chinese sects such as Chan — what the Japanese were later to call "Zen" — were established. Chinese people dressed in foreign clothing and Chinese men married women from Central Asia. The Tang dynasty was a cosmopolitan empire where people from all over the world would mingle — Persian and Jewish traders, Arabic scholars and travelers, conjurers from Syria and acrobats from Bactria.

The Song dynasty, 960–1279, was another period of economic prosperity and cultural flourishing. A number of important technological inventions were made at this time, including gunpowder and the compass. Making creative use of the invention of paper-making technology, the Song were the first to issue bank notes. Paper money helped spur trade, although it also caused inflation. This was when large manufacturing industries were established which produced consumer items for a market that included the whole of the country. The economic changes provided ordinary people with new opportunities. Poor people could rise in the world and rich people could become richer still. Often, members of the newly affluent middle class would establish themselves as patrons of the arts. Scholars and connoisseurs of culture would gather in gardens and private retreats to view works of art or to recite poetry and drink tea, and there were lively, if more plebeian, entertainment quarters in all major cities. During the Song dynasty, literacy increased, books became readily available, and the study of the sciences, mathematics, and philosophy made great strides.

In military terms, the Song emperors were far less successful. Like all Chinese dynasties they were menaced by tribes attacking them from the north, in this case by the Jurchen, a people from whom the Manchus would later claim their descent. In 1127, the Jurchen captured the Song capital of Kaifeng and forced the emperor to retire. In an audacious move, the Song elite relocated their court to the southern city of Hangzhou, just west of present-day Shanghai. Although they had lost much of their territory, and the move was a source of great embarrassment, the economy continued to develop. China's population doubled in size during Song, above all since farming expanded and since new species of rice came to be used. The Song strengthened their navy and built ships that could travel to Southeast Asia and trade with the islands of present-day Indonesia. They strengthened their army too, and began using gunpowder as a weapon. Yet the military setbacks continued. The Song dynasty came to a final end in 1279 when the Mongols under Kublai Khan overran Hangzhou, deposed the emperor and established a new dynasty, the Yuan, 1271–1368. Read more: *The Mongol khanates* at p. 101.

Despite their spectacular success as conquerors, the Yuan dynasty lasted less than one hundred years and, in 1368, the Mongols were replaced by the Ming, a dynasty once again led by Chinese people. The Ming dynasty lasted until 1644. The Ming dynasty too enjoyed economic success. There was now a China-wide market for consumer goods such as fabrics and foodstuffs, as well as for prestige items like porcelain and furniture. Since many of these items were produced in large number, many objects from the Ming period, such as vases and tea cups, are still with us today, fetching high prices at auctions around the world. During the Ming period, gardens became a fashionable setting for social and cultural life. In Hangzhou and in the neighboring city of Suzhou, rich merchants competed ferociously with each other in establishing and extending their gardens. Meanwhile, the Chinese state returned to its Confucian roots after the Mongolian interruption. Administrators were once again selected according to their knowledge of the Confucian classics.

During the Ming dynasty, relations with the rest of the world were rather more complicated than during the Yuan. The Ming rulers had little knowledge of the steppe and little appreciation for trade. Or rather, the Ming dynasty was a time when the issue of foreign trade was hotly contested between various court factions. The group most strongly in favor of trade were the eunuchs, the emasculated courtiers who made up the staff of the imperial palace. The most successful trader among them was Zheng

He, 1371–1433. He brought thousands of vessels with him on no fewer than seven far-flung journeys of exploration and trade which took his fleet to Southeast Asia, the Indian Ocean, and even to the east coast of Africa (see map on p. 8).

A giraffe in Beijing

The Chinese emperors were avid collectors of exotic animals. In their zoos, they had Asian species like elephants, tigers, and camels, and African species like zebras and gazelles. In 1414 the imperial collection received its most exotic creature yet when a giraffe arrived in Beijing, all the way from East Africa. Considering how difficult it is to transport such a large animal such a long distance, we may well wonder how it got there. It was Saifuddin Hamza Shah, the ruler of Bengal, who had decided to impress the emperor by giving him this gift which he, in turn, had received as a tribute from the ruler of Melinda in today's Kenya. The animal was picked up by a ship sent from the fleet that Zheng He commanded in the Indian Ocean, and subsequently transported to Beijing.

When it arrived the giraffe caused general amazement. Checking their encyclopedias, Confucian scholars decided that it must be a unicorn, a mythological creature that traditionally was said to have "the body of a deer, the tail of an ox, and the hooves of a horse," and to be of such a gentle disposition that "it only ate grass and never hurt a living being." When they learned that the animal in the Somali language was known as *girin*, that settled the matter. To Chinese ears, *girin* sounded very much like *qilin*, the Chinese name of the unicorn. Presenting it as a gift was a way for the officials to ingratiate themselves with the court. The appearance of a *qilin* was regarded as proof of the virtue of the reigning emperor.

Despite the excitement caused by the giraffe, all foreign trade and travel were outlawed by imperial decree only a decade later. New decrees in 1449 and 1452 restricted foreign commerce even further, and each new law had increasingly severe penalties attached to it. The ban was eventually extended to all coastal shipping so that "there was not an inch of planking on the seas." In the end, the anti-commercial attitude of the Confucian scholars defeated the entrepreneurial curiosity of eunuchs like Zheng He. Restricting international trade was a way for the Confucians to impose their outlook on the country, but it was also a way to enhance their power at the expense of their opponents at court.

Read more online: https://hdl.handle.net/20.500.12434/e1f1ffa9

Yet, soon after Zheng He returned from these journeys, foreign travel was banned and all ocean-going ships destroyed. The Confucians at court, in their wisdom, decided that foreign contacts on this scale were too disruptive of the Chinese way of life. Although the policy on foreign trade would continue to fluctuate in response to various power struggles, China increasingly closed itself off from the rest of the world. Not coincidentally perhaps, extensive work on the structures known as the "Great Wall of China" took place at this time.

The Great Wall of China does not exist

When Yang Liwei, China's first astronaut, returned to earth on October 16, 2003, he reported to a disappointed Chinese public that the Great Wall was not in fact (as folk wisdom had it) visible from outer space. Yet, from the ground, the wall certainly has a very tangible presence. At Badaling, its most photographed section, conveniently located some 80 kilometers northwest of Beijing, there are millions of visitors every year. The wall, tourist guides tell us, is all together 21,196 kilometers long and thereby the largest man-made structure in the world, although, alas, several sections of it are in a sad state of disrepair. It was Qin Shi Huang, the First Emperor of China, who began work on the wall in the third century BCE, we are informed. It was then greatly extended in the late Ming dynasty.

And yet we can, on good authority, reject these observations as incorrect. It is not just that the wall is invisible from outer space; the Great Wall of China itself does not exist! Or rather, while walls of various kinds have been constructed in northern China at least since the sixth century BCE, they were never thought of as one coherent structure built with one purpose in mind. There are many walls, but no Great Wall. The ramparts that the First Emperor built quickly fell to ruin, and during the Tang and Song dynasties no similar fortifications were constructed. This is why there are many gaps between the structures and why walls in several places run parallel to each other. This is also why it is quite impossible to say how long the wall actually is. GPS technology does not help us here, since we first have to decide what to measure.

The Great Wall of China was constructed not in China, but in Europe. It was built, beginning in the seventeenth century, in the minds of European readers of the letters which Jesuit missionaries in China began sending back. The Jesuits were appealing to the long-established European fascination with things "Oriental" in order to generate support for their missionary project. In China, the most wondrous thing of all, they explained, is "the Great Wall." Naturally, subsequent European visitors insisted on being shown the attraction. After the Communists came to power in 1949, they adopted the European idea of the Great Wall as a national emblem, and a symbol of China's independence and self-reliance.

Read more online: https://hdl.handle.net/20.500.12434/9b9ffaf7

The Qing dynasty, 1644–1912, which replaced the Ming, was the last imperial dynasty. It was established by the Manchu tribes which overran Beijing in 1644, and who, in subsequent decades, proceeded to conquer the rest of the country. In contrast to the Mongols, the Qing emperors adopted many institutions from their predecessors such as the bureaucracy and the entrance examinations, and also many customs, such as the elaborate rituals which the emperors were required to perform. Yet the Qing were, at the same time, intensely proud of their Manchu heritage. Manchu princes were taught how to ride a horse and shoot arrows; at the imperial court in Beijing, visitors were often treated to displays of equestrian arts or, in winter, to skating competitions. The

Qing rulers were Confucians in the ceremonial sense of all emperors, but they were at the same time great patrons of Buddhist temples, especially of the form of Buddhism practiced in Tibet.

Two of the Qing emperors had particularly long and successful reigns. Emperor Kangxi ruled for sixty-one years, between 1661 and 1722, and his grandson, Emperor Qianlong, ruled for almost as long, from 1735 to 1796. These hundred-plus years were a time of great military expansion. This was when Taiwan was incorporated into the empire, together with vast areas to the north and the west, including much of Mongolia, Tibet, and Xinjiang.

Chinese pirates in Taiwan

Koxinga, 1624–1662, known in China as Zheng Chenggong, was a scholar, a pirate, and a Ming loyalist. He was born in Japan, the son of a Chinese father and a Japanese mother. At the age of seven, he moved to China where he successfully sat for the imperial exams. When Manchu tribes began their takeover of the country in 1644 and eventually established their own Qing dynasty, Koxinga continued to fight for the Ming cause. In 1656, partly helped by a big storm, he managed to destroy the Qing navy and continued on to the island of Taiwan. In the eyes of the new regime, he was an outlaw and a pirate.

In the early part of the seventeenth century, Taiwan was controlled by the Dutch East India Company. Read more: *De Vereenigde Oostindische Compagnie* at p. 34. Undaunted by the power of the Europeans, Koxinga laid siege to their major fortification, Fort Zeelandia, in the city of Tainan, eventually defeating them in 1661. Yet only a year later, when conducting raids in the Philippines, he contracted malaria and died, aged only thirty-seven. In 1683 the Qing army defeated Koxinga's descendants, claiming Taiwan as a part of the Chinese empire.

In today's Taiwan, there are temples dedicated to Koxinga, and he is remembered as a hero and as something of a saint. After 1949, when Guomindang, the Chinese nationalists, were defeated by Mao's Communists, they took refuge in Taiwan, just as Koxinga once did. And just like him, they regarded the island as a staging-post for a reconquest of the mainland. Yet Koxinga has been remembered in other ways as well. Taiwanese people who want to remain independent from China, emphasize that Koxinga effectively turned the island into a self-governing territory. To them, he is an independence fighter. The only Taiwanese who refuse to acknowledge Koxinga's memory are the original inhabitants, the aborigines, which make up about 2 percent of the island's population. As a result of Koxinga's occupation, they were pushed off the best agricultural land and their lucrative trade with the Dutch came to a halt.

When Chinese leaders in Beijing today insist that "Taiwan is an eternal part of the motherland," they are wrong. First, there were only aborigines on the island; then came the Portuguese, the Spaniards, and the Dutch. Only after that came the Chinese — and Koxinga, in the latter part of the eighteenth century, was the first Chinese ruler of the island.

Read more online: https://hdl.handle.net/20.500.12434/6a9acc1b

The Chinese waged war, if less successfully, in Vietnam and Burma as well, and stopped the Russians from advancing southward from Siberia.

> ### Treaties with the Russians
>
> To the Chinese, the Russians were not Europeans as much as yet another Asian tribe that made trouble for them on their northern frontier. This was particularly the case from the 1640s onward when Russia's imperial expansion through Siberia took them all the way to the Amur river basin, an area just north of the Manchu heartlands. Once they had conquered all of China in the 1680s, the Manchus decided to deal with this threat. It was clearly impossible for Russia to defend a territory this far away from Moscow, and in 1685 the Chinese forced them to back off. The two countries concluded a treaty, signed at Nerchinsk in 1689, which established a common border between them. In exchange for territorial concessions, the Russians obtained access to Chinese markets and the right to establish a Russian church in Beijing.
>
> The official version of the Treaty of Nerchinsk was written in Latin, with Russian and Manchu translations. Interestingly, there was no official Chinese text, and there were no Confucian scholars present at the negotiations. Throughout the talks, the Chinese treated the Russians with a surprising amount of respect. The tents of the two delegations were, for example, placed next to each other to symbolize their equal status, and the treaty itself made no reference to the Russians as tribute bearers. These concessions may be one reason why the treaty was never translated into Chinese. The Manchu rulers wanted peace on their northern borders, but they were not prepared to publicly renounce their belief in China's pre-eminence.
>
> A further treaty between China and Russia was signed at Kyakhta in 1727. Here, the earlier border was confirmed and new borders were drawn up which separated Mongolia — now under Chinese control — from Russia. The treaty led to a revival of the caravan trade — the Russians buying Chinese tea in exchange for furs. This was the first time the new European science of cartography was used in this part of the world.
>
> *Read more online:* https://hdl.handle.net/20.500.12434/2989c0dd

Even if the state treasury suffered as a result of these extensive campaigns, the economy of the country as a whole was thriving. Both Kangxi and Qianlong were patrons of scholarship and the arts. Kangxi's name is associated with a great character dictionary which helped to standardize the Chinese language. And on Qianlong's orders a great anthology of all Chinese books was compiled — containing some 3,450 works in 36,000 volumes.

> ### Yuanmingyuan — a Disneyland for one person
>
> The Forbidden Palace, in the center of Beijing, was not actually where the Chinese emperors lived. Rather, for most of the Qing dynasty, the emperors spent most of their time at Yuanmingyuan, an enclosed palace compound northwest of the capital.

Yuanmingyuan consisted of a wealth of separate buildings — palaces, temples, pagodas, pavilions, libraries, and tea-houses — set in a series of gardens that were connected through meandering paths and waterways. More than anything, Yuanmingyuan resembled a theme park, not too different from today's Disneyland. At Yuanmingyuan too, there were environments designed to transport the visitor to various exotic locations. There were rural scenes with rice paddies depicting the lives of Chinese peasants, gardens copied from Suzhou and Hangzhou, replicas of temples from Tibet, street scenes from Beijing, and even a set of European-style palaces. Instead of Disneyland's annual 15 million-plus visitors, however, Yuanmingyuan was intended for the amusement of only one person and his family — the emperor of China, his women, children, and the eunuch courtiers who attended to their needs.

Yuanmingyuan, much like Disneyland, was an idealized environment that expressed a particular view of the world. Walking through or rowing around his gardens, the emperor could experience times past and times future, exotic animals, flora and fauna, high mountains, oceans, the countryside, and the city, but also the world of learning and culture. Moreover, the emperor was the undisputed ruler of the whole thing! Everyone obeyed his will and everything was easy for him to manipulate. This was not least the case since the architects, much as the architects at Disneyland, made frequent use of models and miniaturization. Many of the buildings were built in slightly smaller versions than the originals, and even many of the trees, using bonsai techniques, were smaller than the real thing. Just like Disneyland, Yuanmingyuan was filled with mechanical devices. There were mechanical birds that flapped their wings and fountains that sprayed water at designated hours. In addition, the emperor had a vast collection of astronomical instruments, music boxes, and toys such as violin-playing monkeys, pecking hens, and waltzing rope-dancers. Yuanmingyuan was a play-house world. Read more: *The European destruction of Yuanmingyuan* at p. 192.

Read more online: https://hdl.handle.net/20.500.12434/4addcea9

Yet the Qing policies on foreign trade closely mirrored those of the Ming. During the Qing period too there were prohibitions and controls on such activity.

George Macartney at Qianlong's court

The Chinese tribute system did not only include Asian countries but a few European countries as well. There was so much for the Europeans to buy in China, and so many people to sell Europe-made goods to, yet the Chinese were very reluctant to grant them access. The official Confucian view was that only farmers, not merchants, contributed to the wealth of a nation. Besides, they worried about the social and cultural consequences of a foreign presence in the country. Eventually, trade was only allowed with one city, Guangzhou in the south, known as "Canton" to the foreigners. However, the British in particular regarded this as an unacceptable affront, and they dispatched a series of embassies to Beijing to try to convince the emperor to open up the country to their merchants. The most famous such embassy was led by George Macartney in 1792. Macartney made the six-month journey loaded with samples of British-made goods and with presents for the emperor. The idea was to set up an exhibit at the imperial court where Chinese officials could learn about British achievements. It would even be possible to order more British merchandise from a catalog that Macartney planned to hand out.

Once they arrived in Beijing, however, the British were required to go through the same ceremony as all tribute bearers. This included the *ketou*, the "three prostrations, and knockings of the head," which was the traditional way in which visitors showed their submission to the imperial throne. Macartney, however, refused to go through with the ritual. To him, the *ketou* reeked of religious worship, and he found it degrading to his country and himself. This, to the Chinese officials, made no sense. They could never understand why the British had made the long journey, and brought along all those presents, only to refuse to go through with the last set of formalities. The British were told in no uncertain terms that if they refused to *ketou* they might as well go home. They never got a trade deal with China.

Read more online: https://hdl.handle.net/20.500.12434/8a8ba62a

The overland system

The Chinese government, as we mentioned above, organized foreign relations in two distinct ways, depending on the degree of threat posed by the foreigners they confronted. Political entities to the south and the east of China never posed serious challenges since the land borders in these areas were well protected. Political entities to the north and the west were an entirely different matter. Here, land was only sparsely populated, the borders diffuse and impossible to secure with certainty. The result was an international system which took two quite distinct forms. Perhaps we could talk about the "overland" and the "tribute" systems respectively. Although there was a considerable overlap between the two — in particular, many of the overland states were also tribute bearers — the systems were nevertheless governed by quite different institutions, rules and norms.

It is easy to explain the attraction which China held for the peoples on the steppes. They were predominantly pastoralists who followed their herds — of goats, sheep and horses — to where they could find pasture. Nomads are always potentially on the move, and since they never stay long enough in one place, they cannot accumulate many resources. The Chinese, by contrast, were overwhelmingly farmers and some were city-dwellers, meaning that they lived sedentary lives and stayed in one place. Every Chinese family had a home, be it ever so humble, where they gathered possessions which they were prepared to defend with their lives. And, of course, some Chinese families were very wealthy indeed. To the nomads this constituted an obvious temptation. The nomads were interested in all kinds of resources as long as they were portable — gold and silver, animals, and women and children who could be turned into slaves.

It was always difficult for the Chinese to defend themselves against these threats. The steppes were easily crossed by the nomads on their swift horses, but they were far more difficult for the Chinese armies to cross on foot. Deserts like the Gobi and the Taklamakan constituted obstacles for both parties, but they were far more likely to keep the Chinese in than the nomads out. The borders which separated China and the peoples of the steppes were difficult not only to defend, but even to define. Moreover, the peoples of the steppes were ferocious warriors. Although they, initially at least, had little by means of military technology and few inventions of their own, they had access to the best horses in the world. On the back of a horse, they could cover large distances very quickly and attack an enemy at full speed, wielding their spears and firing off arrows with high precision. The perennial question for the Chinese was how best to deal with enemies such as these. The most obvious option was to pursue a defensive strategy, and this is what the Chinese did for much of their history. One way to do this was to build walls. Read more: *The Great Wall of China does not exist* at p. 26.

Impressive as these physical structures no doubt were, a defensive strategy never worked all that well. The Mongols soon learned how to besiege a city using catapults and various ingenious siege engines. For that reason, it was better for the Chinese to go on the offense, and this is what the emperors did on numerous occasions. The first Han emperor undertook large military campaigns which were continued by his successors. The Chinese built fortified towns on the steppe, moved convicts there and encouraged ordinary people to migrate to the frontier. Yet these settlements provided yet another target which the nomads could attack. And the nomads were infuriatingly difficult to defeat. They simply retreated across the steppe and would outrun, or ambush, any Chinese soldiers that came in pursuit of them. If the Chinese managed to hold on to territory they laid claim to, the nomads could indeed be pushed further and further away, yet this only meant that they would return on some other occasion to raid and pillage.

If defense was impossible and offense difficult, the question was what to do. The option which the imperial court eventually arrived at was to engage the peoples of the steppes in various ad hoc arrangements designed to give them a stake in the system. By establishing common institutions there was a chance that the nomads would gradually come to see things China's way. The most obvious option was to conclude a treaty. This was a strategy which the Chinese tried in relation to the Russians. Read more: *Treaties with the Russians* at p. 28.

Another strategy, used in relation to Tibetans and Mongols in particular, was to incorporate elements of the foreign culture into the practices of the Chinese state. Thus Tibetan-style Buddhism was a common point of reference during the Qing dynasty and Mongolian influences could be found everywhere. For example, the Qing emperors constructed an exact replica of the Potala palace in Lhasa at their summer retreat, and they established Tibetan temples in Beijing to which high-ranking Buddhist monks were invited. Whenever such cultural measures were unlikely to work, the Chinese government tried more hands-on tactics. They would, for example, give away imperial princesses as wives or consorts to the rulers on the steppes in order to bring their respective families closer together; or they would engage in elaborate gift exchanges in order to establish relationships of mutual dependence; or, in cases where the emperors were particularly desperate, they would even place themselves in the subordinate position of tribute bearers to the foreigners.

> ### Khotan to the Khotanese!
>
> Xinjiang is the westernmost province of China, a so-called "autonomous region," which borders Kazakhstan and other Central Asian countries. Its population is 43 percent Uyghur, who speak a Turkic language and practice Islam, but Han Chinese are almost as many — 41 percent — and the remainder are Kazakhs and other ethnic groups. Less than 5 percent of Xinjiang is suitable for human habitation; the rest consists of deserts and mountain ranges. Although various Chinese dynasties, including the Han, conducted military campaigns here, it was conquered only in 1759, and it is only since 1884 that Xinjiang came to constitute a Chinese province. Xinjiang literally means "new province" in Chinese. The Uyghurs themselves call their country "East Turkestan" or "Uyghuristan."
>
> Two thousand years ago, a Buddhist kingdom, Khotan, was established here. The caravan trade made Khotan prosperous, and thanks to rivers running from the Himalayas straight into the desert, it was possible to grow fruit and cereal. The people of Khotan cultivated silk and carved jade; they were devout Buddhists, loved literature and, according to visitors, they spent a lot of their time singing and dancing. Some spoke Chinese, others Tibetan and Indian languages. In 1006, the Khotan Kingdom fell to Muslim invaders.
>
> Reacting to attempts to make the region increasingly Chinese, Uyghur nationalists have recently made demands for independence. In July 2009, thousands of Uyghurs clashed with Han Chinese and some 200 people died, although Uyghur nationalists argue that the real death toll was considerably higher. Rioting has repeatedly taken place since and Xinjiang nationalists have been blamed for terrorist attacks throughout China. There have been reports that fighters from Xinjiang have joined Al-Qaeda, and in 2006, the U.S. army captured twenty-two Uyghurs in Afghanistan and sent them to the prison camp at Guantanamo Bay.
>
> In 2018, the Chinese authorities admitted to imprisoning Muslims in internment camps, which they referred to as "re-education centers." The aim of the camps is to replace Islam with Chinese values. Altogether, up to one million people have been detained. Recently, shops in Xinjiang have been forced to sell alcohol and tobacco; university students have been forbidden to fast during Ramadan; women wearing veils have been barred from public transportation or have had their clothes forcibly removed.
>
> *Read more online:* https://hdl.handle.net/20.500.12434/14fb6e88

The tribute system

In addition to these rather cynical methods, the imperial authorities relied on rituals to pacify the foreigners. These rituals applied to all foreigners, but they became particularly important in relation to foreigners to the south and the east of the country. Despite the official Confucian doctrine which said that China was self-sufficient in all things, many Southeast Asian merchants discovered the Chinese to be interested not only in spices and hardwoods but also in speciality items such as rhinoceros horns and ivory. And there was, of course, no end to the things which the foreigners might buy from the Chinese. During the Ming dynasty, much of this commerce was rather informally organized, but during Qing the city of Guangzhou, known as "Canton," in the south, became the one port through which all trade had to take place.

Since there was no way for foreigners to enter China except as tribute bearers, tribute bearers were what all foreigners who arrived in China became. This included foreign merchants. Trade was considered a lowly occupation in China and merchants were, officially at least, regarded as an inferior social class. Confucian scholars pointed out that, whilst farmers toiled in the fields, merchants got rich without breaking a sweat. Lacking an economic rationale for the activity, the imperial authorities instead interpreted foreign trade in cultural terms. China, they argued, was the most sophisticated country in the world and, by comparison, everyone else was a "barbarian." Barbarians, however, were not to be feared as much as pitied, and the fact that they had showed up on China's doorstep proved that they were willing to learn from the Chinese. As such they were to be treated benevolently. By coming to China, and by submitting themselves to the rules prescribed by the tribute system, the foreigners assumed their designated place in the Chinese order of things.

A detailed protocol regulated these visits. Each mission was not to exceed one hundred men, of whom only twenty were allowed to proceed to the capital while the rest remained at the border. On their way to Beijing, each delegation was fed, housed and transported at the emperor's expense; and once they arrived they stayed in the official "Residence for Tributary Envoys," where they were given a statutory amount of silver, rice, and other foodstuffs. Both coming and going, they were accompanied by imperial troops who both protected them and controlled their movements. The foreign visitors were debriefed by court officials who inquired about the conditions obtaining in their respective countries. The gifts which they brought along, the rules stipulated, were to consist of "products native to each land." Often, these were quite humble items — the representatives of a monastic community in Tibet, for example, might only give a few bottles of yak milk. In each case the emperor spent far more on the gifts he gave the foreigners in return. This was one of the ways in which the emperor showed his benevolence.

The highlight of the mission was the audience with the emperor. On the chosen day, the visitors were woken up as early as 3 a.m. and taken to the imperial palace where they spent hours waiting, sipping tea and eating sweetmeats. At long last, they were accompanied into a large hall where many other delegations had already assembled. There were other foreign envoys too, but also delegations from all over China, and state officials of various ranks. Then the emperor appeared and all the visiting delegations were required to perform a *ketone* — a "kowtow" — to symbolize their respect and their submission. Read more: *George Macartney at Qianlong's court* at p. 29.

The emperor graciously accepted their tributes, spoke kindly to them, and gave gifts in return. Then the delegations exited the hall one by one, again while kowtowing. The audience was thereby concluded. During the following days, the delegations were given more gifts and repeatedly wined and dined, even if the emperor himself no longer made an appearance. Then the foreigners were quite unceremoniously told that it was time for them to leave. They were accompanied back to the port where they had entered the country and reminded that they should come back again in the stipulated number of years.

During the Ming dynasty there were altogether 123 states which participated in these ceremonies, although many of the entities in question showed up only once and some of the more obscure names on the list may indeed have been fictional. During the Qing period, the records became more accurate, with a core group of states regularly undertaking missions. These included Korea, Siam, the Ryukyu Islands, Annam, Sulu, Burma, Laos, Turfan, but also the Portuguese, the Dutch, and the British. The Europeans were represented by their respective trading companies.

De Vereenigde Oostindische Compagnie

Trading with Asia was a lucrative business, but also a risky one. It was a long journey to India and back, and any number of things could happen on the way. In order to pool the risks, merchants would at first only invest in a portion of a ship. Their portions came to be known as "shares." Later they invested not in individual ships, but in the businesses which organized the shipping. This is how the first "joint-stock companies" came to be established. These are the origins of the first business corporations.

Another way to deal with risk was to ask for a monopoly on the trade with a particular part of the world. European kings were happy to sell such monopolies as a way to raise revenue. This is how "East India companies" came to be established in one country after another. The English East India Company, 1600, and the Dutch Vereenigde Oostindische Compagnie, VOC, 1602, were the most famous ones, and it was the VOC that ruled the waves. The company bought tea and porcelain in China, established trading posts all over Asia, and founded a fully-fledged colony in today's Indonesia. At the Beurs, the stock exchange in Amsterdam, not only VOC shares could be bought, but all kinds of other shares too. The Amsterdam Beurs was a veritable one-stop-shop for financial services. You could buy maritime insurance, organize bank transfers, cash checks, and trade currencies. "Dutch finance" is the origin of today's financial service industry.

Dutch traders are also the ones who came up with many of the place names we find today on a world map. Zeeland is a Dutch province and that is why two islands east of Australia came to be known as "New Zealand." Australia itself was for a long

> time known as "New Holland," and New York was called "New Amsterdam." In fact, Harlem is a Dutch city and not only a part of Manhattan — although the Dutch spell it "Haarlem." In the nineteenth century, Chinese laborers came to work in "the Dutch West Indies." That is why there are, to this day, people in the Caribbean who speak both Chinese and Dutch.
>
> *Read more online:* https://hdl.handle.net/20.500.12434/6f48caee

In general, the closer the country was located in relation to China, the more often it had to present itself at the imperial court. The Koreans were put on a three-year cycle and they were thereby the most frequent visitors. Since they had to travel so far, the Europeans were supposed to make an appearance only every seventh year, but these regulations were, in practice, never followed. All in all, the Portuguese only made four visits to the imperial court, the Dutch also four, and the British three. The Russians showed up as well, altogether some twelve times, but since they were a part of the overland system — they came from the north after all — particular rules applied to them.

One may wonder why the foreigners agreed to submit themselves to these exacting requirements. The answer is that they wanted to trade with the Chinese. Playing along with the imperial rituals, the envoys who went to Beijing would sometimes find ways to buy and sell things on the sly, but more importantly, their compatriots who remained at the border would set up temporary markets where trade would be brisk for a few weeks. The profits earned in this fashion were more than sufficient to justify the trouble of the journey. Once they had appeared in Beijing, moreover, their countrymen who regularly traded in the city of Guangzhou in the south would be free to pursue their activities as before. In addition, there were political gains to be made. Whenever a new king ascended the throne of a state that was a member of the tribute system, he would send an envoy to China. If the envoy was granted an audience, the authority of the ruler who sent him was impossible to dispute. He was, after all, recognized by the emperor of China himself. Returning home, the diplomat would bring the emperor's official seal with him as a sign of this new status.

The tribute system was unquestionably hierarchical. It was China that dictated the terms, and no one else was in a position to influence the logic that constituted the system. The rituals all emphasized submission to the imperial throne, yet the relationship entailed obligations on both sides. Just like a dutiful son, the foreign visitor should be obedient and respectful, and just as a virtuous father, the emperor should care about those who enjoyed his benevolence. Politically speaking, the imperial center controlled the periphery only in the loosest possible sense. Most obviously, the imperial authorities made no attempts to interfere with the independence of states that came to visit them. Read more: *Chinese pirates in Taiwan* at p. 27.

Moreover, if a state decided not to show up, there was not all that much that the Chinese authorities could do. As long as the foreigners were not making trouble, the imperial authorities much preferred to leave them alone. The units of the system were hierarchically ordered but, at the same time, quite free to govern themselves.

A Japanese international system?

Once the first contacts were established with China in the fifth century CE, the inhabitants of the islands of Japan maintained a close relationship to the Asian mainland. It is unclear how the Japanese first came into contact with China, but it is easy to imagine that Japanese fishermen were washed up somewhere on the shores of the Asian mainland after a storm. When they eventually made it back to Japan, they had amazing stories to tell about all the wonders they had seen. Hearing such tales, the local rulers dispatched better-organized delegations, and soon the Japanese embarked on regular study-visits. Eventually, the Japanese imported an entire culture from China, including arts and technology, religion, a writing system, political and social thought, and associated political and social institutions. The Japanese often changed these imports to fit their own needs, and many of the changes were radical enough, but Japanese society was nevertheless profoundly altered as a result of the interaction. Yet Japan was a tribute-bearing state, and an official member of the Chinese-run international system, only for a few hundred years. Once the Mongols tried, and failed, to invade the country at the end of the thirteenth century, relations could not continue as before. Read more: *Kamikaze* at p. 115.

The Japanese did not want anything to do with an aggressive and expansionist China. Although informal commercial contacts continued and thrived, no more official delegations were dispatched to the Chinese court. The imported Chinese culture continued to evolve, but in a distinctly Japanese fashion.

Among the institutions borrowed from China was that of an emperor, yet the emperor of Japan was nowhere near as powerful as his Chinese counterpart. Instead, real power in the country was in the hands of various local and regional leaders, who had a strong and largely independent position in relation to each other. Japan was decentralized, with many different centers vying for political power. There was, for example, a fundamental tension between the leaders who controlled the Kanto region, where today's Tokyo is situated, and the leaders who controlled the Kansai region, the area around today's Osaka and Kyoto. During the Kamakura period, 1185–1333, power was taken over by military leaders, the *shoguns*, for whom Kanto was their center. The emperor, residing in Kansai, was a figurehead, a symbolic leader, and for most of the country's history he was more or less ignored. An emperor in the sixteenth century even had to sell his own calligraphy in order to pay his household expenses. Yet the power of the *shogun* was quite limited as well. This was particularly the case during the Sengoku period, 1467–1573, which was Japan's own version of China's Warring States period. The Sengoku period was a time of lawlessness, heroism, and political intrigue with vast armies of samurai pitted against each other.

> ### The samurai in fact and fiction
>
> The samurai, or what the Japanese refer to as *bushi*, first rose to prominence during the Kamakura period, 1185–1333. They were soldiers who helped enforce the peace and secured people's property, but the samurai were also known to practice and to support the arts. Many art forms which today we think of as quintessentially Japanese were first developed among them — including Nō theater, tea ceremony, haiku poetry, and, of course, martial arts such as archery and swordsmanship. Many samurai were Zen Buddhists, a version of the Buddhist teaching which emphasized meditation and stoicism in the face of death.
>
> During the Sengoku period, 1467–1573, the samurai made up the foot soldiers of the vast armies that were pitted against each other. Once the wars were over, some of them became bureaucrats in the new Tokugawa regime, while others came to work for various regional rulers, or *daimyos*. A few of them became *ronin* — masterless samurai — who roamed the roads of Japan looking for work and for adventure. During the Tokugawa period, the samurai class made up perhaps 10 percent of Japan's population. The samurai were abolished in 1873 when Japan established a conscripted army. Their titles and privileges were exchanged for government bonds.
>
> According to the code of the samurai, loyalty is the supreme value, and a good samurai should unquestioningly follow the wishes of his master, even if it implies certain death. *Seppuku* — what some non-Japanese refer to as "harakiri" — is the inevitable fate of a samurai who fails to live up to his obligations. Yet *bushido*, understood as a distinct chivalric code, was only developed at the end of the nineteenth century. The Bushido ideals provided a means of instilling loyalty in a by now largely urbanized, and increasingly unruly, Japanese population.
>
> Since 1945, the world of the samurai has been a staple of Japanese films and TV dramas. The most artistically significant examples of this output are the films directed by Akita Kurosawa. His leading actor, Toshihiro Mifune, with his physical style of acting, has come to personify the way the samurai talked and carried themselves. Kurosawa has both influenced and been influenced by cowboy movies. Kurosawa's *The Seven Samurai* (1954) was made into *The Magnificent Seven* in 1960, and his *Yojimbo* (1961) was made into *A Fistful of Dollars* (1964), starring Clint Eastwood. In both cases, entire scenes were lifted from Kurosawa's work.
>
> *Read more online:* https://hdl.handle.net/20.500.12434/6f7c08f4

The Sengoku period ended in the year 1600 after the Battle of Sekigahara when one of the military leaders, Tokugawa Ieyasu, decisively defeated the others. This inaugurated the Tokugawa period, 1600–1868 — also known as the "Edo period" — which brought peace to the country but also economic development and great social and cultural change. In the 1630s, the Tokugawa rulers banned foreign trade, and limited contacts with the rest of the world. Foreign missionaries were expelled, Japanese people were banned from building ocean-going ships, and Japanese people abroad were not allowed to return home. Japan was a *sakoku*, a "closed country," and trade was limited to a few ships per year which entered at the only accessible port, Nagasaki in the far south. According to the official rhetoric, Japan was self-sufficient and its people should not waste their precious silver on luxury items from abroad. Yet, unofficial contacts of various kinds continued, not least silk trade with merchants in Korea and the Ryukyu Islands.

> ### The Ryukyu Islands as the center of the world
>
> The Ryukyu Islands are a chain of islands that extends from the southernmost Japanese island of Kyushu, all the way to Taiwan. From the fifteenth until the nineteenth century the islands constituted an independent kingdom which played a central role in the trading networks of East Asia. From their capital on Okinawa, the largest island in the group, the Ryukyu kings dispatched tribute-bearing missions not only to China, but also to Korea and Japan where their colorful clothes and exotic gifts met with much amazement. Read more: *Processions through Japan* at p. 39. During the Ming era, Ryukyu merchants also traded in Chinese ports, and they traveled to Southeast Asia where they exchanged Chinese products for spices, rhinoceros horn, ivory, and frankincense.
>
> During the Ming dynasty, 1368–1644, many Chinese people settled on the islands, some working as officials for the Ryukyu government. The importance of the islands increased dramatically once the Chinese authorities decided to limit trade with the rest of the world and to ban ocean-going ships. Since Ryukyu merchants were exempt from these rules, they could increase their share of the now even more lucrative Chinese market. In 1609, the islands were invaded by soldiers from Satsuma in southern Japan. Although they maintained their independence even after this date, the islanders were forced to start paying taxes to the Japanese. During the *sakoku* period, when Japan also banned foreign trade, merchants from Satsuma continued to transport their wares to China via the Ryukyus. The Ryukyu Islands were formally annexed by Japan in 1879. The last Ryukyu king, Shō Tai, died in Tokyo in 1901.
>
> During World War II an intense battle, the Battle of Okinawa, was fought there in which some 75,000 Japanese and 15,000 American soldiers died. The ferocity of the fighting contributed to the American decision to use the atomic bomb in order to speed up Japan's surrender. Although America's occupation of Japan ended in 1952, it took until 1972 before Okinawa was returned to Japan. The United States still maintains a number of military installations there. The American military presence has been a source of considerable controversy, not least as a result of several highly publicized rape cases involving American soldiers.
>
> *Read more online:* https://hdl.handle.net/20.500.12434/e1bf34d6

Although Japan was now pacified — historians often talk about a *Pax Tokugawa*, the "Tokugawa peace" — the country was not a unified whole. Instead, various regional rulers, known as the *daimyo*, continued to affirm their independence, each one ruling a region, or *han*, of their own. The number of *han* varied over time, but for most of the

Tokugawa period there were at least 250 of them. The Tokugawa family controlled the largest of these regions and also the largest cities, but over something like three quarters of the *han*, they had no direct influence. The *daimyo* raised their own taxes, had their own armies, police forces, legal and educational systems, and they pursued independent social and economic policies. In fact, each *han* even had its own currency, and at the end of the Tokugawa period there were hundreds of separate forms of exchange in circulation. While the *shoguns* in Edo reserved the right to put down peasant rebellions wherever they occurred, their military power was restricted by the fact that they could not tax people outside of their own lands.

The question of how best to characterize Japan during this period is a difficult one. The most obvious answer is to see Japan as an ordinary state, yet this description is surely incomplete. The Tokugawa government was not fully sovereign since it did not have full control over the country's territory and it had no foreign policy. Perhaps Japan is better described as an international system — a mini-system — in its own right. If we see Japan as an international system we need to explain why it was so peaceful. One reason was a small set of regulations which applied equally to the country as a whole, involving, for example, restrictions on military installations. Yet the most spectacular feature of the Tokugawa system was the institution of *sankin-kōtai*, "alternate attendance," according to which the *daimyo* were required to spend every second year in Edo, where the *shogun* was able to keep a close watch on them. Moreover, during the year they spent at home, taking care of the business of their respective *hans*, they were required to leave their wives and children in Edo, where they effectively would serve as the *shogun's* hostages. If a *daimyo* in some way misbehaved, it was easy for the *shogun* to seek retribution against his family.

Processions through Japan

One of the institutions that kept Japan unified during the Tokugawa period was the system of "alternate attendance," *sankin kotai*. According to the rules of the system, the 250-plus *daimyo*s had to move once a year, either from their own capital to Edo, or from Edo to their own capital. These movements took the shape of long processions which, in the case of the larger *han*, could include up to 2,500 people, and which for distant regions might take up to fifty days to complete. Aware of the attention they attracted, the *daimyo* and their retainers did their best to put on a good show. The lance-bearers were particularly admired and the tallest and most handsome men were usually picked for this job. In fact, much of what we today think of as paraphernalia belonging to the samurai class — helmets, swords, and equipment for horses — was originally produced not for use in battles, but for these ceremonial occasions. Worried about a build-up of military forces in Edo, and concerned about the costs involved, the *shoguns* periodically sought to restrict the number of soldiers a *daimyo* could assemble, but the restrictions had little effect. For the *han*, it was a matter of prestige to send as many men as possible. Sometimes they would hire temporary laborers to swell the ranks of the procession just as it entered a large city.

During the *sakoku* period, when Japan was closed off from the outside world, there was still a trickle of foreign merchants who had official permission to visit the country. Showing up in Nagasaki in the south, they made the long journey on foot to Edo. Much as the processions which took the *daimyos* back and forth to the capital, the processions of these foreigners attracted much attention. There were delegations of merchants from Korea and the Ryukyu islands, but also from the Dutch East India Company. Read more: *The Ryukyu islands as the center of the world* at p. 38.

Read more online: https://hdl.handle.net/20.500.12434/2a7a1229

Further reading

Barfield, Thomas J. *The Perilous Frontier*: *Nomadic Empires and China, 221 B.C. to AD 1757*. London: Wiley-Blackwell, 1992.

Crossley, Pamela. *A Translucent Mirror*: *History and Identity in Qing Imperial Ideology*. Berkeley: University of California Press, 1999.

Elliott, Mark C. *Emperor Qianlong*: *Son of Heaven, Man of the World*. London: Longman, 2009.

Huang, Ray. *1587, A Year of no Significance*: *The Ming Dynasty in Decline*. New Haven: Yale University Press, 1982.

Jansen, Marius B. *The Making of Modern Japan*. Cambridge: Belknap Press, 2002.

Johnston, Alastair Iain. *Cultural Realism*: *Strategic Culture and Grand Strategy in Chinese History*. Princeton: Princeton University Press, 1998.

Kang, David C. *East Asia Before the West*: *Five Centuries of Trade and Tribute*. New York: Columbia University Press, 2010.

Perdue, Peter C. *China Marches West*: *The Qing Conquest of Central Eurasia*. Cambridge: Belknap Press, 2010.

Toby, Ronald P. *State and Diplomacy in Early Modern Japan*: *Asia in the Development of the Tokugawa Bakufu*. Stanford: Stanford University Press, 1991.

Waldron, Arthur A. *The Great Wall of China*: *From History to Myth*. Cambridge: Cambridge University Press, 1992.

Timeline

475–221 BCE	The Warring States period. Warfare between seven separate states. Many schools of Chinese philosophy established.
221 BCE	Qin Shi Huang, the First Emperor, establishes the Qin dynasty. Lasts only 15 years.
206 BCE–220 CE	The Han dynasty, established by Liu Bang.
618–907	The Tang dynasty, with Xi'an as its capital.
629	The monk Xuanzang starts his journey to India.
960	The Song dynasty is established.
1127	The Song move their court to Hangzhou.
1279	The Mongols overrun the Song and establish the Yuan dynasty.
1368	The Ming dynasty is established.
1405	Zheng He embarks on his first voyage to Southeast Asia and the Indian Ocean.
1414	A giraffe arrives in Beijing from Melinda on the coast of East Africa.
1600	The Battle of Sekigahara. The Tokugawa shogunate is established.
1633	First legislation which restricts Japanese interactions with the rest of the world.
1644–1912	The Qing dynasty, established by Manchu armies which invade China.
1868	The Meiji Restoration. The Tokugawa shogunate falls and the Japanese emperor is restored.

Short dictionary

bushi, Japanese	Collective term for Japanese martial arts and the ethical code of the samurai.
daimyo, Japanese	Literally, "big name." Title given to the rulers of Japan's semi-autonomous provinces during the Tokugawa period.
dao, Chinese	Literally, "the way." Collected wisdom regarding morality, longevity and prosperity associated with Daoism.
fajia, Chinese	"Legalism," one of the main schools of Chinese political philosophy, developed during the Warring States period. The Legalists advocated ruthless and authoritarian policies.
han, Japanese	Semi-autonomous province during the Tokugawa period. Ruled by a *daimyo*.
hanren, Chinese	Name for the Chinese people. Named after the Han dynasty.
ketone, Mandarin Chinese, from the Cantonese *kautau*	"Kowtow." Ceremonial Chinese greeting. "Three prostrations and nine knockings of the head."
Pax Tokugawa, Latin	"The Tokugawa peace." Term used by historians for the pacification of Japan which took place during the Tokugawa period.
ronin, Japanese	"Masterless samurai," a samurai working for himself or for any master ready to employ him. *Ronin* are commonly featured in samurai movies.
sakoku, Japanese	Literally, "closed country." The severe restrictions on interactions with foreign countries imposed by the Tokugawa shoguns, 1633–1853.
sankin-kōtai, Japanese	"System of alternate attendance." The system whereby *daimyos* were required to spend every second year in Edo, the Tokugawa capital.
shogun, Japanese	Military leader and de facto ruler of Japan during the Tokugawa period.

Think about

The warring states period
- How should we describe the earliest Chinese states?
- Why was the Warring States Period such a culturally dynamic period in Chinese history?
- How did the First Emperor come to power?

The development of the Chinese state
- What is "the Mandate of Heaven"? How is this mandate gained and lost?
- In what ways are the different dynasties similar to each other? In what ways are they different?
- How should we best describe the bureaucracy of the Chinese empire?

The overland system
- Which political entities were included in the overland system?
- Why did the Chinese empire have such problems dealing with the societies of the Central Asian steppes?
- Which solutions did the Chinese empire come up with? How efficient were they?

The tribute system
- Which states were included in the tribute system?
- Give a brief description of how the tribute system worked.
- Why did political entities from so far away agree to come to China? In what ways did the system benefit China?

A Japanese international system?
- Can Tokugawa Japan be described as an "international system"?
- Describe relations between the shogun, the emperor and the daimyos.
- What were the features of the so-called sankin kotai system?

Map of India from Abraham Ortelius, *Theatrum orbis terrarum* (Antverpiae: Apud Aegid. Coppenium Diesth, 1570). p. 211, https://archive.org/details/theatrumorbister00orte

3. India and Indianization

India, just as China, is not a country as much as a world in itself. Indeed, it is often referred to as a "subcontinent" which includes not only India, but today's Pakistan, Bangladesh, and Sri Lanka as well. The history of India is long, as long as China's. The first human settlements there go back at least 9,000 years. In the valley of the Indus River, the first organized states were established some 5,000 years ago. The ancient city of Harappa, in today's Pakistan, traded with Egypt and Mesopotamia, made goods in copper and bronze, and used an early form of writing. India has always surprised visitors with the enormous size of its population. There are more than two thousand separate ethnic groups here, often with their own language and customs. In addition, India is the origin of two world religions, Hinduism and Buddhism, and of smaller religions too, such as Jainism and Sikhism. By 2024, it is estimated that India will overtake China as the country with the largest population in the world.

Although both China and India have a long history, India's is more difficult to summarize. From the third century BCE, China called itself an empire and although various dynasties replaced one another, it is possible to tell the history of China as a story of one specific political entity. In the case of India, there is no single political subject about which a story can be told. Instead, various states and empires have replaced one another in the course of the millennia. These different units have been independent and often at war with each other, although there have also been periods when most, or at least much, of the subcontinent has been united. Today India is a country, but throughout most of its history, it would best be described as an international system. At the same time, it was an international system which was held together by a strong sense of shared identity — based above all on Hindu practices and beliefs.

A further similarity with China is that India too has constantly been menaced by invasions. The invaders have typically swept down from the northwest, across the mountain passes of what today are Afghanistan and Pakistan. The reason for the invasions was always the same: the extraordinary wealth of the Indian subcontinent. In India everything grew in great abundance; in the fertile rice fields of the south it was possible to gather two, sometimes three, harvests per year. The surplus agricultural goods financed an elaborate hierarchy of social classes and powerful states with rulers

© 2019 Erik Ringmar, CC BY 4.0   https://doi.org/10.11647/OBP.0074.03

famous for their ostentatious displays of wealth. In the Classical period — roughly during the first millennium of the Common Era — India must have been the richest country in the world. And well after that — during the Mughal period — India continued to be known as the *emporium mundi*, the world's greatest hub for trade and manufacturing. In India it was possible to find whatever one wanted and this was why everyone desired to be there. Those who had nothing to sell, like the invading armies coming from the northwest, took what they wanted by force.

The Mughals were one of these invaders. Originating in the region which today is Uzbekistan, they established themselves in India in 1526. During the following three hundred years they were to rule almost all of the subcontinent. The Mughals were Muslims and their culture was to have a profound impact on Indian society. Yet Hindu traditions remained strong. Even the most powerful of foreign conquerors had to make compromises with Indian ways of life, and eventually they blended in with the traditional culture. In addition, India has exercised a powerful influence over the rest of Asia, and over Southeast Asia in particular. Starting in the first centuries of the Common Era, Indian cultural practices, and ideas regarding society and religion were disseminated all around the Indian Ocean, leading to new cultural combinations. We can talk about this as a process of "Indianization." It is because of this Indianization that today's Thailand is a Buddhist country, that Angkor Wat in Cambodia was originally built as a Hindu temple complex, and why a majority of people in Indonesia are Muslims. The influence of Indian culture on non-Indians remains strong to this day — although the impact is now felt on a worldwide scale.

Vedic India

The first written records of Indian history are the *Vedas*, a large body of religious texts dating from around 1500 BCE. The *Vedas* are based on secret oral teachings provided by gurus (religious teachers) and they heavily emphasise rituals, including sacrifice of various kinds. Because of the importance of the *Vedas*, this early stage in the history of the subcontinent is often known as the "Vedic period." The *Vedas* are written in a rather cryptic language and are difficult to decipher. The Upanishads, commentaries on the *Vedas*, which originated some time around 500 BCE, provide more comprehensive, and comprehensible, statements of this early version of Hinduism.

The followers of the *Vedas* were the Indo-Europeans sometimes known as "Aryans." The Indo-Europeans, at least according to one prominent theory, came from Central Asia some time around 2000 BCE and established themselves in northern India, along the plains of the Ganges River, as well as on the Deccan Plateau in central and southern parts of the subcontinent. The Indo-Europeans were originally pastoralists and even though they increasingly turned to farming, cattle breeding continued to be important in their lives. The cow was already at this time a sacred animal. Not that much is known about the Indo-Europeans, but the *Vedas* contain traces of their rituals. Their kings sacrificed horses and they drank *soma*, a potion with magical properties.

Horse sacrifices

One of the rituals described in the *Vedas* is *ashvamedha*, horse-sacrifice. This was a political ritual and it concerned the king's right to rule. First a horse, always a stallion, would be allowed to wander around freely for a year, accompanied by members of the king's retinue. If the horse roamed off into the lands of an enemy, that territory had to be occupied by the king. Meanwhile, any of the king's rivals were free to challenge the horse's attendants to a fight. If they did, and the horse was killed, the king would lose his right to rule. If, on the other hand, the horse still was alive after a year, it was taken back to the king's court. Here it was bathed, anointed with butter, decorated with golden ornaments and sacrificed. Once this ritual was completed, the king was considered as the undisputed ruler of all the land which the horse had covered. All kings in Vedic India performed the *ashvamedha*, and the ritual declined only in the latter part of the Gupta period.

Central Asia, not India, is where the horse originates and the *ashvamedha* is one piece of evidence which locates the Indo-Europeans outside of India. To the people of the steppe, the horse was a sacred animal, and horses were often buried together with dead kings. Horse sacrifices have been carried out all over the Eurasian landmass — in China, Iran, Armenia, among the Greeks and the Romans, even in Ireland. In the Irish ritual, the king had sexual intercourse with a mare who then was killed, dismembered and cooked in a cauldron in which the king proceeded to swim and drink from the broth.

New-age Hindu spiritualists have recently tried to revive the *ashvamedha* ritual, but they use a statue of a horse rather than an actual animal. In other contemporary rituals, live horses are worshiped rather than killed. Apparently, devotion to the horse can help you defeat enemies and clear debts. The first critics of the *ashvamedha* appeared among members of the Charvaka school of philosophy in the seventh century BCE. The Charvakas were skeptics and atheists. They had no doubt that horse sacrifices were invented by "buffoons, knaves, and demons."

Read more online: https://hdl.handle.net/20.500.12434/c84d3ad7

During the first millennium BCE there were a large number of different ethnic groups and tribes located on the plains of the Ganges River. They formed *janapada*, or "nations," which gradually came to be associated with a particular piece of territory. All major geographical regions of contemporary India can be traced back to these Vedic nations. Already these early societies were divided into distinct social classes. The priests, or *brahmins*, formed the leading class; the warriors, or *kshatriya*, came next, then craftsmen and merchants, and finally the servant class. These four main groups were later subdivided into a multitude of different castes, each one responsible for a certain task and governed by its respective rules. The caste system as a whole was maintained through religious sanctions. You were born into a caste, into a certain job, and a social position, and there was almost nothing you could do about it. This was the world which the gods had ordained. Later indigenous religions, such as Buddhism, Jainism and Sikhism, gained adherents by rejecting this rigid view of society.

Around 600 BCE, the large number of *janapada* had been reduced to sixteen major ones, known as *mahajanapada*, "great nations." The military competition between them forced each state to protect itself against its neighbors. This, in turn, required more powerful armies. But more powerful armies required a more powerful economic base, and more efficient state machinery. This is how — much as in China, and roughly at the same time — military competition came to encourage economic and political change. Much as in China, the competition also produced something akin to a philosophical revolution. The courts of the ruler of each *mahajanapada* became centers of scholarship and learning, visited by wandering teachers eager to offer advice. Religion was discussed but many philosophical schools developed too, including rationalists, materialists and atheists. In addition, advances were made in sciences like astronomy and mathematics.

Indian mathematics

The number system which the world uses today originated in India in the first centuries of the Common Era. The numbers are usually referred to as "Arabic" since the Europeans obtained them from the Arabs, but in the Middle East, they are known as "Indian" since the Arabs obtained them from India. Mathematics emerged as a separate field of study in Vedic times, but it was in the Gupta period that the greatest advances were made. Indians learned from Greek mathematicians but they made seminal contributions of their own. They were the first to make use of decimals and the number zero. They used negative numbers too and they beat Pythagoras to his famous theorem. Indian mathematicians calculated the value of π, *pi*, with a very high degree of precision, and determined the circumference of the earth and the timing of lunar and solar eclipses. In the fifteenth century, Kerala, in the far south, was home to a school of mathematics which developed trigonometric functions.

In India, mathematical knowledge always developed in conjunction with its practical application. Already the Harappa civilization, some 2,500 years BCE, used geometry in order to calculate the size of fields. In Vedic culture, maths was used to determine the size of altars and for deciding when to engage in various religious rituals. Likewise, the notions of zero and infinity both have their origins in religious speculations. The world as we know it contains no "nothing"; everything we see around us is something. Yet in Buddhist philosophy, nothingness is a key concept and the goal of meditation is to empty one's mind. Nothingness, to a Buddhist, is real. Meanwhile, the Jains were fascinated by very large numbers. They told stories of gods who appeared millions of times, millions of years apart. The better you can understand the infinite, they argued, the better you can understand the divine.

The history of mathematics is a great example of a civilizational exchange. The Indians learned maths from the Greeks and taught it to the Arab world, who in turn taught the Europeans. At each stage, the knowledge was transformed and improved upon. To this day only some 10 percent of all the manuscripts on Sanskrit science have been published and much remains to be properly studied. There may be many surprising discoveries to be made.

Read more online: https://hdl.handle.net/20.500.12434/df19743e

It was in the late Vedic period, between 500 and 200 BCE, that the great epic poems, the *Mahabharata* and the *Ramayana*, were composed.

The *Mahabharata*

The *Mahabharata* is an epic poem that recounts the story of the dynastic struggles over the throne of Hastinapur, a kingdom in northern India, in the thirteenth and fourteenth centuries BCE. Hastinapur was ruled by the Kuru clan which had two competing branches, the Kaurava and the Pandava. The struggle culminated in the battle of Kurukshetra in which the Pandavas were victorious. The length of the epic is extraordinary — more than 200,000 verses and a total of 1.8 million words. Despite its format, the *Mahabharata* is regularly performed all over India, with sleep and food breaks both for the audience and the cast. The epic is regarded as a historical account, as a moral tale, but also as a basic statement of the principles of Hinduism. There are love stories here too, tales of deceit and revenge, and some great fight scenes.

The principal figure in the epic is Krishna, who is the god of compassion, tenderness, and love, but he is also an embodiment of the universal being. The way he is depicted reflects these varying roles — sometimes he is a god-child playing the flute, sometimes a prankster stealing butter, or a lover surrounded by adoring women. In a part of the *Mahabharata* known as the *Bhagavad Gita*, Krishna is a chariot-driver who gives a lecture to Arjuna, a disciple, in which he explains the difference between just and unjust wars and the importance of loyalty to one's family. We also find religious themes concerning the relationship between the soul of each individual and the soul of the world. Indeed, the warlike setting can itself be interpreted allegorically — the relevant battle concerns not political power but the moral struggles of human life.

The *Mahabharata* has had a profound influence on Indian culture and it continues to inspire playwrights and artists to this day. It has had an impact on the Bollywood film industry too. Read more: *Curries, Bollywood and the Beatles in India* at p. 63. This is obvious, for example, in the narrative techniques used in Indian movies with their many side-stories, back-stories, and stories-within-stories. Indian movies too are rather long-winded and they make heavy demands on the ability of the audience to follow an elaborate plot.

Read more online: https://hdl.handle.net/20.500.12434/c4c2e1d2

The leaders of the *mahajanapadas* also needed political advice. This was provided in works such as the *Arthashastra*.

Arthashastra

The *Arthashastra* is a manual on statecraft allegedly written by Kautilya, also known as Chanakya. Kautilya was an adviser to Chandragupta, the first king of the Maurya Empire, in the third century BCE. The *Arthashastra* is a "mirror of princes,"

> a book of secret advice given directly to a ruler by one of his advisers. As such it is a contribution to the same genre as Niccolò Machiavelli's *The Prince*. Both books describe politics as a ruthless game of power, yet the *Arthashastra* is by far the more cynical. A king, Kautilya explained, has to lie and deceive, torture, imprison and kill, and these acts must sometimes be carried out also against the innocent and for no other reason than to intimidate others. Friends and family members are targets too — in fact, one should be particularly suspicious of friends and family. It is better to be feared than loved.
>
> The manuscript of the *Arthashastra* was rediscovered only in 1905. The find produced a sensation since it showed a very different image of ancient India than the one commonly held at the time. It is the only text from the Vedic period which does not deal with religious or philosophical matters. Kautilya's society was thoroughly secular and ruled by people who worshiped martial virtues, not gods. In the early part of the twentieth century, this was a description particularly appreciated by nationalists who advocated armed resistance against the British. It is said that the *Arthashastra* is taught in military academies in Pakistan to this day — as a way to better understand the mindset of Indian politicians. And much as Sunzi's *Art of War*, the advice contained in the *Arthashastra* has been peddled by manuals on "how to get ahead in business."
>
> *Read more online:* https://hdl.handle.net/20.500.12434/19306c71

Politics, its author suggested, is a dog-eat-dog world in which only the most ruthless rulers survive. Another text from this period is the *Manusmriti*, the "Code of Manu," a legal code and manual of statecraft.

As far as religious thought is concerned, two quite distinct traditions developed. In the western part of the Ganges River valley — towards today's Pakistan — a priest-led culture flourished, as originally described in the *Vedas*, which focused on rituals and on the secret teachings conveyed by gurus. Here the emphasis was on the sacrifices which the gods required and the rewards you might get if you performed them correctly. This is the religious tradition which later came to be known as Hinduism. The leading social class, the *brahmins*, were the keepers of these rituals and the wisdom the traditions contained constituted the spiritual basis of their secular power. However, in the eastern part of the Ganges plains — towards today's Bangladesh — the emphasis was rather on ascetic practices, on meditation and on the spiritual development of each individual. Much-debated questions here included the nature of consciousness and the notion of the self. How can the self remain the same from one moment to the next or from one lifetime to another? In order to investigate such questions, ascetics engaged in practices which later developed into yoga and meditation.

It was in this environment that two schools arose which later were to become full-fledged religions — Jainism and Buddhism. The Jains are famous for their doctrine of *ahimsa*, or "non-violence," which not only made them renounce war but also turned them into vegetarians. Jainism preaches universal love, non-attachment to worldly possessions, and it emphasizes the importance of devotional practices. Much later, in the twentieth century, the idea of *ahimsa* would inspire the methods employed by Mahatma Gandhi, the leader of the Indian independence movement. There are still between four and five million Jains living in India today.

Buddhism was founded by Siddharta Gautama, a prince born in the small kingdom of Shakya, in today's Nepal, most likely in the fifth century BCE. At first he lived the regular, pleasure-seeking life of a prince; he married and had children. Yet at the age of twenty-nine, legend has it, he left his palace one day and encountered first an old man, then a sick man and finally a decaying corpse. Realizing that sickness, old age and death awaited also him, he decided to change his way of life. He engaged in various ascetic practices before eventually settling on a "middle way," a life of moderation and detachment, which eventually brought him to enlightenment. Siddharta became a "Buddha," meaning "the awakened one." The world is an illusion, the Buddha taught, and through our desires and ceaseless striving we make ourselves unhappy. In fact, the self is an illusion too. Enlightenment is a matter of being released from suffering and from our notion of a self. This way we no longer have to be reborn.

Soon the Buddha started telling others about his spiritual discoveries and this is how the religion which bears his name came to be established. Buddhism spread quickly along the trade routes of inner Asia and across the Indian Ocean.

Buddhas of Bamiyan

In Bamiyan, a valley in central Afghanistan, two gigantic Buddha statues were constructed in the sixth century CE. Hewn directly out of the sandstone cliff, they were 35 and 53 meters tall respectively, and the largest standing Buddha statues in the world. The Bamiyan Buddhas were wonderful examples of the eclectic blend of cultural influences that characterized Bactria — the Buddhas were Indian enough, but they were wearing Greek clothing.

Introduced to Afghanistan in the fourth century BCE, Buddhism flourished during the Kushan Empire. At the time Bamiyan was a hub on the caravan routes which connected India, Central Asia, and China. From the monasteries constructed here, Buddhist influences spread far and wide. A Chinese pilgrim, Xuanzang, who visited Bamiyan in 630, mentioned "more than ten monasteries and more than a thousand monks" living here. Read more: *Journey to the West* at p. 23. The hermit monks had dug caves for themselves in the rock face, each one painted with brightly colored frescoes. Xuanzang also noted that two enormous Buddha statues were "decorated with gold and fine jewels."

The statues were destroyed by the Taliban government in March 2001. To the Taliban they were "idols," and they were angry that the international community allocated funds for maintaining the statues while the Afghans themselves were starving. The destruction was carried out in stages and it took weeks to complete. Initially, the statues were fired at using anti-aircraft guns and artillery but eventually, they were dynamited. Public opinion worldwide was outraged by this act of cultural vandalism.

Various proposals have been made for reconstructing the statues, using what can be recovered of the original stones. In 2013, the foot section of the smaller Buddha was

> rebuilt with iron rods, bricks, and concrete, but the work was halted after protests from UNESCO. Some have felt that the niches should be left empty as a monument to the fanaticism of the Taliban. In June 2015, the statues were temporarily recreated by means of hologram images projected onto the cliffs. There is no doubt what the Buddha would have said regarding the destruction of the statues. "Nothing in this world is forever," he would have pointed out, "everything must pass."
>
> *Read more online:* https://hdl.handle.net/20.500.12434/05553d6c

Before long there were Buddhists from Afghanistan in the west to Japan in the east. Today Buddhism is a world religion with an estimated 500 million followers, including a growing number in Europe and North America. Yet there are many kinds of Buddhists. Some engage in spiritual techniques designed to achieve enlightenment, but most devotees are content to engage in various pious practices — bringing food to Buddhist monks or praying and burning incense at temples. Curiously for a religion, Buddhism has no notion of a god. It is also a very egalitarian faith. Buddhism acknowledges no separate social classes, no castes, and few distinctions are made between the roles of men and women. This egalitarian ethos has always been part of its appeal.

Classical India

One invasion which was to have a profound impact on India was one that never happened. In 326 BCE, Alexander the Great and his armies moved into the Punjab, in the northwestern corner of the subcontinent. Alexander was a Greek statesman and general who had already successfully fought the Persians and continued eastward from there. In this way he created a vast, if short-lived, empire which stretched from Europe all the way to India. India, the Greeks believed, was where the world ended and by conquering it, Alexander would come to rule the whole world. Once in Punjab, however, his troops rebelled and he was forced to turn back. Alexander died in Babylon shortly afterwards, only thirty-three years old. Yet remnants of his army lingered on in the valleys of what today is Afghanistan. They founded communities here where Greek culture, language and arts came to blend in with local traditions.

The chaos left by Alexander's failed invasion provided an opportunity for others to assert themselves. This is how the first India-wide state, the Mauryan Empire, came to be established. The Mauryans overthrew the various *mahajanapada* kingdoms and between 322 and 180 BCE, they ruled an empire which for the first time encompassed almost all of India — only the southern tip of the subcontinent remained outside of their control. The most famous of the Mauryan kings was Ashoka, 304–232 BCE, also known as "Ashoka the Great." Ashoka was a ruthless ruler, or rather, this was how he began his career. In order to become heir to the throne, legend has it, he killed no fewer than ninety-nine of his brothers, and once he had assumed power he continued to be both selfish and cruel. Yet he eventually came to regret his behavior. Above all, the spectacular bloodshed which took place at the battle of Kalinga in 260 BCE, in which, reputedly, no fewer than a quarter of a million soldiers died, made him change his ways. Remorseful and disgusted with his previous way of life, Ashoka converted to Buddhism, gave away his possessions to the poor and took up vegetarianism.

He proceeded to reform the Maurya state in line with his new Buddhist beliefs. Ashoka planted trees along the roads, dug wells and canals for irrigation, built resthouses for travelers and hospitals for the sick. He instructed his officials to keep an eye out for the welfare of the poor, the aged and the widowed. He replaced the traditional hunting parties — a favorite pastime of all previous Indian rulers — with religious pilgrimages. Ashoka also introduced writing to India and put up a large number of pillars made in stone on which he declared himself to be the ruler of the country and explained his policies and aspirations to his people.

Pillars of Ashoka

Ashoka the Great, 268–232 BCE, renounced violence, converted to Buddhism, and started a number of projects to improve the lot of the poor, the aged and the widowed. In addition, he put up pillars all over his empire, often in city-squares or along major thoroughfares, on which he explained his policies and his aspirations. Today there are still thirty-three of these pillars in existence. Darius, the king of Persia, had put up similar monuments where he had boasted about the battles he had won and the number of enemies he had killed. Ashoka, however, inverted this message. His pillars express his promise to rule his people with compassion and benevolence, to renounce violence and make sure that every one of his subjects was happy and well-fed. The text is written in a colloquial style, using local languages instead of the Sanskrit employed at court. The pillars were also a way of spreading his presence throughout the empire, uniting it, and making every subject aware of who their ruler was.

The only problem was that people, in general, were unable to read. For that reason, to make them understand what the pillars said, a public official was posted at the foot of each one of them. The officials explained the message, but at the same time, they also gathered information about the state of the country and the grievances of the population. This information was then used by the government in devising new policies. Along the borders of Ashoka's empire, there were pillars written in foreign languages such as Aramaic and Greek. They announced that whoever was traveling this way now had entered the lands governed by the great and benevolent king Ashoka.

Read more online: https://hdl.handle.net/20.500.12434/4dbf402d

Ashoka's religious conversion was crucial for the dissemination of Buddhism not only in India but throughout Asia. His own son is said to have been the first Buddhist missionary to Sri Lanka. Yet the state that Ashoka created barely outlived him. After his death, the subcontinent was once again invaded by various armies coming from Central Asia. In 185 BCE, the Mauryan Empire was no more.

The most successful of the new wave of invaders were the Kushans who established themselves in northern India during the first four centuries of the CE. The Kushan Empire stretched into Central Asia too and it included Bactria, in today's Afghanistan. Bactrian culture at the time was a curious mixture of Buddhist influences, Zoroastrianism, and the Greek traditions which the army of Alexander the Great had left behind. The Kushans produced works of art in the Greek tradition. Gold coins featuring Greek text were minted and enormous statues were erected in which the Buddha was wearing a Greek toga. Read more: *Buddhas of Bamiyan* at p. 51.

During the Kushan Empire, trade flourished with Central Asia, but also with places much further afield — Egypt, the Aksumite Kingdom and Rome.

The Ark of the Covenant

The Steven Spielberg movie *Raiders of the Lost Ark*, 1981, finishes with a memorable scene. Throughout the movie, Indiana Jones, played by Harrison Ford, has been in pursuit of the Ark of the Covenant, the gold-covered wooden chest which, according to the Hebrew Bible, contains the stone tablets with the original version of the Ten Commandments ("Thou shalt not kill," etc.). Avoiding capture by German soldiers and outsmarting a French competitor, Indiana Jones eventually brings the Ark back to the United States. Once there, however, it soon disappears into an enormous government warehouse where it will presumably never again be found.

Compare this story to the one Coptic Christians in Ethiopia tell. The Ark of the Covenant, they insist, is not at all lost, and it is not in a government warehouse in the United States. It can instead be found in the Church of Our Lady Mary of Zion, in Axum, in the Tigray province of Ethiopia. It was brought here by Menelik I, the son of King Solomon and the Queen of Sheba after he had paid a visit to his father in Jerusalem. And the Ark of the Covenant has been there ever since. Since it is associated with such awesome powers, however, only one person — a guardian monk — is allowed to see it.

There are striking similarities between the Hollywood version of this tale and the Coptic version. In both cases, the Ark is a source of divine power. The divine object, moreover, has been appropriated by an imperial power and brought to the very center of the empire. This feat has in both cases been accomplished by a young hero. The Covenant is in both cases hidden from public view, yet this does not mean that it has stopped radiating its divine power. Whether the Ark in question actually exists is a far less important question. It is the myth, conveyed by the legend and the movie, which provides legitimacy to the empire.

Read more online: https://hdl.handle.net/20.500.12434/11e66a50

In the second century, the Kushans brought tributary gifts to the emperor in China and they sent missionaries who helped translate Buddhist scriptures into Chinese. Much of what we know about the Kushan Empire is contained in eyewitness accounts left by Chinese visitors. One such traveler, Xuanzang, was a Chinese monk who traveled to India early in the seventh century in order to find more authentic versions of Buddhist texts. Read more: *Journey to the West* at p. 23.

He returned home with many manuscripts but also with the Bactrian version of the images of the Buddha. This is how Buddha statues everywhere came to wear Greek togas.

In the fourth century, the rulers of the Gupta dynasty, 319–605, came to dominate the northern parts of the Indian subcontinent. The Gupta Empire was a proper state, with a bureaucracy, a tax system and salaried officials. The Gupta kings issued coins stamped with their images, thus spreading their images throughout the kingdom and informing ordinary people who their ruler was. The economy was flourishing and so were new production techniques — metallurgy in particular. At the time India was the world's largest producer of iron. Enormous iron pillars were cast together with Buddha statues in copper. The sciences made great strides too. It was at this time that Indian mathematicians invented the number zero. Zero sounds as though it might be insignificant, but it was to revolutionize mathematics. They also determined that π, *pi*, was equal to 3.14 plus a long string of digits. Indian astronomers calculated the exact number of days in a year and also the circumference of the earth with astonishing precision. Read more: *Indian mathematics* at p. 48.

It was during the Gupta period that many of the things we today think of as quintessentially "Indian" first came to be established, including Indian music, architecture, sculpture and paintings. It was also then that Hinduism came to be institutionalized and given set texts, rituals and prayers. And it was during the Gupta period that the images of the Hindu gods received their iconic forms — Vishnu with his four arms; the dancing Shiva; Ganesh, the elephant god; Hanuman, the monkey god, and so on. The power of the Gupta Empire ensured that these new images would be disseminated across a vast area. The *Kama Sutra* was also compiled at this time, notorious as a sex manual but also a discussion of social relationships and family life.

The *Kama Sutra*

Foreigners often regard Indian culture as "spiritual," but many of its cultural practices, such as meditation and yoga, concern the body rather than the soul. This is true also of the wisdom contained in the *Kama Sutra* which is known as a sex manual, but which above all is a manual on how to lead a complete, long and satisfying life. It discusses sex to be sure, but also the nature of love and the requirements of family life.

The author of the *Kama Sutra*, Vatsyayana, was a philosopher who lived in the second or third century BCE, but next to nothing is known about him. It is when you are young, he tells us, that you should seek bodily pleasures but as the years pass you should concentrate on spiritual matters in order to escape the cycle of rebirths.

Sexuality can be given a religious interpretation too. A man and a woman in a close embrace symbolize *moksha*, "liberation," the final release from the dualities which characterize human life. If nothing else, this interpretation provides an excuse for reading the book.

The teaching conveyed by the *Kama Sutra* is depicted in the thousands of statues that decorate the temples of Khajuraho, in Madhya Pradesh in central India. The statues show men and women in various sexual positions but also scenes from everyday life — women putting on makeup, musicians making music and farmers going about their daily chores. Sexuality, the collection of statues tells us, is a regular part of human life.

Today the production and distribution of pornography is a punishable crime in India. Bollywood, the Indian film industry, excels in evocative dance numbers but has traditionally refrained from undressing actors and actresses. Read more: *Curries, Bollywood and the Beatles in India* at p. 63. Prostitution as such is legal in the country, but brothels and pimping are not. India is estimated to have over half a million prostitutes. The trafficking of young girls is an often-reported problem, in particular among members of vulnerable minority groups.

Read more online: https://hdl.handle.net/20.500.12434/8eecd7c7

Nalanda, a very old university

The Buddhist monastery complex at Nalanda, in today's Indian state of Bihar, was a center of learning founded in the fifth century. Archaeological excavations which began in 1915 have revealed temples, lecture and meditation halls, libraries and gardens, together with a trove of sculptures, coins, seals and inscriptions. Subjects taught here included the *Vedas*, logic, Sanskrit grammar, medicine, fine arts, astronomy, mathematics, politics, and epistemology. Above all, however, it was a center of Buddhist learning which flourished under the Gupta Empire. Read more: *Indian mathematics* at p. 48. Much of our knowledge of Nalanda comes from the writings of Chinese monks who came here to study in the seventh century. At the height of its prominence, the university had some 2,000 professors and 10,000 students who all were accommodated in dormitories. Nalanda was the first educational institution to conduct entrance exams. The fortunes of the university declined after the Gupta rulers and in the 1190s it was destroyed by invading armies from Central Asia.

Al Quaraouiyine, in Fez, Morocco, is sometimes said to be the oldest university in the world, founded in 859. Read more: *Ibn Rushd and the challenge of reason* at p. 84. The oldest universities in Europe — Paris and Bologna, founded in the thirteenth century — are thus far younger. Nalanda, however, is the oldest of all. Since 2014 Nalanda University is once again accepting students. Led by Amartya Sen, a Nobel Prize-winning economist, and with economic support from various Asian countries, its aim is to once again become Asia's leading center of learning. Subjects taught here today include ecology, history, economics, and languages. Buddhism is taught too but features less prominently on the curriculum than once was the case. The hope is that Nalanda University will help contribute to the economic development of Bihar, one of India's poorest regions.

Read more online: https://hdl.handle.net/20.500.12434/21c2a54a

When the Gupta Empire began to decline early in the seventh century, it was replaced by a number of competing kingdoms, yet none of them was able to conquer the subcontinent as a whole. Contemporary writers described the political situation as one of "fish justice" — a world in which the big fish eat the small. From this state of anarchy two empires eventually arose, albeit in different parts of the subcontinent — the Pala and the Chola. The Pala Empire ruled Bengal and today's Bangladesh. The Pala were Buddhists but they were far more warlike than Ashoka the Great had become. Their army was particularly famous for its war elephants.

War elephants

An "elephantry" is a cavalry equipped with elephants instead of horses. Elephants have been used for military purposes since antiquity. For example, the Indian epic, the *Mahabharata*, from the fourth century BCE, mentions war elephants and elephants were employed by the Persians in their wars with Alexander the Great. *Read more: The Mahabharata at p. 49.* In one famous battle in 1539, the king of Siam killed the king of Burma in one-on-one combat between their respective elephants.

In battle, elephants with their enormous bulk are useful for charging at the enemy, for breaking the enemy's ranks and in general for instilling terror. Generals would often place themselves on top of an elephant in order to get a better view of the battlefield, and archers would sometimes put platforms on the elephants' backs from which they could assault the enemy. Both male and female elephants can be used in battle, but the male is more useful since female elephants tend to run away from males.

The standard tactic for fighting an elephantry is to dodge their charge and attack the *mahout*, the elephant-keeper from behind. Elephants have their limits as a military force since they have a tendency to panic, especially when wounded. The Mongols, who never used elephants themselves, would fight the elephantry of their enemies by setting light to straw tied to the backs of camels. When the burning camels charged, the enemy's elephants would get scared and turn on their masters.

The introduction of muskets in the sixteenth century had only a limited impact on elephants, who were protected by their thick hides. The Mughals continued to rely on them in their conquest of the subcontinent, and Akbar had a famous elephantry. Yet the arrival of battlefield cannons in the nineteenth century made them redundant. Against cannons, you need far better protection. Today elephants are still used for other military tasks such as transporting equipment and supplies.

Read more online: https://hdl.handle.net/20.500.12434/f98fcd58

The Pala had skilled diplomats and traded with communities as far away as in China and the Middle East. It was then that Islam was introduced into India and that Indian science and mathematics were exported to the Muslim world. Read more: *The translation movement* at p. 80.

The Pala rulers were patrons of architecture and they took over from the Guptas as sponsors of the Buddhist university in Nalanda. When their empire declined in the twelfth century, it meant the end of the last Buddhist rulers in the subcontinent.

The Chola dynasty, 300 BCE–1279, meanwhile, dominated the entirety of the eastern coast, where a substantial part of the population were Tamil speakers. Although the Chola Kingdom dates from the third century BCE, it was only in the latter half of the ninth century that it became an empire. The Chola kings, much as the Guptas before them, were the leaders of a centralized state with a professional and disciplined bureaucracy. They constructed great buildings, including many temples, and they too were patrons of the arts. It was then that a body of literature written in Tamil first came to be developed. Ordinary people in the Chola Empire were fishermen, seafarers and traders who maintained close contacts with lands beyond the subcontinent — from the Maldives islands in the south to the Indonesian archipelago in the east. The Indian influences which reached Southeast Asia during this period were more than anything the Chola version of Indian culture. In the tenth century, the Chola invaded Sri Lanka. Today's ethnic division of Sri Lanka — where Tamils constitute some 11 percent of the population — dates from the Chola period.

Indianization

Although India was repeatedly invaded by foreign armies, Indian empires themselves never expanded beyond the subcontinent. Despite this fact, India has had a profound impact on societies elsewhere. This power has been civilizational rather than political and it has relied on exchange rather than on the force of arms. This process is often referred to as "Indianization." Indianization, in other words, refers to the process whereby the cultural practices of the Indian subcontinent, together with aspects of its political and social system, came to influence the rest of Asia — Southeast Asia most directly, but China, Japan and Central Asia too. Since Indianization was never a matter of official policy, it is difficult to say exactly when the process began and how it developed. What is clear, however, is that Indian influences spread along trade routes, both in Central Asia and in the Indian Ocean. In the Indian Ocean, thanks to the monsoons, it was quite easy to cover even large distances. Since the winds changed with the seasons, a trader in southern India could set sail for, say, the Malacca Peninsula in the summer and then return home in the winter when the direction of the winds changed.

In the third century CE, there were already well-established contacts between ports all around the Indian Ocean. This was where Indian merchants came to settle. With the trade and the traders came various Indian religious practices but also ideas regarding politics and society, together with some of the institutions required to implement them. In Southeast Asia, a strong Indian influence is detectable from the eighth century, and it was to continue for at least five hundred years. This was when Hinduism spread, followed by Buddhism and then Islam. This was also how the Pali and Sanskrit languages were exported, together with Indian music, theater and dance, food, ways of dressing, and much else besides.

> ### Thaipusam
>
> Thaipusam is a religious festival celebrated by the Tamil community in India and by the Tamil diaspora worldwide. The festival commemorates the occasion when Parvati, the Indian goddess of fertility and love, gave her son Murugan, the god of war, a spear in order to defeat a fiendish demon. The festival thus celebrates the victory of good over evil, light over darkness, and wisdom over ignorance. Devotees pray to Murugan in order to overcome the obstacles they face in life.
>
> To outsiders, Thaipusam is a gruesome spectacle. The people who participate in the festivities perform the *kavadi aattam*, the "burden dance," in which they bring offerings to their god. In the most basic version, they carry a pot of milk to the temple, but many devotees take the sacrifice far further. They pierce the skin on their backs with hooks from which they hang bottles of milk, and some pull large carts by means of hooks attached to their bodies. Many also pierce their tongues and cheeks with skewers, reminders of the spear which Parvati gave to her son.
>
> To withstand the pain, the devotees engage in all sorts of mind-altering activities — fasting, praying, chanting and drumming. In order to recuperate once the hooks and skewers have been removed, they rub their wounds with holy ash. Today ambulances are on standby during the ceremony, but remarkably few devotees need medical attention. The *kavadi aattam* is an endurance test by which the devotees demonstrate the power of their faith. Not surprisingly, the most demanding feats attract mainly young men, and you do not necessarily have to be a Tamil in order to participate. During Thaipusam celebrations in the Tamil diaspora in the United States, devotees undertake long walks on foot, carrying pots of milk, but no piercing or skewering is involved.
>
> *Read more online:* https://hdl.handle.net/20.500.12434/a34a0c2f

Many aspects of Indian society were highly elaborate and urbane and thereby quite alien to the agricultural and rather rustic traditions of Southeast Asia. Not surprisingly, a local ruler who could surround himself with the trappings of Indian culture was quite automatically regarded as both powerful and legitimate. In addition, the rulers of Southeast Asia were eager to adopt any institution or technique that might help them strengthen their hold on power. This included Indian manuals on statecraft, political institutions, and the Indian legal system.

There were many Indianized states throughout East Asia. This is a small sample:

- Langkasuka, 200s–1500s, the oldest kingdom in the Malay Peninsula thought to have been created by descendants of Ashoka the Great. Mixing Hindu, Buddhist and Malay culture, Langkasuka was a part of the Chinese international system and their tribute bearers are mentioned in imperial Chinese records. Read more: *China and East Asia* at p. 13.

- Srivijaya, 650–1377, a kingdom on the island of Sumatra in today's Indonesia, heavily influenced by Indian culture. Srivijaya was a thalassocracy, an empire stretching across the ocean, with strong connections to the Malacca Peninsula and societies bordering on the South China Sea. Srivijaya attracted pilgrims from other parts of Asia and was home to more than a thousand Buddhist scholars.

- Medang, 800s–1100s, was a Hindu-Buddhist kingdom on Java in today's Indonesia. They built the Borobudur, a Buddhist temple complex, and the Prambanan, a Hindu temple complex. The Medang rulers oversaw the translation of Indian texts but the culture included distinct Javanese influences. Medang buildings are known for their bas-reliefs which often contain quotations from Buddhist sutras.

- Champa, 192–1832, was a kingdom located in southern and central Vietnam which adopted Sanskrit as a scholarly language and made Hinduism into a state religion, although Indian influences here too were heavily mixed with local religious lore. In 1832 the Champa were conquered by the Viet, a society with far closer cultural ties to China. There are still people in Vietnam today who speak Chamic, a language related to Malay.

- The Khmer was a Hindu empire that existed between the ninth and thirteenth centuries in today's Cambodia. Its political and religious center was the Angkor Wat, an enormous complex of more than 900 temples. The kings were considered as incarnations of Vishnu, the Hindu god. Read more: *Angkor Wat* at p. 61.

- The Kingdom of Tondo, 900s–1589, was an Indianized kingdom in today's Philippines. They traded with China and participated in the Chinese international system.

- Pagan, 849–1297, was a kingdom in central Burma, predominantly Buddhist but also incorporating Hindu beliefs. They were invaded by the Mongols in 1297 and never recovered.

- Ayutthaya, 1351–1767, a kingdom in today's Thailand. They engaged in extensive trade, sent ambassadors to foreign courts and expanded into the Malay Peninsula. The Ayutthaya kings combined Hinduism and Buddhism and were considered semi-divine. Their armies made extensive use of war elephants. Read more: *War elephants* at p. 57.

- Majapahit, 1293–1527, was another thalassocratic empire, based in Java in today's Indonesia. They had some ninety-eight states paying tribute to them from areas including Malaysia, southern Thailand, the Philippines and New Guinea. Majapahit rose to power in the wake of the Mongol invasion. The

Majapahit built stupas in red brick, statues in terracotta and figurines in gold. Read more: *The Mongol khanates* at p. 101.

- Bali, in today's Indonesia, an island strongly influenced by Hindu culture from the first century. Unusually for Southeast Asia, an Indian-style caste system was in place here, although it was greatly simplified. Hinduism is practiced in Bali to this day but it is combined with many Buddhist beliefs and native religious practices.

Angkor Wat

Angkor Wat is a vast temple complex built by the kings of the Khmer Kingdom between 1113 and 1150. Khmer society as it emerged in the seventh century was originally based on maritime trade and it was from the beginning heavily influenced by Hindu culture. Angkor Wat was dedicated to the Indian god Vishnu, who was the divine sponsor of the kings, and the temple complex was built in accordance with Hindu cosmology. It had a 65-meter-tall tower at its center, replicating Mount Meru, the home of the gods. The tower was surrounded by vast reservoirs, modeled on the seven seas, and the complex as a whole was surrounded by a 5-kilometer-long moat. The temples are noted for their exquisite craftsmanship and their many statues and bas-reliefs depicting the lives of gods and ordinary people. In addition to Angkor Wat itself, there were thousands of smaller temples, scattered in a temple network that covered much of what today is Cambodia and eastern Thailand.

The city of Angkor was abandoned in the fifteenth century and a thick jungle vegetation quickly spread on the site. However, thanks to aerial laser photography, it is now possible to better understand how the city was laid out. Angkor had a vast grid system, with roads, temples, gardens, and squares which were home to some one million people. King Jayavarman VII, 1181–1218, fortified the city to better withstand military attacks. In addition, he built hospitals where medical treatment was free for all subjects. He also turned Angkor Wat into a Buddhist temple, or rather, a Buddhist temple filled with plenty of Hindu gods.

Angkor Wat is a symbol of today's Cambodia. It appears on the country's flag, stamps and money. The temple complex, which only had a few thousand annual visitors in 1993, now attracts some three million tourists. Concerns have been raised regarding the environmental impact of mass tourism.

Read more online: https://hdl.handle.net/20.500.12434/0e5e06af

It is at the same time clear that the indigenous people of Southeast Asia were far more than the passive recipients of these influences. For one thing, they often traveled to southern India themselves. Southeast Asian rulers would place orders for specific goods with Indian producers or they would convince Indian craftsmen to come and settle at their courts. Before long they produced their own versions of Indian products. Cultural practices too were first adopted and then adapted to suit local needs. For example: although the indigenous rulers were often keen on the idea of castes, they were not, with the exception of Bali, able to impose the system on society at large. In the Khmer Kingdom, for example, the caste system was implemented only within the temple compound of Angkor Wat itself. Clearly this way of organizing social relations, with its many fine-tuned gradations between classes, was a poor fit in Southeast Asian societies where next to everybody was a farmer. This also shows that there were limits to how far Indian cultural references could spread. In many cases, it was only the local elite that was thoroughly steeped in Hinduism.

We see the same mixing of cultural references when it comes to religious practices. For one thing, the nuclear family was always more powerful in Southeast Asia than in Indian society itself. Thus in Bali, reincarnation was thought to happen within the family lineage and not randomly in society at large. Women have also played a more prominent role than they did, or do, in India, and the adoption of Indian cultural practices did not change this fact. Or consider the use of Sanskrit. Today languages such as Thai and Burmese are written with letters that remind us of Indian letters, but they have been greatly modified and the writing systems are entirely different.

Shadow puppets

One of the arts spread through the Indianization of Southeast Asia is shadow puppetry. Shadow puppets have a long history in India and different parts of the subcontinent have their own versions of the art. The shows are usually staged during Hindu festivals and stories drawn from the Indian epics feature prominently. Read more: *The Mahabharata* at p. 49. Sometimes the shows are performed by families of itinerant puppeteers.

The art has been picked up all over Southeast Asia. In Indonesia, it is known as *wayang* or *wayang kulit* and is common in Java and Bali. In Javanese, *wayang* means "shadow," "imagination" or "spirit," and *kulit* means "skin" — the puppets here are usually made of leather. The flat puppets have movable joints that are animated by rods, and a skilled puppeteer can make the shadows walk, dance, fight, nod, and laugh. In Bali, the performance typically starts at night and continues until dawn. A complete troupe of *wayang kulit* performers also includes singers and *gamelan* players — the *gamelan* is an ensemble of musicians who play various traditional percussion instruments. Shadow puppets have been popular in Cambodia, Thailand, Laos, and Malaysia too. Here the performances are staged during temple festivals and storylines from Indian epics are common. The shadows are cast using oil or halogen lights onto a cotton cloth background.

There is concern regarding the future of shadow puppetry. The art is well documented in museums, and it is commonly performed for tourists, but it is rather more uncertain whether it will survive as a genuinely popular form of entertainment. There is today a lot of competition from other forms of shadow plays — movies, television, YouTube clips. In 2003, UNESCO designated *wayang kulit* as an example of a "masterpiece of oral and intangible heritage of humanity."

Read more online: https://hdl.handle.net/20.500.12434/bf4e1a05

This mixing of religions was further facilitated by the fact that neither Hinduism nor Buddhism are monotheistic faiths. A religion with only one omnipotent God will always reject the possibility of there being other competing divinities. For Buddhism and Hinduism, there were no such problems, and both religions happily borrowed references from each other. You could be a Buddhist part of the day, or part of your life, and a Hindu the rest of the time. Or, more likely, you would not make a sharp distinction between the two.

"Indianization" is consequently a contested term. Indeed, the first ones to use it were Indian nationalists in Bengal in the 1920s, at the time when India was still a British colony. Inspired by French excavations of Angkor Wat and other ancient temple sites, they began to speculate regarding the existence of an ancient "greater India" which had spread out over much of East Asia. Read more: *Angkor Wat* at p. 61.

This had not been an empire, they explained, but rather a civilization. India had brought progress and prosperity to its neighbors but not, like the British, through military conquest, but instead through trade and peaceful exchange. Yet, as we have seen, while Indian traditions certainly were widely disseminated they were often diluted or completely reconfigured in the process. If we go on using the term, we should think of Indianization as a process of *hybridization* — such as when two plants interbreed to form a unique combination. Indianization is not the spread of Indian culture as much as the creation of a new species of culture which draws heavily from India but which at the same time is adapted to local traditions and needs. Indian culture has continued to have a profound impact on other societies, but in the twenty-first century, its influence is nothing short of global.

Curries, Bollywood, and the Beatles in India

Indian culture continues to fascinate non-Indians to this day. Indian food provides one example. When the British colonial administrators returned home from India they often took recipes with them. The first reference to "currey" appeared in 1747, and in 1810 an Indian entrepreneur, Sake Dean Mahomed, opened the Hindoostanee Coffee House, the first curry house in London. Curries are now a staple of the British diet — more common than roast beef and tastier than pies and mash. Curries found their way to other parts of the British Empire too. In Jamaica, curried goat is a favorite dish and in Guyana they eat crab curry. In South Africa "bunny chow" is popular — a hollowed-out loaf of bread filled with curry. Curries are eaten outside of the former empire too. In Japan, *karee raisu* — a thick curry stew of potatoes, carrots, onions and chicken — is common in school canteens.

Indian movies provide another example of the worldwide appeal of Indian culture. The Indian movie industry, with its center in Mumbai — the city the British called "Bombay." — is often referred to as "Bollywood." It is the largest movie production center in the world with an output of close to two thousand movies per year. And it is not only Indians who are watching. Bollywood movies are popular throughout the subcontinent, in Southeast Asia, and they have a following in the Middle East and Africa too. Posters of Indian actresses can be seen at car repair garages in Nigeria and women in West Africa have been known to wear saris as a way to model themselves on the movie stars they are watching. In terms of global ticket sales, Bollywood far outsells Hollywood.

India has also had a strong spiritual influence on the rest of the world. Or rather, Europeans and North Americans have often considered Indian culture to be "spiritual." As such the country has attracted people looking for religious experiences. In February 1968, the Beatles traveled to India to take part in a meditation course at the *ashram* (spiritual hermitage) of Maharishi Mahesh Yogi, an Indian guru. The Englishmen wrote a number of songs here. Following the Beatles' lead, all rock stars of any stature for a while had to have their own gurus. Indian spiritual practices such as yoga and meditation have now entered the mainstream and are no longer identifiably Indian.

Read more online: https://hdl.handle.net/20.500.12434/e432346b

The Mughal Empire

Between the tenth and the twelfth centuries, another great wave of invasions swept through northern parts of the Indian subcontinent. Once again these were led by nomads coming from Central Asia, but this time they were Muslims who spoke a Turkic language. Between 1206 and 1526, a Muslim state — the Sultanate of Delhi — dominated much of northern India. Here Indian traditions mixed with Islam and new contacts developed between India and the thriving, if politically fragmented, Abbasid Caliphate. Read more: *The Umayyads and the Abbasids* at p. 78.

The Delhi sultanate was one of the few states that successfully defended itself against the Mongols. As former raiders on horseback themselves, they clearly knew how to deal with them.

The Sultanate of Delhi was weakened by uprisings and eventually, it was overthrown. Yet the rulers who overthrew them also had their origin in Central Asia. The Mughal Empire, 1519–1857, was a Muslim kingdom that started out in today's Uzbekistan. Its first ruler, Babur, 1526–1530, was a thirteenth-generation descendant of Genghis Khan's son Chagatai and also a relative of Timur Lenk, who, in the fourteenth century, had created a vast, if short-lived, empire in Central Asia. Babur tried his best to live up to the traditions of his family. Born in the fertile Fergana Valley in today's Uzbekistan, he settled in Samarkand where he surrounded himself with a small band of retainers. Pushed out of Samarkand by the advancing Uzbeks, he moved on to Afghanistan and eventually settled in Kabul. From here his armies began making incursions in India. The Mughal soldiers used guns to great effect. Historians sometimes talk about the "gunpowder empires" of Asia — which in addition to the Mughals included the Ottomans and the Safavids of Persia. Read more: *The Ottoman Empire* at p. 91.

Babur's battle tactics also explain much of his success. While guns had been used in India before, they had never been combined with a rapidly moving cavalry. "The

Indian defenders were amused by our muskets," Babur recalled in his autobiography, "but they stopped making jokes when they saw what our weapons could do." From the beginning, Babur treated the people of India leniently, more as his subjects than as his prey. And yet, he remained homesick for Samarkand until the end of his life.

There were eighteen subsequent rulers of the Mughal Empire. Babur was succeeded by his son, Humayun, 1530–1540 and 1555–1556. His name means "the lucky one," but he was clearly quite inappropriately named. He lost the Mughal throne and was exiled to Iran, but with Persian support he eventually reconquered it. Humayun died at only forty-eight years old, when falling down a staircase — according to one version, while running to get to Friday prayer on time. After his unexpected death, it was unclear who would succeed him, but eventually, his son Akbar, 1556–1605, did. Akbar was thirteen years old at the time of his accession and he was to rule India for the next fifty years. Akbar was the emperor who more than all others put his mark on the empire. When he captured the state of Gujarat in 1573 — a major victory — he was only thirty-one years old. This was a time of great expansion in world trade, and Mughal India was its hub. Read more: *A mountain of silver* at p. 184.

Akbar loved hunting, horse riding, and archery, and although he remained illiterate all his life, he had a library of some 24,000 volumes written in Sanskrit, Urdu, Persian, Greek, Latin, and Arabic. Persian culture was influential at Akbar's court, with Persian-style music, poetry and illuminated manuscripts as primary art forms.

Akbar also strengthened the institutions of the Mughal state. He embarked on far-reaching administrative reforms and imposed uniform rules on the bureaucratic systems. He reformed the military too, organizing the cavalry into the same units of ten soldiers which had been a feature of Genghis Khan's armies. He also established an elephantry. Read more: *War elephants* at p. 57.

Akbar was constantly on the move, and much as his ancestor Genghis Khan before him, he took his bureaucrats with him wherever he went. He made a serious attempt to conquer all of the Indian subcontinent, and in the end, only a small tip in the very south of India remained outside of his control. Akbar took a strong interest in questions of religion. He held religious disputations at his court where Muslim scholars debated with Hindus, Jews, and Christians. He even tried, if unsuccessfully, to amalgamate the faiths of the country into one state religion.

Din-e Ilahi

Din-e Ilahi, "the religion of God," was a system of religious beliefs introduced by the Mughal emperor Akbar in 1582. Akbar took a deep personal interest in religious matters. He founded an academy, the Ibadat Khana, "the House of Worship," in 1575, where representatives of all major faiths could meet to discuss questions of theology. Listening to these debates, Akbar concluded that no single religion captured the whole truth. His idea was to combine Islam and Hinduism into one faith, but also to add aspects of Christianity, Zoroastrianism, and Jainism.

Din-e Ilahi emphasized morality, piety, and kindness. Just like Sufi Islam, it regarded the yearning for God as a key feature of spirituality, just like Catholicism it took celibacy to be a virtue, and just like Jainism, it condemned the killing of animals. As for its rituals, Din-e Ilahi borrowed heavily from Zoroastrianism, making fire and the sun objects of divine worship. Read more: *Zarathustra and Zoroastrianism at p. 76.* The new religion had no scriptures, no priests, and in fact it never had more than a handful of followers — mainly the members of Akbar's closest circle of advisers.

Din-e Ilahi is best viewed as a state religion with the emperor himself at its center. As a single authority on all matters, Akbar was not only going to interpret and apply the religious law but to make it. Din-e Ilahi was his solution to the thorny problem of how a Muslim ruler could govern a predominantly Hindu society. Yet the Din-e Ilahi was fiercely opposed by many Muslims clerics who declared it a heretical doctrine. Although the new religion did not survive its founder, it triggered a strong fundamentalist reaction among India's Muslims. According to rumors, the Muslim call to prayer, "Allahu akbar," meaning "God is the greatest," was interpreted by Akbar himself as "God is Akbar."

Read more online: https://hdl.handle.net/20.500.12434/52310d8c

In order to improve relations with his Hindu subjects, he abolished the *jizya*, the tax imposed on all non-Muslims. He also took several Hindu wives.

Akbar's oldest son Jahangir, 1605–1627, replaced him in 1605. Jahangir means "conqueror of the world" and he tried his best to live up to the name, although he is remembered more vividly by posterity for his active love life. The economy of the country remained strong, and so did the Mughal administration. Jahangir also encouraged religious debates and tolerance of other faiths. Shah Jahan, 1628–1658, was Akbar's grandson. He took an interest in architecture and left a number of prominent buildings to posterity. He constructed the Red Fort in Delhi and made Agra into his capital. He also commissioned the Taj Mahal as a monument to commemorate his beloved wife.

Taj Mahal

The Taj Mahal, located on the south bank of the Yamuna river in the city of Agra, just south of New Delhi, is one of India's main tourist attractions. It was commissioned by the Mughal emperor Shah Jahan, the grandson of Akbar the Great, and completed in 1653. The Taj Mahal is a mausoleum built to house the grave of Shah Jahan's favorite wife, Mumtaz, who lost her life at the age of thirty-eight while giving birth to the couple's fourteenth child. Shah Jahan never recovered from the loss and dedicated the Taj Mahal to her memory. Her grave is found in a crypt under the building. Apparently, Shah Jahan had planned to build a black version of the mausoleum as a tomb for himself on the other side of the river. A bridge would have connected the two monuments. Yet no black Taj Mahal was ever built and after his death, Shah Jahan was instead buried beside Mumtaz. For good measure, two more of Shah Jahan's wives are also buried on the premises.

Some 20,000 craftsmen from all over India are said to have worked on the site, and it took twenty years to complete. It is a masterpiece of Mughal architecture, incorporating many Persian influences, and elaborately decorated throughout — apart from the graves themselves which, in accordance with Muslim custom, are left unadorned. Around the mausoleum is a vast Persian-style garden, and in front of the tomb is a raised water tank with a reflecting pool. As the tourist guides never tire of repeating, it is a monument dedicated to love. The Taj Mahal was famously described by the Indian author Rabindranath Tagore as "the tear-drop on the cheek of time."

If nothing else, the Taj Mahal is a great source of income. It is visited annually by some eight million tourists, not least by couples who like to pose for photos in front of the iconic facade. The buildings have recently turned yellow as a result of acid rain but various attempts have been made to restrict environmental pollution in the area.

Read more online: https://hdl.handle.net/20.500.12434/8bb03535

In addition, Shah Jahan is famous for the Peacock Throne and the Koh-i-Noor diamond. It was on the Peacock Throne, in the Red Fort, that the Mughal emperors were seated on ceremonial occasions. The Peacock Throne is said to have cost twice as much as the construction of the Taj Mahal itself.

The fourteen subsequent emperors were less distinguished and less colorful. A particularly controversial ruler was Aurangzeb, 1658–1707. The empire continued to expand during his reign and the economy remained strong. The Mughal Empire at the time had some 150 million subjects and an economy responsible for perhaps a quarter of the world's output. However, relations between the Muslim rulers and their Hindu subjects deteriorated. Aurangzeb reintroduced the *jizya* and he was notorious for destroying Hindu temples. During the rule of his descendants, the Mughal hold on the country weakened considerably. There were revolts against higher taxes and discontent regarding religious matters. Various regional rulers rose up to compete with the imperial center. This was also when the next wave of invaders appeared, this time traveling by boat. The first Europeans to arrive were the Portuguese; then came the Dutch, the French and eventually the agents of the British East India Company. This, however, is a story to which we will return in our last chapter. *Read more: The European expansion* at p. 179.

India as an international system

India, we said, is not a country as much as an international system in its own right. It contains a vast number of ethnic groups, almost as many languages, and separate religions that count millions of adherents. There has always been great political diversity too with many independent states competing with each other. During some periods one state managed to conquer much, or most, of the subcontinent. This is what the Maurya did, the Guptas, and later the Mughals. Yet they all had to make allowances for the diversity of cultures and ethnic groups. And even the most powerful rulers had little power over what was going on in India's hundreds of thousands of villages. The diversity and political fragmentation become even more obvious if we include Southeast Asia in the Indian international system. Southeast Asian societies were really quite different from India and Indian rulers never made any attempts to control them. At the same time, the Indian international system was held together by shared practices and beliefs. This has often been identified as a "Hindu" legacy, but Hinduism itself is an ongoing interaction between diverse traditions rather than a set of fixed practices and beliefs. This has made Hinduism into a rather indistinct religion but it has also made it highly persuasive. It has been easy to mix Hinduism with other traditions. Thus Buddhists could form a new religion without quite breaking with the old, and Islam could make converts among people who maintained much of their traditional ways of life. This explains both India's strong influence on Southeast Asia and its continuing influence in the world at large.

Today many Indian nationalists take a different view of Hinduism. Indian nationalism became a coherent movement at the end of the nineteenth century to oust the British occupiers. Read more: *The European expansion* at p. 179.

For this to be possible, Indian nationalists claimed, the country had to be united. Yet unity, some of them maintained, could never be achieved in a society as diverse as India. These nationalists envisioned a far simpler world — a society only by and for Hindus. And Hinduism, moreover, should be strictly defined, not as an ongoing interaction between diverse traditions, but as a definite set of practices and beliefs. This notion is often referred to as *Hindutva*. Not surprisingly, nationalists of a *Hindutva* persuasion have their own interpretation of Indian history. Other cultures and religions are regarded as foreign impositions, and times when they were prominent are considered to be periods of division and weakness. This even applies to a ruler such as Ashoka the Great whom Indian nationalists dislike since he converted to Buddhism and rejected the caste system.

Much the same is true of the *Hindutva* view of the Sultanate of Delhi and the Mughal Empire. The Mughals, Hindu nationalists explain, were invaders who ruined the country and imposed a foreign religion on its people. The divisions created in this way made the country an easy prey for European colonizers. The half-century rule of emperor Aurangzeb is regarded as particularly disastrous. Aurangzeb, Indian schoolchildren are taught, "hated Hindus." Instead it is the Gupta period which is identified as the age of Indian greatness. During the Gupta Empire the country developed economically, it was politically centralized, and Hinduism was officially promoted. There are still *Hindutva* nationalists in India today. Indeed, the country is run by them. And history textbooks continue to be rewritten in order to make India less pluralistic and Hinduism into a less forgiving faith. The *Hindutva* vision for the future is of a new Gupta Empire — one nation united under one set of Hindu gods.

Yet Hinduism was never a culture as much as a civilization. It never built walls or sought to define itself in distinction to other traditions. Instead, Indian society reached out to others and engaged them in trade and exchange, both along the caravan routes of Central Asia and between the ports in the Indian Ocean. Indian society was always open to the world and the world was always open to Indian civilization. This is how India became rich and admired.

Timeline

1500 BCE	The *Vedas* are written.
500–200 BCE	Works such as the *Mahabharata, Ramayana, Arthashastra,* and *Manusmriti* are written.
480 BCE	Possible date of birth for Siddharta Gautama, the Buddha.
322 BCE	Chandragupta establishes the Mauryan Empire.
260 BCE	The Battle of Kalinga. King Ashoka converts to Buddhism.
319–590	The Gupta dynasty conquers most of the Indian subcontinent.
630	The Chinese pilgrim Xuanzang visits Bamiyan.
925	Armies of the Chola Empire invade Sri Lanka.
1113	Work begins on Angkor Wat in today's Cambodia.
1206–1526	Sultanate of Delhi. Founded by invaders from Central Asia.
1526	Babur establishes the Mughal Empire.
1556	Akbar the Great becomes Mughal emperor.
1653	The Taj Mahal is completed by Emperor Shah Jahan.
1810	The first curry restaurant, the Hindoostanee Coffee House, opens in London.
1857	The Indian Uprising is defeated by the British. The official end of the Mughal empire.

Short dictionary

ahimsa, Sanskrit	Literally, "not to injure." The doctrine of non-violence and compassion associated with the Jain religion and with Mahatma Gandhi.
allahu akbar, Arabic	"God is the greatest." Incantation featured in Muslim calls to prayer.
ashvamedha	the Vedic version of horse sacrifices whereby a king came to be designated a legitimate ruler.
brahmin, Sanskrit	The priestly, and highest, cast in the Indian caste system.
Hindutva, Hindi	"Hinduness." Name for Indian nationalists who emphasize Hindu traditions.
janapada, Sanskrit	Small kingdoms in northern India during Vedic times.
jizya, Arabic	The tax imposed by Muslim rulers on their non-Muslim subjects.
kavadi aattam, Tamil	Literally, the "burden dance." Sacrificial offering and endurance test practiced among devotees of the Indian god Murugan.
kshatriya, Sanskrit	The military caste in the Indian caste system. Regarded as the second-highest cast after the brahmins.
mahajanapada, Sanskrit	Name for the sixteen large janapadas that emerged in northern India at the end of the Vedic period.
moksha, Sanskrit	"Liberation" from the cycles of rebirth. Cf. "nirvana" in Buddism.
wayang, Javanese	Literally, "shadow" or "imagination." Term for shadow puppet theater. Also known as *wayang kulit*.

Think about

Vedic India
- What were the *Vedas* and what do we know about their origin?
- Compare the cultural flourishing of Vedic India with the Warring States Period in China.
- Who was Siddharta Gautama and how did he acquire a world-wide following?

Classical India
- Give an account of the career and achievements of Ashoka the Great.
- Why has the Gupta dynasty come to be thought of as quintessentially "Indian"?
- What characterizes the culture and history of Afghanistan?

Indianization
- What role has the Indian Ocean played in establishing trade relations?
- Why did Indian culture have such a huge impact on Southeast Asia?
- Why is "Indianization" a contested term?

The Mughal Empire
- Why is Akbar often considered to be the greatest of the Mughal emperors?
- How did the Mughals, who were Muslim, manage to rule a predominantly Hindu society?
- Describe some of the cultural achievements of Mughal India.

India as an international system
- How do Indian nationalists define their country?
- Why is their definition considered as a threat by other ethnic and religious groups?
- Why have many features of Indian culture had such a powerful impact on foreigners?

Map of the Ottoman Empire from Abraham Ortelius, *Theatrum orbis terrarum* (Antverpiae: Apud Aegid. Coppenium Diesth, 1570), p. 219, https://archive.org/details/theatrumorbister00orte

4. The Muslim Caliphates

After the death of the Prophet Muhammad in Medina in 632, his followers on the Arabian Peninsula quickly moved in all directions, creating an empire which only one hundred years later came to include not only all of the Middle East and much of Central Asia, but North Africa and the Iberian Peninsula as well. This was known as the "caliphate," from *khalifah*, meaning "succession." Yet it was difficult to keep such a large political entity together and there were conflicts regarding who should be regarded as the rightful heir to the prophet. Thus, the first caliphate was soon replaced by a second, a third and a fourth, each one controlled by rival factions. The first caliphate, the Rashidun Caliphate, 632–661, was led by the *sahabah*, the "companions" who were the family and friends of the prophet and who were all drawn from Muhammad's own Quraysh tribe. The second caliphate, the Umayyads, 661–750, moved the capital to Damascus in Syria. And while it did not last long, one of its offshoots established itself in today's Spain and Portugal, known as al-Andalus, and made Córdoba into a thriving, multicultural center.

The third caliphate, the Abbasids, 750–1258, presided over what is often referred to as the "Islamic Golden Age," when science, technology, philosophy, and the arts flourished. The Abbasid capital, Baghdad, became a center in which Islamic learning combined with influences from Persia, India and even China. These achievements came to an abrupt halt when the Mongols sacked the city in 1258. From then on it was instead Cairo that constituted the center of the Muslim world. Yet the caliphs in Cairo too were quickly undermined, in this case by their own soldiers, an elite corps of warriors known as the Mamluks. The next Muslim empire to call itself a "caliphate" was instead the Ottoman Empire, with its capital in Istanbul, the city the Greeks had called "Constantinople." Although the Ottomans were Muslims, they were not Arabs but Turks, and they had their origin in Central Asia, not on the Arabian Peninsula.

Despite the continuing story of political infighting and fragmentation, the idea of the caliphate continues to exercise a strong rhetorical force in the Muslim world to this day. During the caliphates the Arab world experienced unprecedented economic prosperity and a cultural and intellectual success which made them powerful and admired. Not surprisingly perhaps, the idea of restoring the caliphate is still alive among radical Islamic groups who want to boost Muslim self-confidence.

© 2019 Erik Ringmar, CC BY 4.0   https://doi.org/10.11647/OBP.0074.04

The Arab expansion

After the death of the Prophet Muhammad in 632, the various families, clans and, tribes that made up the population of the Arabian Peninsula seemed prepared to return to their former ways of life, which included perpetual rivalries and occasional cases of outright warfare. Yet a small but influential group of the prophet's followers, the *sahabah*, sought to preserve the teachings which he had left them and to keep the Arabs united. This, the *sahabah* believed, could best be achieved if their energies were directed towards external, non-Arab targets. Moreover, they were on a mission from God. The *sahabah* were the custodians of the revelation as given to Muhammad and their task was to spread the word and convert infidels to the new faith. The new leader of the community must consequently, many felt, combine the qualities which had characterized Muhammad — to be a religious leader but also a politician and military commander. In 632, it was the prophet's father-in-law, Abu Bakr, who best exemplified these qualities, and he was elected to be the first caliph of what later came to be known as the *rashidun*, or "rightly guided," caliphate. During his short rule, 632–634, Abu Bakr consolidated Muslim control over the Arabian Peninsula, but he also attacked the southern parts of Iraq, occupied by the Persians, and the southern parts of Syria, occupied by the Byzantines.

The term *jihad*, "holy war," is often used to describe this military expansion, yet political control, not religious conversion, was its main objective. The expansion may best be explained not by a religious but by a military logic. Since the troops of the caliphate were paid by the spoils of war — by what they could lay their hands on in the lands they conquered — the army could only be maintained as long as it continued to be successful. "Raids" is consequently a better term for many of these engagements than "battles," even if the raids eventually turned into permanent occupations. Thus when the advance of the Muslim forces throughout Europe was eventually halted at the Battle of Tours in 732, this was regarded as a major triumph by European observers but merely as a temporary setback by the Arabs themselves. They simply retreated in order to fight another day. Moreover, since their occupation in many cases was quite superficial, it was often easy enough for the local population to reassert their independence. As a result, in several cases the Arabs had to reconquer the same territory over and over again.

The secret behind this astounding military success was a lightly armed and highly mobile fighting force. Although Muhammad and his immediate followers were merchants and city-dwellers, most of the population of the Arabian Peninsula were Bedouins. Mobility was key to survival in the harsh environment of the desert, and thanks to horses and camels, the Bedouins could cover large distances with great speed. Once they were formed into an army their horses could be used for swift attacks and their camels for transporting supplies. The neighboring empires — the Greeks in Byzantium to the west and the Persians to the east — were both stationary by comparison. As soon as the Arabs had mastered the basics of siege warfare, these sedentary societies were easily defeated.

Moreover, the Arabs were able to benefit from the fact that Byzantines and Persians had been each other's worst enemy for centuries. After decades of relative peace, the wars between the two superpowers flared up again in the beginning of the seventh century, with devastating effects for both parties. Thus, when the Arab forces began their incursions from the south, both Byzantines and Persians were already considerably weakened. Yet, it was far more difficult for the Arabs to expand their territorial control wherever they encountered people who resembled themselves. This was the case in northern Africa where the Berbers, after some costly engagements, were not defeated as much as bought off and incorporated into the new Arab elite.

During the reign of the second caliph, Umar, who succeeded Abu Bakr in 634 and ruled for ten years, these military campaigns were dramatically extended. The caliphate now became an imperial power. It occupied the eastern parts of the Byzantine Empire, including Syria, Anatolia, and Egypt in the 630s; and then all of the Persian Empire in the 640s, including present-day Afghanistan, Azerbaijan, Armenia, and Georgia. Umar's greatest achievement, however, was to give an administrative structure to the new state. Clearly, the institutions once appropriate for the cities of Mecca and Medina were not appropriate for the vast political structure which the caliphate now had become. Umar's answer was the *diwan*, a state bureaucracy with a treasury and separate departments responsible for tax collection, public safety and the exercise of *sharia* law. Coins were minted by the state and welfare institutions were established which looked after the poor and needy; grain was stockpiled to be distributed to the people at times of famine. The caliphate engaged in several large-scale projects, building new cities, canals and irrigation systems. Roads and bridges were constructed too and guest houses were set up for the benefit of merchants or for pilgrims going to Mecca for the *hajj*. Umar, the second rightly guided caliph, has always been highly respected by Muslims for these achievements and for his personal modesty and sense of justice.

Although the occupation of lands outside of the Arabian Peninsula happened exceedingly quickly, converting the occupied populations to the new faith took centuries to accomplish, and in many cases, it never happened. As a result of its military victories, Islam became a minority religion everywhere the Arabs went and forced conversions were for that reason alone unlikely to prove successful. Moreover, conversions were financially disadvantageous to the authorities. Since non-Muslims were required to pay a tax, the *jizya*, which was higher than the tax for Muslims, a change of religion meant a loss of tax revenue for the caliphate.

Instead, the various non-Muslim communities, known as the *dhimmi*, were allowed to practice their religion much as before. As the new Arab rulers saw it, monotheistic religions such as Christianity, Judaism and Zoroastrianism were precursors of Islam, which the teachings of the prophet had made redundant.

The military success of his followers, in their own eyes, had proven the viability of the new faith. Other religions were regarded as the colorful remnants of an older order, but not as threats to Islam itself. Indulging them, the Arab rulers allowed them to govern their respective communities in accordance with their own customs.

> ### Zarathustra and Zoroastrianism
>
> Zoroastrianism, just as Christianity, Judaism, and Islam, is a monotheistic religion. Zoroastrians call their deity Ahura Mazda, translated as "enlightened wisdom." Zoroaster, or Zarathustra, who founded the faith, was born northeast of the Caspian Sea most probably sometime around 1200 BCE. He was the author of the *Yazna*, a book of hymns and incantations. After the fourth century of the Common Era, Zoroastrianism was the official and publicly supported religion of the Sasanian Empire, located in today's Iran.
>
> Like other monotheistic religions, Zoroastrianism grapples with the question of how a belief in one almighty god can be combined with the existence of evil. The Zoroastrian answer is that good and evil are choices that confront human beings, not entities that compete for power. Questions of correct conduct are a crucial part of their faith. Zoroastrian rituals rely heavily on fire which is regarded as a holy force. Fire temples, attended by priests, were constructed throughout the Sasanian Empire. Zoroastrianism had a powerful influence on the other monotheistic religions of the Middle East, and many of its main themes — questions of the afterlife, morality, issues of judgment and salvation — feature prominently in Judaism, Christianity, and Islam too. Moreover, Zoroastrianism was the first religion that regarded people as equals before God and gave every believer the opportunity to attain salvation.
>
> Although the conversion took several centuries to accomplish, some 95 percent of Zoroastrians eventually switched to Islam. There are still Zoroastrians today, but not many. In Iran, an official census has counted less than 30,000. Yet the Persian new year, Nouruz, which was central to the Zoroastrian faith, is still the most important holiday in Iran. On occasions when the mandatory fasting required during Ramadan has come into conflict with the eighteen days of festive celebrations required by Nouruz, the Zoroastrian tradition has prevailed.
>
> *Read more online:* https://hdl.handle.net/20.500.12434/b7bffe6e

Christians, for example, could continue to drink alcohol and eat pork. Though the *dhimmi* lacked certain political rights that came with membership in the community of Muslim believers, they were regarded as equal with Muslims before the law and they were not expected to become soldiers in the caliphate's armies.

In 644, Umar was assassinated by a slave during a *hajj* to Mecca, apparently in revenge for the wars which the Arabs had waged against the Persian empire. This time, the problem of succession became acute. The question of who should take over as caliph raised issues concerning the proper distribution of power among the small elite of the prophet's Arabian followers. The most obvious choice was Ali, Muhammad's son-in-law, who had married Fatimah, the only one of the prophet's children who survived him. Yet it was instead Uthman ibn Affan who became the third caliph. Uthman too was an early convert to Islam and one of the prophet's closest companions but — and probably more importantly as far as the question of succession was concerned — he was a member of the Umayyads, one of Mecca's oldest and best-established families.

Once elected, Uthman dispatched military expeditions to recapture regions in Central Asia which had rebelled against Arab rule. He also made war on the Byzantine Empire, occupying most of present-day Turkey and coming close to besieging Constantinople itself. Rather more surprisingly for a military force largely made up of Bedouins, Uthman constructed an impressive navy which occupied the Mediterranean islands of Crete, Rhodes, and Cyprus and made raids on Sicily. At the end of the 640s, when the Byzantine attempt to recapture Egypt failed, all of North Africa came under the caliphate's control.

Despite these military advances, it was difficult to maintain peace between the various factions of the caliphate's elite. Indeed, the rich spoils which the Arab armies encountered in countries such as Syria and Iraq constituted a new source of conflict. During Umar's reign the soldiers had been paid a stipend, been quartered in garrisons well away from traditional urban areas, and been banned from taking agricultural land. During Uthman's leadership these policies were reversed. This led to resentment as a new land-owning Arab elite came to replace traditional leaders. Uthman was also accused of favoring members of his own family when it came to appointing governors to the new provinces. Another source of conflict was Uthman's attempt to standardize the text of the Quran and thereby to force all believers to accept his interpretation of its message.

Resentment against these policies was channeled into support for Ali, Muhammad's son-in-law, and before long an uprising against Uthman was underway. In 656, three separate armies marched on Medina, laid siege to Uthman's house and killed him. Now it was finally time for Ali to become the new leader. He remained in power for five years, 656–661, but his rule was undermined by continuous conflicts. Uthman's followers wanted revenge and insisted that Ali should punish the people who had murdered him. This, however, was difficult for Ali to do since it was thanks to them that he had come to power. In addition, Uthman's relatives and associates in the provinces wanted to protect their assets and their new landholdings. The result of these conflicts was the First Fitna, the first civil war between Muslims, which broke out in 657. Ali's forces met the forces of the Umayyads at Siffin, in today's Syria, but instead of a military confrontation, Ali decided to settle the matter by means of negotiations. This led some of his supporters to abandon his cause, and in 661 he was murdered by one of them. Muawiyah, the leader of the Umayyads, now established himself as the new caliph. However, this succession was disputed by Husayn, Ali's son, and once again war broke out. In the year 680, Husayn was ambushed and killed together with all of his family.

This is the historical origin of the split between the Sunni and the Shia, the two largest denominations of Muslims in the world today. According to Shia beliefs, Ali had been designated as the prophet's immediate successor, and his son and Muhammad's grandson, Husayn, was thus the rightful heir. Shia Muslims continue to believe that the caliphate was taken away from them by the Umayyad family and that authority in the Muslim world is illegitimately exercised to this day. They even blame themselves for Husayn's killing, since too few of his followers came to his support. On the day of his death, Ashura, a festival of mourning and repentance is celebrated by Shia Muslims. The processions held in Karbala, Iraq, where Husayn died, are the most spectacular, with millions of believers attending. These festivals have often been the targets of violence by non-Shia groups. Although only about 10 percent of all Muslims are Shia, they constitute today around 30 percent of the population of the Middle East.

The Umayyads and the Abbasids

The Umayyad Caliphate, 661–750, was a time of military consolidation rather than expansion, but it was above all a time when the caliphate established itself as a proper empire, ruled by institutions and bureaucratic routines. Muawiyah, who had been governor of Syria, began by moving the capital to Damascus. It was here that the caliphate's first coins were minted, instead of copies of Byzantine originals. It was also then that a regular postal service was set up, a requirement for disseminating information, instructions and decrees across the empire. And crucially, Arabic was made into the official language of the state, replacing Greek and assorted other languages. Greek had been spoken by administrators throughout the Middle East since the days of Alexander the Great — for close to a thousand years — but from the Umayyad Caliphate onward you had to know Arabic if you aspired to an administrative career. As a result, territories in which no Arabic speakers had previously existed, such as Egypt, were Arabized for the first time. And with Arabization, in many cases, came conversion to Islam.

Yet no amount of administrative reorganization could stop political conflicts from tearing this caliphate apart too. In the middle of the eighth century, the Umayyads were challenged by new regional elites, in particular by the governors of Iraq, a fertile and rich part of the empire. Before long a new civil war, the Second Fitna, broke out. In 750 the Umayyads were decisively defeated and the Abbasid Caliphate, 750–1258, took their place. The Abbasids claimed descent from Abbas, Muhammad's youngest uncle. Their first capital was Kufa, in southern Iraq, but in 762 they constructed a new capital in Baghdad. It was soon to become the largest and richest city in the world and a great center of culture and learning.

In Baghdad many cultures mixed freely and, much as elsewhere in the Muslim world, the *dhimmi* were given the right to run their own affairs. During the Abbasid Caliphate, the influences from Persia and Central Asia were strong. Persians, or rather Arabized Persians, were employed in the administration of the caliphate as advisers and judges, and Persian scholars and artists populated the caliph's court. Cultural influences did not only come from Persia, however, but also from far further afield. From the Indians the Arabs learned about the latest advances in mathematics. Read more: *Indian mathematics* at p. 48.

Through exchanges with China, the Arabs came to master the secrets of paper-making and soon a paper mill was established in Baghdad. Since paper is far cheaper to produce than parchment or papyrus, it was suddenly possible to gather far larger collections of books. Libraries were established throughout the caliphate which contained hundreds of thousands of volumes. At the time, the caliph's library in Baghdad had the largest collection of books in the world.

> ### Arabian Nights
>
> *One Thousand and One Nights* is a collection of folktales compiled in Baghdad during the Islamic Golden Age. It is often known in English as *The Arabian Nights* from the first English-language translation in 1706, which rendered the title as "The Arabian Nights' Entertainment." The work was not written by a single author but instead assembled over many centuries by various translators and editors. Caliph Harun al-Rashid was in charge of one of the main editions, and he also featured as a protagonist in some tales. Other stories retell plots popular in Indian, Persian and Arabic folklore and include love stories, tragedies, poems, and burlesques. There are murder mysteries too and horror stories featuring jinns, ghouls, sorcerers, and magicians. Many of the tales — such as "Aladdin's Wonderful Lamp" or "Ali Baba and the Forty Thieves" — were not part of Harun al-Rashid's original compilation but were instead added by European translators.
>
> All the editions of *The Arabian Nights* share the same framing device. This is the story of a Persian king who despairs at the infidelity of women. In order to make sure that his wife remains faithful he decides to marry a succession of virgins and have each killed on the day after their wedding night. Eventually, the king's vizier, whose duty it is to provide the women, cannot find any more virgins for the king. This is when Scheherazade, the vizier's own daughter, offers herself as the next bride. On the night of their marriage, Scheherazade begins telling him a story, but without finishing it. Curious to hear the conclusion, the king postpones her execution. Each night, as soon as one story had ended, she begins telling a new one, and in this way, the king is forced to let her live. The ruse is repeated for 1,001 consecutive nights. In the end, Scheherazade's life was spared.
>
> *Read more online:* https://hdl.handle.net/20.500.12434/6941bc5f

During the Abbasid Caliphate, the Arab world received influences from Byzantium too. Indeed, since Byzantium remained the caliphate's greatest military enemy, competition with this remnant of the Roman Empire was intense. One cultural expression of their rivalry was the so-called "translation movement" which began during the reign of the founder of the Abbasid Caliphate, al-Mansur, 754–775. Compared to the Greeks, the Arabs were social upstarts and although their cultural sponsorship was paying off handsomely, they had none of the historical prestige of the Greeks. Indeed, the Arabic language had until recently been spoken mainly by Bedouins in the desert and it lacked much of the technical terminology required to express philosophical and scientific ideas. All too aware of these deficiencies, the Abbasid caliphs embarked on a vast project of translating Greek books into Arabic.

The translation movement

With the fall of Rome, the cultural heritage of classical Greece was lost to Western Europe and next to no Europeans knew how to read Greek. Instead, the texts survived in translations into Arabic. The Abbasid Caliphate sponsored these translations and the caliphs took a personal interest in the project. The translations were often carried out by Syrian Christians, who spoke both Greek and Arabic, and they often used Syriac as an intermediary language. The translators would send for manuscripts from Byzantium, or they would go there themselves to look for books. They were handsomely rewarded for their efforts — a translator might be paid some 500 golden dinars a month, an astronomical sum at the time.

There were two main circles of translators in Baghdad, centered on the scholars Hunayn ibn Ishaq and al-Kindi. Having mastered Arabic, Syriac, Greek, and Persian, Hunayn translated no fewer than 116 works, especially medical and scientific texts, but also the Hebrew Bible. His son and nephews joined him as translators in his workshop. Hunayn was notable for his method which began with literal translations on which he based subsequent, rather loose paraphrases of the original text. Hunayn also wrote his own books, some thirty-six works altogether, of which twenty-one were concerned with medical topics. Hunayn may also be the author of *De scientia venandi per aves*, a book on falconry much admired in the Middle Ages.

Al-Kindi was Hunayn's near-contemporary and the head of a rival circle of translators. Although al-Kindi knew no Greek himself, his collaborators did, and he spent time overseeing and editing their work. The members of the al-Kindi circle were the first to translate many titles by Aristotle and other Greek philosophers. Al-Kindi also wrote his own books. In *On First Philosophy*, he gave an impassioned defense of why translations from Greek were necessary. The truth is the truth, he insisted, regardless of the language in which it is expressed. Al-Kindi is said to have introduced Indian numerals to the Islamic world, and he was a pioneer in cryptography. He also devised a scale that allowed doctors to assess the potency of the medication they gave patients.

Read more online: https://hdl.handle.net/20.500.12434/8394a664

Despite its glories and successes, Baghdad was not the only center of the caliphate. Indeed, in Iraq itself, Basra and Samarra were important hubs, and in Central Asia different cities were run by increasingly assertive local rulers. Much like the caliphs in Baghdad, they wanted not only political power but also the reputation of running an intellectually and culturally sophisticated court. Thus the library of the rulers of Shiraz, in Persia, was reputed to have a copy of every book in the world, and the library in Bukhara, in today's Uzbekistan, had a catalog which itself ran to thousands of volumes — besides, the library provided free paper on which its users could take notes. Meanwhile, the local rulers of Afghanistan made that part of the Abbasid Caliphate into a center of learning. The leading scholar here, Abu Rayhan al-Bīrūnī, went to India and returned with books on astronomy and mathematics which he synthesized and expanded. Read more: *Indian mathematics* at p. 48.

As the power of these regional centers grew, the Abbasid rulers in Baghdad became correspondingly weaker. They lost power over North Africa, including Egypt, in the eighth century, and in the tenth century, they controlled little more than the heartlands of Iraq. Even in Baghdad itself, the caliphs lost power to the viziers, their prime ministers. Interestingly, the city seemed to benefit culturally from the political fragmentation and the new influences it provided. The *majlis*, or salon, was a particularly thriving institution. In the drawing-rooms of the members of the elite, scientists, philosophers and artists would meet to gossip, debate and exchange ideas. Here Muslims, Jews and Christians could mingle freely and often the political elites, including the caliphs themselves, would participate in the proceedings. The *majlis* provided a free intellectual atmosphere in which different opinions on matters of philosophy, religion and science thrived. This is how Muhammad al-Razi's chemical discoveries — including the discovery of alcohol — became known, together with al-Farabi's synthesis of the philosophies of Plato and Aristotle.

The glories of Baghdad, together with the Abbasid Caliphate itself, came to an abrupt end with the Mongol invasion of 1258. What the Mongols did to Baghdad counts as one of the greatest acts of barbarism of all time. A large proportion of the inhabitants were killed — estimates run into several hundreds of thousands — and all the remarkable cultural institutions were destroyed together with their contents. Survivors said that the water of the river Tigris running through the city was colored black from the ink of the books the Mongols had thrown into it, and red from the blood of the scholars they had killed. The caliph himself was rolled up in a carpet and trampled to death by horses. Baghdad never recovered from the devastation.

The Arabs in Spain

Although the Umayyads were decisively defeated by the Abbasids in 750, they were given a new and surprising lease of life — in the Iberian peninsula, on the westernmost frontier of the Arabic world. As the caliphate in Damascus was about to fall, a branch of the Umayyad family fled across North Africa and established itself in the city of Córdoba, in present-day Spain, or in what the Arabs referred to as "al-Andalus." The Arabic incursion into Spain had started already in 711, with a small party of raiders, predominantly Berbers, making their way from Morocco to Gibraltar — or *Jabal Ṭariq* as they called it, "the mountain of Tariq," named after their commander. In the end, all of present-day Spain and Portugal were occupied, except for a few provinces close to the Pyrenees in the north. In 756, the Umayyads established a new caliphate for themselves at Córdoba. They were greeted as saviors by the Jewish community who had suffered from persecution under the Visigoths, the previous rulers, and by many ordinary people too who had suffered under heavy taxation.

The Caliphate of Córdoba, 929–1031, was the high point of Arabic rule in Spain. This was, first of all, a period of great economic prosperity. The Arabs connected Europe with trade routes going to North Africa, the Middle East and beyond, and industries such as textiles, ceramics, glassware, and metalwork were developed. Agriculture was thriving too. The Arabs introduced crops such as rice, watermelons, bananas, eggplant, and wheat, and the fields were irrigated according to new methods, which included the use of the waterwheel. Córdoba was a cosmopolitan city with a large multi-ethnic population of Spaniards, Arabs, Berbers, Christians and a flourishing community of Jews. In Córdoba, much as in the rest of the Arab world, the *dhimmi* were allowed to rule themselves as long as they stayed obedient to the rulers and paid their taxes. The caliphs were patrons of the arts and fashion and their courtiers took up civilized habits such as the use of deodorants and toothpaste.

Deodorants and the origin of flamenco

Abu l-Hasan, 789–857, nicknamed "Ziryab" from the Arabic for "blackbird," was a musician, singer, composer, poet, and teacher, who lived and worked in Baghdad, in Northern Africa, and during some thirty years also in al-Andalus in Spain. More than anything he was a master of the *oud*, the Arabic lute, to which he added a fifth pair of strings and began playing with a pick rather than with the fingers. Many good musicians assembled at the court in Córdoba, but Ziryab was the best. He established a school where the Arabic style of music was taught for successive generations, creating a tradition which was to have a profound influence on all subsequent Spanish music, not least on the flamenco.

The first references to flamenco can be found only in the latter part of the eighteenth century and then it was associated with the Romani people. Yet it is obvious that the flamenco is a product of the uniquely Andalusian mixture of cultures. The music does indeed sound Romani but at the same time also Arabic, Jewish, and Spanish. According to one theory, the word "flamenco" comes from the Arabic *fellah menghu*, meaning "expelled peasant." The *fellah menghu* were Arabs who remained in Spain after the fall of Granada in 1492. Some of them joined Romani communities in order to escape persecution. The Arabs and the Roma must have enjoyed themselves playing guitar and dancing together.

As for Ziryab, he was also ninth-century Córdoba's leading authority on questions of food and fashion. He was said to have changed his clothes according to the weather and the season, and he had the idea of wearing a different dress for mornings, afternoons and evenings. He invented a new type of deodorant and a toothpaste and promoted the idea of taking daily baths. He also made it fashionable for men to shave their beards. In addition, Ziryab popularized the concept of three-course meals, consisting of soup, main course, and dessert, and he was the person who introduced the asparagus to Europe. If a society's level of civilization can be determined by its standard of hygiene, Ziryab had a profoundly civilizing impact on southern Spain.

Read more online: https://hdl.handle.net/20.500.12434/f2a0fb14

Córdoba was an intellectual center also. The great mosque, completed in 987 and modeled on the Great Mosque of Damascus, was not only a place of religious worship but also an educational institution with a library which contained some 400,000 books. The scholars who gathered here did cutting-edge research in the medical sciences, including surgery and pharmaceuticals. They reacted quickly to intellectual developments that were coming out of Baghdad and from other places in the Arab world.

Yet this caliphate too proved difficult to keep together. In the first part of the eleventh century, it fell apart as rivalries, a coup and a fully-fledged civil war — the Fitna of al-Andalus — pitted various factions against each other. In 1031, the caliphate disintegrated completely and political power in the Iberian peninsula was transferred to the *taifa* — the small, thirty-plus kingdoms which all called themselves "emirates" and all to varying degrees were in conflict with one another. This was when the Christian kingdoms in the north of the peninsula began to make military gains. Christian forces captured Toledo in 1085, and the city soon established itself as the cultural and intellectual center of Christian Spain.

The Toledo school

Once Toledo was captured in 1085, it became the most important city in Christian Spain and its cultural and intellectual center. Christians from al-Andalus took their refuge here, but intellectually speaking the city served more as a bridge than as a spearhead. The scholars who settled in Toledo were often Arabic-speaking, and they relied on Arabic sources in their work. When they came into contact with western Christendom, where Latin was the only written language, it became necessary to translate this material. In the first part of the twelfth century, Raymond, the archbishop of Toledo, set up a center in the library of the cathedral where classical texts were translated, together with the commentaries and elaborations provided by Arabic authors. This was an exciting task since the Arabs had access to many works, including classical Greek texts, which Europeans had heard about but never themselves read. This included works by Galen, Ptolemy, Aristotle, and many others. Gerard of Cremona was the most productive of the translators, completing more than eighty-seven works on statecraft, ethics, physiognomy, astrology, geometry, alchemy, magic and medicine.

The translation movement of Toledo in the twelfth and thirteenth centuries thus parallels the translation movement of Baghdad in the ninth and tenth centuries. The Arabs translated the classics from Greek into Arabic, and now the same texts were translated from Arabic into Latin. From Toledo, the classical texts traveled to the rest of Europe where they were used as a textbook at a newly established institution — the university. Read more: *Nalanda, a very old university* at p. 56. This is how Albertus Magnus and Thomas Aquinas at the Sorbonne came to read Ibn Rushd and Ibn Sina, how Roger Bacon at Oxford became inspired by the scientific methods of Ibn al-Haytham and how Nicolaus Copernicus in Bologna read the works of Greek and Arabic astronomers. Renaissance means "rebirth" and what was reborn more than anything was the scholarship of classical antiquity — as saved, translated and elaborated on by the combined efforts of the scholars of Baghdad and Toledo.

Read more online: https://hdl.handle.net/20.500.12434/b733cd75

This is not to say that the various Christian kingdoms had a common goal and a common strategy. Rather, each Christian state, much as each Muslim, was looking after its own interests and waging wars with other kingdoms quite irrespective of religious affiliations. Thus some emirs were allied with Christian kings, while kings paid tribute to emirs, and they all employed knights who killed on behalf of whoever paid the highest salary. Quite apart from the military insecurity of the *taifa* period, this competition had positive side effects. The *taifa* kings sponsored both sciences and the arts. This is how small provincial hubs such as Zaragoza, Sevilla and Granada came to establish themselves as cultural centers in their own right.

Enter the Almoravids. Read more: *North Africa* at p. 131.

The Almoravids were a Berber tribe, originally nomads from the deserts of North Africa, who had established themselves as rulers of Morocco, with Marrakesh as their capital. After the fall of Toledo, they invaded al-Andalus and a year later, in 1086, they had already successfully occupied the southern half of the Iberian peninsula. However, they never managed to take back Toledo. In 1147, at the height of their power, the Almoravids were toppled and their leader killed by a rival coalition of Berber tribes known as the Almohads. The Almohads were a religious movement as well as a military force, and their rule followed strict Islamic principles: they banned the sale of pork and wine and men and women were forbidden to mix in public places. They burned books too — including Islamic tracts with which they disagreed — and insisted that Christians and Jews convert to Islam on pain of death.

Ibn Rushd and the challenge of reason

Ibn Rushd, also known as "Averroes," was a scholar and a philosopher born in Córdoba in al-Andalus in 1126. He is famous for his detailed commentaries on Aristotle, whose work he strongly defended against those who regarded him as an infidel. Ibn Rushd, that is, defended reason against revelation. Or rather, he regarded revelation, as presented in the Quran, as knowledge suitable above all for the illiterate masses. Ordinary people are literal-minded, and they need miracles in order to believe. Miracles do indeed happen, Ibn Rushd argued, but they must correspond to the laws which govern the universe. If not, the universe will become arbitrary and unintelligible.

The works of Ibn Rushd came to have far-reaching influence on intellectual developments in Europe, in particular on the thinking of Thomas Aquinas. Aquinas, the Church Father whose *Summa Theologica* laid the foundations for all theological debates in the European Middle Ages, asked himself the very same questions as Ibn Rushd. He too wanted to know how to reconcile reason with revelation. Aquinas too was a great fan of Aristotle, and although he disagreed with many of Ibn Rushd's specific arguments, his general conclusions were basically the same. Aquinas always referred to Ibn Rushd with the greatest respect, calling him "the Commentator," much as he called Aristotle "the Philosopher."

The seminal contribution which Ibn Rushd made to the intellectual development of Europe had no counterpart in the Muslim world. Here Ibn Rushd left no school and no disciples, and his works were barely read. It was only at the end of the nineteenth century that he was rediscovered. The immediate reason was a book by the French Orientalist Ernest Renan, *Averroès et l'Averroïsme*, 1852, in which Renan made a strong case for Ibn Rushd's importance. Translating Renan's book into Arabic, Muslim intellectuals discovered exactly what they had been looking for — an Arab who had made a seminal contribution not only to Arabic civilization but to the civilization of the world. To some contemporary Muslim intellectuals, the work of Ibn Rushd has become a symbol of a rationalistic intellectual tradition, in tune with modern society, liberalism and a scientific outlook on life.

Read more online: https://hdl.handle.net/20.500.12434/deab0a1f

By 1172, the Almohads had conquered all of al-Andalus. Under these circumstances many of the inhabitants preferred to flee — Christians to the north, while Jews fled east to Cairo and the Fatimid Caliphate, where the rulers were far more accepting of members of other religions.

Mosheh ben Maimon

Mosheh ben Maimon was a scholar, judge and medical doctor, born into an influential Jewish family in Córdoba in 1135. He is known as "Musa Ibn Maymun" in Arabic and as "Moses Maimonides" in Latin. Ben Maimon was trained both in the Jewish and the Arabic intellectual traditions, and he wrote in Judeo-Arabic, a classical form of Arabic which used the Hebrew script. Ben Maimon is most famous as the author of the fourteen-volume *Mishneh Torah*, a sprawling collection containing all the laws and regulations that govern Jewish life. The *Mishneh Torah* is widely read and commented on to this day.

In 1148, when the Almohad rulers of al-Andalus imposed their harsh reforms on their subjects, Christians and Jews were required to either convert or be killed. Ben Maimon and his family escaped to Egypt, which at the time was run by the Fatimid caliphs, a far more tolerant regime. In Cairo, he established himself as an interpreter of the Torah and as a teacher in the Jewish community. This is also when he wrote his most famous philosophical work, *Guide for the Perplexed*. We are knowledgeable about Ben Maimon's life thanks to the Cairo Geniza, a collection of up to 300,000 fragments of manuscripts discovered in the synagogue in Cairo. Since Jews were afraid to throw away any piece of paper which may have the name of God written on it, they ended up with a very large collection of scraps of papers of all kinds. The papers were kept in a "geniza," a storage room, and the Cairo Geniza, once the historians investigated it, turned out to include much of Ben Maimon's personal notes and correspondence.

Ben Maimon is buried in Tiberias, in today's Israel. On his death, as the story goes, he wanted to be buried in the land of his forefathers. Yet Ben Maimon would no doubt have objected to being made into an Israeli citizen after his death. More than anyone Ben Maimon symbolizes the tight connection that always has existed between Muslim and Jewish traditions. Meanwhile, the Jewish community in Cairo which as recently as in the 1920s comprised some 80,000 people has dwindled to

> fewer than 200 members today. There is a tradition among them that Ben Maimon's body never was transferred to Tiberias and that he still is buried in Cairo.
>
> *Read more online:* https://hdl.handle.net/20.500.12434/685232b7

Yet Almohad rule in al-Andalus did not last long. In 1212, at the Battle of Las Navas de Tolosa, the Christian princes managed, for the first time, to put up a united front against them. Córdoba fell to the Christian invaders in 1236 and Sevilla in 1248. From this time onward only Granada, together with associated smaller cities such Málaga, remained in Muslim hands. Here, however, the multicultural and dynamic spirit of al-Andalus continued to thrive for another 250 years. Wisely, after Navas de Tolosa, Granada allied itself with the Christian state of Castile. Although this friendship occasionally broke down, the Emirate of Granada, as it came to be known, continued to pay tribute to Castile in the form of gold from as far away as Mali in Africa. Read more: *Golden Stool of the Asante* at p. 138.

Today the most visible remnant of the Emirate of Granada is the Alhambra, the fortress and palace which served as the residence of the emir. It is famous above all for its courtyards, its fountains and its roses. Yet in 1492, Granada too fell to the Christians and the last Emir of al-Andalus — Muhammad XII, known as "Boabdil" to the Spaniards — was forced out of Spain. The Christians, much as the Almohads before them, were on a mission from God, and they ruled the territories they had conquered in a similarly repressive fashion. The Alhambra Decree, issued three months after the fall of Granada, forced the non-Christian population to convert or leave. As a result, some 200,000 Muslims left for North Africa, while an equal number of Jews preferred to settle in the Ottoman Empire to the east. This was the end of Muslim rule and the end of the cultural and intellectual flourishing of southern Spain.

A caliphal international system

The Fatimid Caliphate, 909–1171, is usually considered as the last of the four original caliphates which succeeded the prophet Muhammad. The Fatimids were originally Berbers from Tunisia but claimed their descent from Fatimah, the prophet's daughter. They were Shia Muslims, which make them unique among caliphs. In 969 they moved their capital to Cairo and from here they ruled all Muslim lands west of Syria, including the western part of the Arabian Peninsula, Sicily and all of North Africa. Fatimid Cairo displayed much the same multicultural mix and intellectual vigor as the capitals of the other caliphates. The Fatimids founded the al-Azhar mosque here in 970, and also the al-Azhar University, associated with the mosque, where students studied the Quran together with the sciences, mathematics, and philosophy. Al-Azhar University is still the chief center of Islamic learning in the world and the main source of *fatwas*, religious rulings, and opinions.

Yet the Fatimid Caliphate was not actually an empire, if we by that term mean a united political entity that imposes its authority on every part of the territory it claims to control. Much as the other caliphates, it had barely established itself before it began to fall apart. First, the Fatimids lost power over the Berber homeland where the Almoravids and Almohads took over; Sicily was next to break off, first establishing its own independent emirate and then, in 1072, the island was occupied by Vikings from France.

Kitab Rujar and the Emirate of Sicily

The Arabs did not only invade Spain but also Italy, or at least the southern Italian island of Sicily. In 831, Sicily was wrestled from the Byzantines and an emirate established here, with Palermo as its capital. It lasted, albeit in an increasingly weakened form, until 1072. Much as in Spain, the Arab occupation transformed a provincial backwater into a flourishing economic and cultural center. Land reform reduced the power of the old aristocracy and increased the productivity of agriculture; the irrigation systems were improved and the Arabs introduced new crops such as oranges, lemons, pistachios, and sugarcane. In the eleventh century, Palermo had a population of 350,000, making it the second-largest city in Europe after Córdoba in al-Andalus. In 1091, the Normans captured the island. The Normans were Vikings from France who started out as mercenaries working for Byzantine kings, but who before long began making war on their own behalf. Yet in sharp contrast to the situation in Spain after the *Reconquista*, the Normans did not try to destroy Arab Sicily. Instead, Arab scholars and artists were given new commissions and Arab bureaucrats continued to be employed by the new rulers. Visitors were astonished to learn that even the king's own chef — a key position for anyone interested in poisoning his majesty — was an Arab. The result was a blend of Arabic, Byzantine and Norman influences which is still on display in some of Palermo's churches.

The court of the Norman king Roger II, 1130–1154, was particularly splendid. Although its official language was French, the king spoke Arabic fluently, and the administration communicated with its subjects in Latin, Greek, Arabic, and Hebrew. People were encouraged to convert to Christianity, but Islam was tolerated. The geographer Muhammad al-Idrisi, was one of the scholars employed at Roger's court. In 1154, after fifteen years of research, he produced the *Kitab Rujar*, the "Book of Roger," a description and a map of the world. The original copy of *Kitab Rujar* was lost in the 1160s and the Norman court was destroyed soon after that. Next Sicily came under the power of the Catholic church. The persecution of Arabs began in the 1240s and Byzantine influences were wiped out too. By the 1330s, Palermo was once again a provincial backwater — now with only 50,000 inhabitants.

Read more online: https://hdl.handle.net/20.500.12434/ce76893e

In the end the caliphs were really only in control of their heartland in the Nile River Valley.

In addition, the Fatimid caliphs became increasingly dependent on mercenaries, known as mamluks, meaning "possession" or "slave." The mamluks were bought or captured as children, often from the Caucasus or Turkish-speaking parts of Central Asia. From here they were taken to Cairo where they were housed in garrisons together with other captives, brought up in the Muslim faith and taught martial arts — archery and cavalry in particular. The mamluks served as soldiers and military leaders but also as scribes, courtiers, advisers, and administrators. As it turned out, however, it was not a good idea to give slaves access to weapons. The mamluks ousted the Fatimids and took power in Egypt in 1250. They continued to rule the country, as the Mamluk Sultanate, until 1517, when the Ottomans invaded.

Saladin and the Crusaders

Richard Coeur-de-lion, or "Lionheart," 1189–1199, was an English king, yet he is famous above all as one of the commanders of the Third Crusade. In 1099, during the First Crusade, the Europeans had captured Jerusalem and established a Christian kingdom there. In 1187, however, the Europeans were decisively defeated at the Battle of Hattin, and Jerusalem retaken by the Muslims. It was to relieve them, and to try to get Jerusalem back, that Richard set off for the Holy Land. On his way there he occupied Sicily in 1190, Cyprus in 1191, and once he arrived he retook the city of Acre. The Europeans established a new kingdom here which was to last until 1291. Read more: *Rabban Bar Sauma, Mongol envoy to the pope* at p. 113. But that was as far as Richard got. The various European commanders were quarreling with each other; they lacked the soldiers and the patience required for a successful campaign. Despite repeated attempts, Richard never recaptured Jerusalem.

The person who more than anyone else stopped the Europeans was An-Nasir Salah ad-Din Yusuf ibn Ayyub, 1174–1193, known as "Salah ad-Din" or "Saladin." Saladin was of Kurdish origin but had made his career with the Fatimids in Cairo where he rose to become vizier. In 1171, he turned on his employer and established a dynasty of his own, the Ayyubids, 1171–1270. It was Saladin and the Ayyubid armies that defeated the Crusaders at Hattin, took Jerusalem back, and successfully defended themselves against the onslaught of the foreigners.

Richard Lionheart and Saladin are the original "knights in shining armor." Despite an abundance of high-quality scholarship on the Crusades it is difficult to separate facts about them from all the fiction. Walter Scott, the British author, published a highly romanticized account of their rivalry in 1825, and in the twentieth century, Hollywood has produced a number of similar versions. According to the Europeans, Richard brought Christianity and civilization to the Middle East. According to the Arabs, Saladin defended Muslim lands against a barbarian invasion. Reading and fantasizing about them ever since, political leaders both in Europe and in the Muslim world have found their respective role models.

Read more online: https://hdl.handle.net/20.500.12434/d34b96c8

The Mamluk sultans ran a meritocratic regime which rewarded the talented and the hardworking rather than the well-connected, but since succession did not follow a family line, the infighting at court was intense. Some rulers ruled for days rather than years and none of them slept comfortably at night. The Mamluks embarked on ambitious architectural projects, constructing mosques and other public buildings in a distinct architectural style of their own.

The result was an international system with unique characteristics — perhaps we could talk about a "caliphal international system." Instead of being an empire, each caliphate was more like a federation where the constituent parts had a considerable amount of independence from the center and from each other. The system as a whole was held together by institutional rather than by military means — by its language, its administrative prowess and by an abiding loyalty to the idea of the caliphate itself. And it was held together by religion too of course. The caliphs were religious leaders of enormous cultural authority. This applied in particular to the caliphs, such as the Fatimids, who had responsibility for the holy sites at Mecca and Medina.

In this international system there were occasional conflicts over boundaries and jurisdictions, but there were no wars of conquest. Political entities beyond the caliphate's borders would occasionally make trouble, and military expeditions would be dispatched to punish them, yet the caliphs much preferred to control the foreigners by cultural means. For example: Baghdad would dispatch missions to the Bulgars, a people living on the river Volga in present-day Russia, in order to instruct them how to properly practice the Muslim faith.

A Viking funeral on the Volga

Ahmad ibn Fadlan was a *faqih*, an expert in Islamic jurisprudence, who accompanied an embassy dispatched in 921 by the Abbasid caliph to the Bulgars who lived along the river Volga, in today's Russia. The Volga Bulgars had only recently been converted to Islam and the purpose of the mission was to explain the tenets of the faith and to instruct them in the proper ritual. This was why Ibn Fadlan came along.

The embassy encountered many interesting peoples along the way, but it is Ibn Fadlan's account of the Vikings which is most famous. In the tenth century, Vikings from today's Sweden relied on the rivers of Russia to travel and to trade, and their commercial contacts reached as far as Constantinople, Baghdad, and the Silk Road. Ibn Fadlan was both fascinated and horrified by these people. "I have never seen more perfect physiques than theirs," he insisted — they are "fair and reddish" and tall "like palm trees," and tattooed "from the tip of his toes to his neck." Yet they were also ignorant of God, disgusting in their habits and devoid of any sense of personal hygiene.

Ibn Fadlan went on to describe a Viking funeral which he personally had witnessed. First, the dead chieftain was placed in a boat, together with his swords and possessions, then a number of cows, horses, dogs, and cockerels were sacrificed. Finally, a slave girl was dressed up as his bride and ritually raped by all the warriors. She too was placed on the funeral pyre, while the members of the tribe banged on their shields to drown out her screams. The boat was then set alight.

In 2007, a Syrian TV station produced a drama series based on Ibn Fadlan's account. The background was the controversy stirred up when *Hollands-Posten*, a Danish newspaper, published cartoons of the Prophet Muhammad which many Muslims regarded as offensive. The publication led to diplomatic protests, a boycott of Danish goods and to demonstrations and rioting in several Muslim countries in

> which some 200 people were killed. It is easy to see why Ibn Fadlan's account might appeal to an Arab audience of TV viewers. He was a sophisticated intellectual, of urbane tastes and refined manners, and the Scandinavians he encountered were little more than savages. The task of today's Muslims too is to explain the true meaning of Islam to Europeans, and perhaps to Scandinavians in particular.
>
> *Read more online:* https://hdl.handle.net/20.500.12434/0378c429

Rulers such as the Bulgars paid tribute and, as a result, the caliphates came to exercise a measure of control over far larger areas than their armies could capture.

Two external incursions temporarily wreaked havoc with these arrangements — the invasions by European Crusaders and by the Mongols. Both had come to Muslim lands from very far away indeed, and they had no respect whatsoever for Islamic civilization or for the idea of the caliphate. Both were also bent on territorial conquest. The Europeans, known to the Arabs as *Faranj*, from "Franks," first arrived in the eastern Mediterranean in the final years of the eleventh century and proceeded to capture Jerusalem and what they regarded as the "Holy Land." Read more: *Saladin and the Crusaders* at p. 88.

They then returned again and again as the First Crusade, 1095–1099, was followed by similar military campaigns in 1145, 1189, 1202, 1213, 1248 and 1270. The *Faranj* established small kingdoms on the territory of the Fatimid Caliphate, and they waged war in a barbaric fashion — the capture of Jerusalem in 1099, and the subsequent massacre of civilians, is only the most notorious example. In 1291, with the fall of the last Crusader state, the Europeans were finally defeated. As far as the Mongols are concerned, they captured and destroyed Baghdad in 1258, yet only two years later, at the Battle of Ain Jalut, they were themselves defeated and their advance stopped. Although the Mongols had been beaten before, they would always come back to exact a terrible revenge. After Ain Jalut, however, this did not happen. It signaled the beginning of the end of the Mongol Empire.

Why empires rise and fall was a question that preoccupied Ibn Khaldun, 1332–1406, a historian and philosopher, who worked first in Tunis, then in Cairo. It is the communal spirit of a people, he argued, which makes a state powerful. This is the spirit that causes a group, such as the Berbers of North Africa, work together even under the harshest of circumstances. Yet, once they have come to power and settled in cities, they lose their communal spirit. Instead, everyone becomes more selfish and the political leaders start fighting each other. Ibn Khaldun's work, the *Muqaddimah*, published in 1377, is sometimes considered the first text on historical sociology.

Ibn Khaldun and the role of *asabiyyah*

Ibn Khaldun, 1332–1406, was a historian and philosopher born in Tunis in North Africa but in a family which for centuries had been officials to the Muslim rulers of Spain. By Khaldun's time, Muslim North Africa was in decline and the once-powerful states had fragmented into a number of competing political entities. It was among these that Ibn Khaldun looked for employment. He was well-read in the Arabic classics, an expert in jurisprudence, and he knew the Quran by heart. He was, by all accounts, extraordinarily ambitious and perfectly convinced of his own intellectual superiority. He was also in the habit of plotting against his employers. The result was a life which alternatively turned him into a statesman and a prisoner.

In 1375, he took a prolonged sabbatical from his political career and settled in the Berber town of Qalat Ibn Salama, in today's Algeria. Here he began writing what at first was meant to be a history of the Berber people but which soon turned into a history of the world, prefaced by a *Muqaddimah*, a "Prolegomenon," in which he laid out his theory of history. Writing as a historical sociologist, Ibn Khaldun sought to explain what it is that makes kingdoms rise and fall. As far as the rise to power is concerned, he emphasized the role of *asabiyyah*, "social cohesion" or "group solidarity." The Berbers provide a good example. They survived in the harsh conditions of the desert only because they stayed united and helped each other out. This sense of solidarity provided them with *mulk*, "the ability to govern," and made them into formidable conquerors. The success of a conqueror, however, would never last long. Once in power, the *asabiyyah* would start to dissipate as the new rulers became rich and began to indulge in assorted luxuries. Instead of relying on the solidarity of the group, the rulers employed mercenaries to fight their wars and bureaucrats to staff their ministries. In five generations, Ibn Khaldun explained, the *mulk* was gone and the state was ripe for a takeover by others.

Read more online: https://hdl.handle.net/20.500.12434/95b70d1f

The Ottoman Empire

The empire which rose to replace the Abbasids as leaders of the Muslim world were the Ottomans. The Ottomans were Turks with their origin in Central Asia, and they spoke Turkish, not Arabic. Remarkably, the same dynasty, the Osmans, was in charge of the empire from Osman I in the thirteenth century until the last sultan, Mehmed VI, in the twentieth. Altogether there were thirty-six Ottoman sultans. Although the Turks too were Muslim and called themselves a "caliphate" — the Ottoman Caliphate, 1517–1924 — their capital was the former Greek city of Constantinople. While they ruled much of North Africa and the Middle East, they ruled much of Europe too — the Balkans in particular and large parts of eastern Europe.

First founded in 1299, the Ottoman Empire began as one of many small states on the territory of what today is Turkey. After having conquered most of their neighbors, the Ottomans moved across the Bosporus and into Europe in the early fifteenth century. Before long they came to completely surround the Byzantines — now reduced to the size of little more than the city of Constantinople itself. As far as the Byzantine Empire is concerned, it claimed a legacy that went right back to the Roman era. In the year 330 CE, emperor Constantine had moved the capital to the eastern city that came to carry his name. Rather miraculously, when the Western Roman Empire fell apart in the fifth and sixth centuries, the Eastern Roman Empire survived. Over the years Constantinople was besieged by Arabs, Persians and Russians, and in 1204 the city was sacked and destroyed by members of the Fourth Crusade. Despite these setbacks, the Byzantine Empire managed to thrive both culturally and economically.

> ### The Byzantine diplomatic service
>
> The Byzantine Empire, 330–1453, was originally the eastern part of the Roman Empire, where Emperor Constantine established a capital, Constantinople, in 330. When Rome was overrun and sacked by various wandering tribes, the empire survived in the east. The Byzantine Empire was to last for another thousand years and at the height of its power, it comprised all lands around the eastern Mediterranean, including North Africa and Egypt. The Byzantines spoke Greek, they were Christian, and they spread their language and their religion to all parts of the empire. An educated person in Egypt or Syria prior to the eighth century was likely to have been Christian and Greek-speaking.
>
> An important reason for the longevity of the Byzantine Empire was its aggressive use of diplomacy. They set up a "Bureau of Barbarians" which gathered intelligence on the empire's rivals and prepared diplomats for their missions abroad. The diplomats negotiated treaties and formed alliances and spent much time making friends with the enemies of their enemies. Foreign governments were often undermined by various underhanded tactics. For example: in Constantinople, there was a whole stable of exiled, foreign, royalty whom the Byzantines were ready to reinstall on their thrones if an occasion presented itself.
>
> Constantinople was thoroughly sacked by the participants in the Fourth Crusade in 1204, an event which left bitter resentment and strong anti-Catholic feelings among all Orthodox Christians. In the thirteenth century, the Turks began expanding into the Anatolian peninsula, and eventually, the once vast Byzantine Empire came to comprise little but the capital itself and its surrounding countryside. Constantinople fell to the Turks in 1453 and the large cathedral, Hagia Sophia, was turned into a mosque. The fall of Constantinople is still remembered as a great disaster by Greek people while Turks celebrate it as ordained by Allah and foretold by the prophet Muhammad himself.
>
> "Byzantine" is an English adjective which means "devious" and "scheming" but also "intricate" and "involved." Learning about the diplomatic practices of the empire, it is easy to understand why. But then again, their diplomacy served the Byzantines well.
>
> *Read more online:* https://hdl.handle.net/20.500.12434/8fb10ad6

However, in May 1453, after a seven-week-long siege, Constantinople fell to the Ottomans, led by Sultan Mehmed II, henceforth known as "Mehmed the Conqueror." The city was renamed "Istanbul," and the famous cathedral, Hagia Sophia, was turned into a mosque. The defeat was met with fear and trepidation by Christians all over Europe and it is mournfully remembered by Greek people to this day.

Even as Constantinople was renamed "Istanbul," it continued to be a cosmopolitan city. In the Ottoman Empire, much as in the Arab caliphates which preceded it, the *dhimmi* enjoyed a protected status. Known as the *millet* system in Turkish, the Ottoman Empire gave each minority group the right to maintain its traditions and to be judged by its own legal code. It was policies such as these that convinced many Jews to settle here after the Christian occupation of Muslim Spain in 1492. To this day there are Spanish-speaking Jews in the former parts of the Ottoman Empire. Moreover, the city's strategic location at the intersection of Europe and Asia was as beneficial to Ottoman traders as it had been to the Byzantines. The state manipulated the economy to serve its own ends — to strengthen the army and to enrich the rulers — yet the administrators employed for these purposes were highly trained and competent. The state-sponsored projects which the Ottomans embarked on, such as the construction of roads, canals and mosques, helped spur economic development. The empire was prosperous and markets for both consumer items and fashion were established.

Tulipmanias

At the beginning of 1637, a madness seems to have overcome the Dutch. Everyone was buying tulips and the prices of tulip bulbs were skyrocketing. Even the most casual of daily conversations contained references to the prices for various strains, hybrids, and colors. For a while, one single bulb was selling for more than ten times the annual income of an ordinary laborer. In the rising market, extraordinary wealth could be accumulated in a matter of days. Soon what was bought and sold was not the tulips themselves, but the right to buy or sell tulips at a certain price at a future date. The Dutch were seized by "tulipmania."

Today we may associate tulips with Holland, but originally the flower grew wild in Anatolia, in today's Turkey. In 1554, the first bulbs were sent from the Ottoman Empire to Vienna and from here the flower soon spread to Germany and the United Dutch Republic. The first attempts to grow tulips took place in Leiden in 1593 and it turned out that the flower survived well in the harsher climate of northern Europe. Soon tulips became a status symbol for members of the commercial middle classes. The flower was not only beautiful and unusual but, given the Ottoman connection, also very exotic. When commercial cultivators entered the market, prices began to rise. This was where the speculation in the tulip market began.

The "Tulip Period" is the name commonly given to the short era, 1718–1730, when the Ottoman Empire began orienting itself towards Europe. It was a time of commercial and industrial expansion and when the first printing presses were established in Istanbul. In the Ottoman Empire too there was a tulip craze. In Ottoman court society, it was suddenly very fashionable to grow the flower, to display it in one's home and to wear it on one's clothes. The tulip became a common motif in architecture and fabrics. In the Ottoman Empire too, prices of bulbs rose quickly and great fortunes were made and lost. This was the first commercialized fad to sweep over the caliphate and the beginnings of modern consumer culture.

Read more online: https://hdl.handle.net/20.500.12434/740ed361

The Ottomans continued to enjoy military success. Selim I, 1512–1520, established a navy which operated as far away as in the Red Sea and the Persian Gulf. He defeated both Persia and the Mamluks in Egypt, dramatically expanding an empire that came to include the holy cities of Mecca and Medina. It was then that the sultans began calling themselves "caliphs," implying that they were the rulers of all Muslim believers everywhere. Suleiman I, known as "the Magnificent," 1520–1566, continued the expansion into Europe. He captured Belgrade in 1521 and Hungary in 1526, and laid siege to Vienna in 1529, but failed to take the city. The Ottoman army responsible for these feats was quite different from the European armies of the time. Like other armies with their roots in a nomadic tradition, they relied on speed and mobility to overtake their enemies but the Ottoman armies were also one of the first to use muskets. During the siege of Constantinople they used falconets — short, light cannons — to great effect. More surprisingly perhaps, the Ottomans had a powerful navy which helped them unite territories on all sides of the Mediterranean. The Ottoman army, much as armies elsewhere in the Muslim world, relied heavily on foreign-born soldiers.

Janissaries and Turkish military music

The janissaries were the elite corps of the Ottoman army, independent of the regular troops and responsible directly to the sultan himself. In a practice known as *devşirme*, or "gathering," the Ottomans would periodically search Christian villages in the Balkans for young boys whom they would proceed to abduct. The boys were taken to the Ottoman Empire, taught Turkish, circumcised and given a Muslim education. The great advantage for the sultans was that these men had no families and their only loyalty was to the sultan himself. By relying on the janissaries to carry out the key functions of the state, it was possible to sideline the traditional nobility. The janissaries were used, to great effect, in all military engagements, including the siege in 1453 when Constantinople was captured. During the reign of Suleiman the Magnificent, 1520–1566, there were some 30,000 janissaries employed by the Ottoman state.

Initially, the janissaries were not allowed to marry or to own property. They lived together in garrisons where they practiced various martial arts and socialized only among themselves. They wore distinct uniforms and were required to grow mustaches but not allowed to grow beards. From the seventeenth century onward, however, they became powerful enough to change many of these rules. The practice of *devşirme* was discontinued in the seventeenth century, mainly since the existing janissaries did not want competition from outsiders.

The janissaries had their own distinct form of music, known as *mehterân*. When marching off to war they would bring their musicians with them. The shrill ululations of the *zurna*, a sort of oboe, struck a fearful mood in the enemy much as the *davul* drums made the janissaries more courageous. Impressed by these effects, European armies too began making use of military bands. Turkish military music suffered when the janissaries' corps was abolished in 1826, but the tradition has recently been revived.

Read more online: https://hdl.handle.net/20.500.12434/4a6911c2

In the case of the Ottomans too, these former slaves eventually established themselves as rulers in their own right. This is how the Ottoman provinces of Egypt, Iraq and Syria came to assume an increasingly independent position, each ruled by its own military commanders.

The Ottomans were skillful diplomats. Despite the official Christian fear of the Turks, the Ottoman Empire was, after 1453, a European power and as such an obvious partner in both alliances and wars. This was particularly the case for any European power that opposed countries which were also the enemies of the Turks — such as the Habsburg Empire and Russia. The French, for example, quickly realized that the Ottomans constituted a force that could be convinced to attack the Habsburgs from the south. During the Thirty Years War in the seventeenth century, the king of Sweden drew the same conclusion. And much later, in the 1850s, Great Britain and France relied on Turkey as an ally in waging war against Russia in the Crimea. At the Congress of Paris, 1856, which concluded the Crimean War, the Ottoman Empire was officially included as a member of the European international system of states.

Yet for much of its later history, the empire was in decline. Economically it suffered when international trade routes, from the sixteenth century onward, were directed away from the Mediterranean. Together with the rest of Eastern Europe it suffered again when, in the nineteenth century, the western parts of Europe began to industrialize and cheap factory-made goods began flooding in. The failed siege of Vienna in 1683 — the second time the Ottomans tried to take the city — is often seen as the symbolic start of the decline. The Ottomans held the city ransom for some two months, during which food was becoming exceedingly scarce and the Austrians increasingly desperate.

Coffee and croissants

All coffee comes originally from Ethiopia where the coffee tree grows wild. By the fourteenth century, the tree was cultivated by the Arabs and exported from the port city of Mocha in today's Yemen. But it was only once the Ottomans occupied the Arabian peninsula in the first part of the sixteenth century that the habit of coffee drinking really took off. The first coffeehouse opened in Istanbul in 1554, and before long sipping coffee, eating cakes and socializing became a fashionable pastime. From the Ottoman Empire, the coffee-drinking habit was exported to the rest of Europe, together with the word itself. "Coffee" comes from the Turkish *kahve*, and ultimately from the Arabic *qahwa*. The first coffee shop opened in Venice in 1645, in London in 1650 and in Paris in 1672.

Vienna has its own and quite distinct café tradition. The Viennese drink their coffee with hot foamed milk and, just as in Turkey, it is served with a glass of cold water. The first coffeehouse in Vienna was opened by a man called Jerzy Franciszek Kulczycki, a Polish officer in the Habsburg army. Since Kulczycki had spent two years as a Turkish prisoner of war, he was well acquainted with the habit of coffee drinking and was quick to spot a business opportunity. Every year, coffeehouses in Vienna used to put portraits of Kulczycki in their windows in recognition of his achievements.

There is a legend that the croissant — the flaky, crescent-shaped pastry that French people, in particular, like to eat for breakfast — first was invented during the

> siege of Vienna. According to one version of the story, the Ottomans were trying to tunnel into the city at night, but a group of bakers who were up early preparing their goods for the coming day heard them and sounded the alarm. The croissant, invoking the crescent shape so popular in Muslim countries, was supposedly invented as a way to celebrate the victory. Unfortunately, however, this story cannot possibly be true. Baked goods in a crescent shape — known as *kipferl* in German — were already popular in Austria in the thirteenth century.
>
> *Read more online:* https://hdl.handle.net/20.500.12434/63788023

In the end the Ottomans were decisively defeated, losing perhaps 40,000 men. And before the end of the seventeenth century they had lost both Hungary and Transylvania to the Austrians. In the nineteenth century, the Ottoman Empire became known as "the sick man of Europe." A number of administrative reforms were tried during this period. After the revolt of the so-called "Young Turks" in 1908 — a secret society of university students — the Ottoman Empire became a constitutional monarchy in which the sultan no longer enjoyed executive powers. The Ottoman Empire ceased to exist in 1922, the Republic of Turkey was founded in 1923, and the caliphate was officially abolished in 1924.

Further reading

Adamson, Peter. *Philosophy in the Islamic World*. Oxford: Oxford University Press, 2016.

Bauer, Susan Wise. *The History of the Medieval World: From the Conversion of Constantine to the First Crusade*. New York: WW Norton & Co., 2010.

Bennison, Amira K. *The Great Caliphs: The Golden Age of the 'Abbasid Empire*. London: I. B. Tauris, 2009.

Casale, Giancarlo. *The Ottoman Age of Exploration*. New York; Oxford: Oxford University Press, 2010.

Faroqhi, Suraiya. *The Ottoman Empire and the World Around It*. London: I. B. Tauris, 2006.

Gutas, Dimitri. *Greek Thought, Arabic Culture: The Graeco-Arabic Translation Movement in Baghdad and Early 'Abbasaid Society*. London: Routledge, 1998.

Jayyusi, Salma Khadra, ed. *The Legacy of Muslim Spain*. Leiden: Brill, 2000.

Menocal, Maria Rosa. *The Ornament of the World: How Muslims, Jews and Christians Created a Culture of Tolerance in Medieval Spain*. Boston: Back Bay Books, 2003.

Ramadan, Tariq. *Introduction to Islam*. New York: Oxford University Press, 2017.

Timeline

632	Death of the Prophet Muhammad in Medina.
657	The First Fitna or Muslim civil war is fought between groups which later would become Sunni and Shia.
661	The Umayyad Caliphate is established in Damascus.
711	Arabs cross into Spain at Gibraltar.
732	The Battle of Tour in central France. The Muslim forces are defeated.
750	The Umayyads are defeated in the Second Fitna. The Abbasid Caliphate is founded and takes Baghdad as its capital.
929	The Caliphate of Córdoba is established by a branch of the Umayyad family.
969	Cairo is founded by the Fatimid Caliphate.
1031	Fall of the Caliphate of Córdoba.
1212	Battle of Las Navas de Tolosa where a coalition of Christian kings defeats the Almoravids.
1258	The Mongols destroy Baghdad.
1453	The Ottomans capture Constantinople and rename it "Istanbul."
1492	Granada falls and the last Muslim ruler leaves for North Africa.
1683	The Ottomans besiege Vienna but fail to take the city.
1922	The Ottoman Empire is dissolved.

Short dictionary

asabiyyah, Arabic	"Solidarity," or "group cohesion." A term used by Ibn Khaldun to explain the military and political success of nomadic peoples like the Berber.
devşirme, Turkish	"Ingathering." The Ottoman practice of kidnapping young boys, mainly in the Balkans, who were brought up as servants of the state. The practice was abolished in the first part of the eighteenth century.
dhimmi, Arabic	Literally, "protected person." Designated non-Muslim residents of a Muslim caliphate. Equivalent to the Turkish *millet*.
Faranj, Arabic	Literally, "Frank." "European." Name given to the waves of armies from Europe who invaded the Middle East from the eleventh to the thirteenth century. Cf. the Thai *farang* and the Malay *ferenggi*.
fatwa, Arabic	A legal opinion on a point of Islamic law given by a legal scholar.
fitna, Arabic	Literally, "sedition," "temptation" or "civil strife." The name given to wars fought between various Muslim groups.
hajj, Arabic	Pilgrimage to Mecca. A religious duty for all Muslims.
jihad, Arabic	Literally, "striving" or "struggle." Any effort to make personal or social life conform to God's guidance. This includes proselytizing and projects that improve the situation of the *ummah*.
jizya, Arabic	The tax which Muslim rulers imposed on non-Muslim subjects.
majlis, Arabic	Literally, "a place of sitting." Name for legislatures in the Islamic world, but also for gatherings that take place in private houses. The *majlis* of the Abbasid Caliphate were centers of intellectual discussion.
millet, Turkish	"Nation." Designated non-Muslim communities which lived in the Ottoman Empire. Equivalent to the Arabic *dhimmi*.
Reconquista, La. Spanish	Literally, "The reconquest." The attempt by Christian princes in northern Spain to occupy al-Andalus. Completed in 1492.
sahabah, Arabic	The companions, disciples, scribes and family of the Prophet Muhammad.
sharia, Arabic	Islamic law based on the text of the Quran, the Islamic tradition and rulings by legal scholars.
taifa, Arabic	The small Muslim kingdoms that were formed all over southern Spain after the fall of the Caliphate of Córdoba in 1031.

Think about

The Arab expansion
- Why did the people of the Arabian peninsula began their military expansion? What explains their success?
- Describe relations between the Arab rulers and the people they conquered.
- What is the origin of the split between the Sunni and the Shia?

The Umayyads and the Abbasids
- What characterized the "Arab Golden Age"?
- Which were the main centers of the Abbasid Caliphate?
- How did the Abbasid Caliphate come to an end?

The Arabs in Spain
- Describe the cultural and intellectual life in the Caliphate of Córdoba.
- Who were the Almoravids and who were the Almohads?
- How did Muslim rule in Spain end?

A caliphal international system
- Who were the Fatimids? Who were the Mamluks?
- What made Sicily into such a cosmopolitan place?
- What unites the Muslim world? What divides it?

The Ottoman empire
- Who were the Ottomans?
- How did the Ottoman Empire become a European power?
- What is the millet system?

Map of Tartaria from Abraham Ortelius, Theatrum orbis terrarum (Antverpiae: Apud Aegid. Coppenium Diesth, 1570), p. 207, https://archive.org/details/theatrumorbister00orte

5. The Mongol Khanates

In the thirteenth and fourteenth centuries, the Mongols created the largest contiguous empire the world has ever known. In 1206, Temüjin, an orphan and a former slave, united the many feuding clans which occupied the steppes to the north of China and took the title "Genghis Khan." Once this feat was accomplished he turned to military conquests abroad. The Mongols' armies were spectacularly successful. Their soldiers, consisting only of cavalry, were fast, highly disciplined and well organized, and they wielded their bows and lances while still on horseback. Since most lands between Europe and Asia were sparsely populated and quite unprotected, the Mongols quickly overran an enormous territory while most of the actual warfare consisted of sieges. Once they had mastered the art of siege warfare, the cities too fell into their hands. The Mongols fought in the jungles of Southeast Asia too, built a navy and tried to invade both Java and Japan. In 1241 they completely obliterated the European armies that had gathered against them and in 1258 they besieged, sacked and burned Baghdad. At the height of their power, the Mongols controlled an area which stretched from central Europe to the Pacific Ocean. It was a territory about the size of the African continent and considerably larger than North America. Although the Mongols counted only about one million people at the time, the lands they once controlled comprise today a majority of the world's population.

The Mongols were known as merciless warriors who destroyed the cities they captured, sparing no humans and occasionally killing also their cats and dogs. Yet apart from their military superiority, they had nothing much to impart to the rest of the world. The Mongols made no technological breakthroughs, founded no religions, built no buildings, and they had not even mastered simple techniques such as weaving, pottery or bread-making. Rather, by conquering such a vast territory, and by unifying it under the same administration, they managed to connect parts of the world which previously had never been connected, or not connected as closely and efficiently. The results were profound and revolutionary. Throughout the land they controlled, the Mongols guaranteed the security of travelers and they encouraged trade by reducing taxes and facilitating travel. During the so-called *Pax Mongolica*, the "Mongol peace," exchanges along the caravan routes of Central Asia became more intense than ever before. This was when Persian businessmen would go to China on regular visits and when a diplomatic envoy from a Mongol khan could visit Paris and take communion with the pope in Rome.

© 2019 Erik Ringmar, CC BY 4.0   https://doi.org/10.11647/OBP.0074.05

The Mongol Empire lasted only some 150 years. The political structure had already begun to crack by the middle of the thirteenth century and by the early fourteenth century it was disintegrating. In 1368, the Mongols lost control over their most prized possession — China. One important reason for the decline and fall of the Mongol empire was the perpetual infighting which took place among Genghis Khan's descendants. When his grandchildren by the middle of the thirteenth century were ready to take over the realm, the question of succession turned out to be impossible to settle. The outcome was a civil war which turned brothers against each other and eventually resulted in the division of the empire into four separate realms — the Golden Horde in Russia, the Ilkhanate in Persia, the Yuan dynasty in China, and the Chagatai khanate in the traditional heartlands of Mongolia. Although these entities were closely related to each other in various ways, there were also constant conflicts between them. In addition, the Black Death, a contagious disease that spread quickly along the caravan routes, decimated the population and made travel and exchange into deadly activities. As a result, at the end of the fourteenth century, the Mongol Empire was once again a small kingdom confined to the steppes north of China. Its last remnant was conquered by the Manchu armies in 1635. Other vestiges of the Mongols and their descendants lived on, most successfully in the form of the Mughal Empire in India, founded in 1526 by Babur who counted himself as a direct descendant of Genghis Khan. Read more: *The Mughal Empire* at p. 64.

From Temüjin to Genghis Khan

The boy who was to become Genghis Khan was born in 1162, not far from the current Mongolian capital of Ulaanbaatar. He was given the name Temüjin. Like all Mongolian boys, Temüjin learned to ride a horse at a very early age, to tend the family's animals and to hunt. His father was a chieftain, and well respected within the society of nomads, but there were many chieftains on the steppes. Indeed, the people we call the Mongols were only one of many nomadic tribes — in addition, there were Merkits, Naimans, Keraits, Tatars, Uyghurs, and so on — and the Mongols were not even the largest group among them. Each tribe was divided into clans and lineages, and many of them were in perpetual conflict with each other — over grazing rights, horses and treasure. They traded with each other, but they also raided each other's camps looking for women to take as wives or for children to capture and keep as slaves. Indeed kidnapping was a common way to obtain a wife, especially for those who were too poor to be considered eligible husbands.

Then disaster struck. Temüjin's father was killed and the family was cast out by their clan who decided that they did not have enough food to feed them. Instead, at the age of only eight, Temüjin had to help his family eke out a living gathering plants on the steppe and hunting in the forest. Remarkably the family survived, although their camp was raided and Temüjin was taken prisoner and made into a slave. At the age of seventeen, he managed to escape his captors and marry a girl, Börte, to whom he had been engaged while his father was alive. Yet Börte too was abducted by a rival tribe. This event, however, was to be the beginning of Temüjin's career as a conqueror. Together with a small band of followers, he attacked the kidnappers and took back his wife. He meted out an act of terrible revenge on her captors — killing the men and enslaving their women and children.

Temüjin's skills as a raider soon attracted wider attention and before long he concluded a treaty with one of the traditional chieftains, which gave him access to a far larger contingent of men. This was the band of warriors which he went on to leverage into an ever-increasing force as every successful raid attracted ever more of a following. The people who were loyal to him he treated as family members, while those who crossed or betrayed him were given no mercy. In 1206, Temüjin called a *kurultai*, an assembly of the leading chieftains, where he was elected *khagan*, khan of khans. He took the name "Genghis Khan" for himself. There is no consensus on what "genghis" actually means and in any case the pronunciation in Mongolian is closer to "chinggis." The people he united came to be called "Mongols" after the name of his own tribe. Genghis Khan was now the supreme leader of perhaps 1 million people and some 15 to 20 million horses, sheep, and goats.

A nomadic state

Once in power, Genghis Khan put in place a legal and institutional framework that would help break the cycle of violence in Mongol society and prevent the kinds of events that had wreaked havoc in his own life. One aim was to abolish the traditional divisions into tribes, clans and lineages. Consequently Genghis Khan abolished aristocratic titles and promoted people according to merit. He was also keen to advance the careers of people from other tribes than his own — or indeed, once the foreign conquests had begun, of people other than Mongols. Genghis Khan also decimalized the army, as it were. That is, he divided the men into groups of ten — known as *arban* — drawn from different sections of Mongol society. Each *arban* was then ordered to live and fight together as loyally as brothers. From the point of view of the government, each group of ten men was treated as a family and thereby as the basic unit not only of military but also of social life. The ten-groups were then multiplied by ten to produce groups of 100, 1,000 and 10,000 soldiers. A group of 10,000 men, that is, soldiers, was known as a *tumen*.

A new legal code, the *yassa*, was also established which criminalized a number of actions, in particular those which Genghis Khan knew to be a cause of conflict. Thus the abduction of wives and the sale of women were declared illegal, together with the enslavement of fellow Mongols. Theft of cattle or horses became a capital crime and anyone who found a lost animal was obliged to return it or be condemned to death as a thief. There were further laws against raiding and looting and regulations for where and during which times of the year animals could be hunted. All children, moreover, were regarded as the legitimate offspring of their parents regardless of the circumstances under which they had been conceived — a provision which helped to recognize children born from mothers who had been taken away as slaves. Freedom of religion was also officially recognized by the Mongol authorities. Although Genghis Khan himself was a Tengrist, there were Muslims, Christians and Buddhists among his subjects. Only complete freedom of religion could prevent conflicts among them.

> ### Tengrism
>
> Tengrism has historically been the predominant religion among the peoples of Central Asia. Tengrism combines animism with shamanism and the cult of ancestors. It worships Tengri, a supreme power that is associated with the sky. Tengri is the force that determines everything from the weather to the fate of individuals and nations. Tengri, say Tengrists, is the unknowable One who knows everything and who judges people's actions as good or bad and rewards them accordingly. Tengrists believe in spirits too. There are spirits of trees, mountains, planets, and ancestors, and they are either evil, benevolent or of mixed temperament. Some shamans have powers that resemble those of spirits, such as the power of prophecy or the ability to cast spells. Genghis Khan was a Tengrist, and so were all Mongol rulers until the early fourteenth century when some of them converted to Islam. To this day it is common for Mongols to refer to their country as *Munkh khukh tengri*, the land of the "eternal blue sky." This is not a weather report as much as the hope of divine protection.
>
> There has been a revival of Tengrism in Central Asia since the fall of the Soviet Union. Or rather, some academics and politicians have sought to promote Tengrism as an indigenous alternative to foreign religions such as Christianity and Islam. Neo-Tengrists are particularly active in Kyrgyzstan where a scientific center for Tengrist studies has been set up in the capital Bishkek. Observers claim that 60 percent of the rural population follow Tengrist traditions. In 2011, a proponent of Tengrism, Kubanychbek Tezekbaev, was put on trial in Kyrgyzstan for inciting religious and ethnic hatred because of statements he made in an interview describing Muslim clerics as "former alcoholics and murderers." Tezekbaev is an outspoken critic of what he sees as the growing influence of fundamentalist Islam in his country, especially among young people. He calls himself a half-Muslim. "I don't fully follow Islam, I just partially follow some Muslim rituals. I am a pure Kyrgyz."
>
> *Read more online:* https://hdl.handle.net/20.500.12434/5167319d

The rules of the *yassa* code were enforced by trials which were held in public and all Mongols, including Genghis Khan himself, were bound by the letters of the law. All important matters, including questions of succession and foreign policy, were to be discussed and decided on in a *kurultai*, the parliament of chieftains.

What more than anything brought the Mongols together, however, was the decision to embark on military conquests. In line with Mongol traditions these were not wars as much as raids as their object was, initially at least, not to occupy land or kill enemies, but to loot — horses and slaves at first, and later grain, treasure, and all kinds of productive resources. This more than anything was how Genghis Khan built support for himself. Every city they captured was looted according to a set formula, with shares for everyone, from the 10 percent given to Genghis Khan and his family down to smaller shares for orphans and widows. Yet the expectations of the Mongol people multiplied over time and no one was ever quite satisfied with what they had already acquired. This is what set the Mongols on the path to loot the whole world.

To the south of the Mongols, between themselves and the Song dynasty in China, were a number of tribes who had managed to establish kingdoms of their own. The most successful of these was the Jurchen who had made war on the Song dynasty and forced them to move their capital to Hangzhou in the south of China. Read more: *The Mughal Empire* at p. 13.

Other neighbors were the Tanguts, a kingdom of Tibetan-speaking people, and the Khanate of Qara Khitai, a kingdom located further west on the steppes towards Russia. Genghis Khan took on these kingdoms and their armies one by one and before long he had defeated them all — the Tanguts in 1210, the Jurchen in 1214 and Qara Khitai in 1218. There were rich spoils of war to be had from these conquests, in particular from the Jurchen who controlled some of the trading routes which brought Chinese merchandise to Central Asia and beyond.

These military successes put the Mongols in contact with the Khwarazmian Empire in the far west. The Khwarazmians were the rulers of Persia, but also of present-day Turkmenistan, Uzbekistan and much of Afghanistan. Yet the Khwarazmians were a city-based state, not a band of nomads, and they laid claims to all the resources and the historical heritage of the Persian states of antiquity. From the Khwarazmian point of view, the Mongols were nothing but an annoyance and initially Genghis Khan was convinced that the Khwarazmians were too powerful to attack. Instead, he dispatched a diplomatic delegation to their court asking for the right to trade. When some of the envoys were killed and others were returned with their faces mutilated, Genghis Khan was outraged. He dispatched another delegation which was treated in much the same fashion. After this experience Genghis Khan had no choice but to attack. And in 1220, after an exceptional ride through the Taklamakan desert, his mounted warriors descended on the city of Bukhara, in today's Uzbekistan, and caught the Khwarazmians by surprise. Genghis Khan gathered the local potentates in the city's biggest mosque and explained to them that he was God's punishment for their sins. Then he killed them all and thoroughly looted the city. The neighboring city of Samarkand was captured in the same fashion. As news of these spectacular attacks reached other parts of the empire, the Khwarazmians lost their self-confidence. Genghis Khan gave them an ultimatum — to surrender without a fight or to be annihilated. Within a year the entire empire was in his hands.

After this spectacular victory, the Mongols were no longer simply a loose federation of horsemen but a proper empire in control of some of the richest cities in the world. They had possessions and thereby responsibilities. They were also suddenly a Middle Eastern power and before long they continued their raids with attacks in the Caucasus. Georgia, a Christian kingdom, was to become a particularly loyal ally. Once the Mongols had established themselves in the Caucasus, in turn, they came into contact with the Kievan Rus, the fledgling Russian state in present-day Ukraine. However, in 1227 an unexpected uprising among the Tanguts forced Genghis Khan to return home. This is also where he died, aged sixty-five years old, under rather mysterious circumstances. Some say that he was wounded in a battle, others that he fell off his horse, or perhaps that he was killed by a Tangut woman he had taken as a concubine. In any case, his body was buried in a grave without markings according to the customs of his tribe. By the time of his death the Mongols controlled the center of the entire Eurasian landmass — from the Pacific Ocean to the Black Sea.

> ### Genghis Khan in today's Mongolia
>
> During the Communist period, 1924–1992, when the Soviet Union exercised a strong influence in the country, textbooks used in Mongolian schools described Genghis Khan as a "reactionary" and an "enemy of the people." However, in commemoration of the eight hundredth anniversary of his birth in 1962, a monument was erected in his honor and an academic conference was held to discuss his life and legacy. The conference ended with applause, cheers, and chants for Genghis Khan. Agents for the KGB, the Soviet secret service, who were present on the occasion, reported the event to Moscow. This resulted in purges within the leadership of the Mongolian Communist Party. Those who had sided with Genghis Khan were regarded as enemies of the Soviet Union.
>
> Since the end of Communism, there has been a strong revival of interest in Genghis Khan in Mongolia and he is now regarded as a national hero. Mongolians are quick to insist that his reputation as a bloodthirsty barbarian is vastly exaggerated. In 2008, a private company erected a 40-meter-tall equestrian statue of him in stainless steel at the cost of 4.1 million U.S. dollars. Entering the statue, visitors can take an elevator to Genghis's head and enjoy a panoramic view of the Mongolian steppe.
>
> In today's Mongolia, Genghis Khan's name and likeness can be found on products ranging from liquor bottles and energy drinks to cigarette packages and candy, as well as on the bills people use to pay for these items. The Mongolian parliament has discussed the risk of trivializing his memory, but the discussions have not so far resulted in any legislation. Since 2012, the first day of the first winter month of the year has been designated as Genghis Khan's birthday and a national holiday. His actual birthday is unknown. According to the customs of his tribe, Genghis Khan was buried in a grave without markings. It is said that 10,000 horses trampled over the ground where he was buried, that a forest was planted over the site or that a river was diverted to cover it. Not surprisingly perhaps the grave has never been located.
>
> *Read more online:* https://hdl.handle.net/20.500.12434/283be8a7

How to conquer the world

The key to the military success of the Mongols was their extraordinary army, which consisted entirely of cavalry — soldiers mounted on the backs of fast Mongolian horses. Although all men up to the age of seventy were conscripted, the army comprised no more than 100,000 men. Often they were divided into several armies that operated independently of each other. What they lacked in numbers, they made up for in terms of speed and mobility. For one thing, they had no supply train. Instead, the soldiers carried strips of dried meat and curd with them in their saddlebags which they could eat while on the move. All soldiers had access to several horses which they switched between. The horses would graze on the land which they covered and they could be milked or tapped for blood to drink or eaten by the soldiers. Dead soldiers would simply be left to decompose where they fell or be picked at by wild animals, in accordance with Mongol custom. In addition, the Mongols had no slow-moving engineering corps. Instead the engineers built what they needed — bridges or assault weapons for attacking city walls — with the help of whatever material they found on the spot. Moreover, the Mongol armies were used to fighting in wintertime when most other armies took time off. And their horsemanship was of course second to none. Each Mongol warrior had been on horseback since he was a toddler and could fire off arrows while in full gallop towards an enemy. Their bows were so tightly strung that it took two men to do it.

Compared with the armies of agricultural empires, the Mongols used entirely different battlefield tactics. They fought sneakily, with no regard for chivalric conduct or fair play. A favorite ruse was to feign defeat and beat a retreat. As the enemies came in pursuit of them, they would be ambushed and picked off one by one. Another ruse was to make an assault at night, and make fires which made the Mongol army look far larger than it really was. They would then proceed to attack from all directions at once. Battlefield tactics such as these required discipline and a high level of coordination. These skills were initially honed during the hunts, known as *nerge*. The Mongol chieftains would organize hunting parties, comprising thousands of participants, which encircled herds of deer and other prey, driving the animals before them as they gradually tightened the circle. As each man quickly learned, any failure of discipline and coordination allowed the prey to escape. On the battlefield these lessons were adapted to military use by commanders who relied on torches, whistling arrows and flags to direct their troops. The chief aim of the Mongol generals was to strike terror in their enemies. To loot a city in a spectacular manner was not only a way of getting one's hands on treasure, but also, and above all, a way of sending a message to the people in the next town that all resistance was futile. By striking terror in their enemies, their will to resist was broken. However, in relation to the cities that surrendered peacefully the message was equally clear: as long as you behave yourselves, and faithfully pay a 10 percent tax, your assets will be safe and your inhabitants protected.

After Genghis Khan's death in 1227, his sons and grandsons continued these wars.

Genghis Khan's family tree

The Mongol Empire at its height spanned much of the Eurasian landmass, but it was not the creation of only one man. When Genghis Khan died in 1227, the Mongols had not yet arrived in Europe, not taken the Middle East and not occupied China. These conquests were for Genghis Khan's successors, his sons, and grandsons, to complete. Family trees are always complicated and difficult to remember, but these are the main branches of Genghis Khan's tree:

- Börte, 1161–1230, Temüjin's wife and grand empress of the empire. Börte was not Temüjin's only wife, but the couple seem to have had very fond feelings for each other. She was his trusted advisor and was given her own lands to manage. Börte gave birth to four sons:

- Jochi, 1181–1227, was not Temüjin's son since he was born too soon after Börte's return to her husband. He was never accepted by his brothers as the legitimate successor to their father. When Genghis Khan divided his empire, Jochi got the westernmost part, a territory that later came to constitute the Golden Horde, in today's Russia.

- Chagatai, 1183–1242, was the leading critic of Jochi and was considered a hothead by his brothers. He inherited the Central Asian parts of the empire from his father, later known as the Chagatai khanate. He was very fond of *airag*. Read more: *How to make kumis* at p. 117.

- Ögedei, 1186–1241, was the third son and successor to Genghis Khan. He expanded the empire into the Middle East, attacked the Jin dynasty in China and moved into Korea. It was during his reign that the Mongols expanded into Europe too.

- Tolui, 1192–1232, was the youngest of Genghis Khan's sons. He inherited the traditional Mongol heartlands from his father. His descendants ruled Mongolia until 1691.

Tolui, in turn, had four sons, but there were intense rivalries and occasionally wars between them.

- Möngke, 1208–1259, improved the administration of the empire. During his reign, the Mongols occupied Iraq and Syria. After his death, a war broke out between his brothers regarding the right of succession.

- Kublai, 1215–1294, was the Mongol ruler who occupied China in 1271 and founded the Yuan dynasty which was to last until 1368 when it was overrun by the Ming. He moved his capital to Beijing.

- Hülegü, 1218–1265, occupied much of Western Asia, including Persia, and was responsible for the sacking of Baghdad in 1258. His forces lost an important battle at Ain Jalut in 1260, against the Mamluk rulers of Egypt. His part of the empire became later known as the Ilkhanate, located in today's Iran.

- Ariq Böke, 1219–1266, was the youngest son of Tolui. After the death of Möngke in 1259, he claimed the throne but was defeated by his brothers. He died aged only forty-five years old. Rumors had it he was poisoned.

Read more online: https://hdl.handle.net/20.500.12434/42aaddfe

In 1235, his son Ögedei, who replaced him, called in a *kurultai* to decide on the future direction of the conquests. After some debate it was decided to make a move on Russia and Europe. Subutai, the leading general, was the one who first discovered Europe in the 1220s. When the new campaign began in 1236, he set his sight on the Volga River, inhabited by the Bulgars, and this was where a three year-long campaign began. The Mongols quickly discovered that the various Russian city-states were divided among themselves, and that they were only weakly defended. In accordance with their custom, they began by dispatching diplomatic envoys, asking the Russians to submit willingly. Only a few cities took up the offer, however, and those that did not were promptly attacked. Ryazan, 200 kilometers southeast of Moscow, was first in line. From here the Mongols moved on to Kiev, the main city in Russia at the time, which was captured in December 1240. In the end, only a few towns, such as Novgorod and Pskov in the north, survived the onslaught. One long-term consequence was that Kiev lost influence throughout Russia and that Moscow gained in prominence. The prince of Muscovy, who sided with the Mongols, acted as an intermediary between the foreign invaders and the various Russian leaders.

Now the Mongol armies suddenly found themselves on the doorstep of Europe. In the spring of 1241, in a two-pronged attack, they simultaneously moved into Poland in the north and Hungary in the south. The Europeans were completely taken by surprise, but eventually a combined army of Czech, Polish and German knights was assembled. Two battles ensued — at Legnica in Poland on April 9, 1241, and at Mohi, Hungary, two days later. On both occasions, the European armies were completely routed.

The Mongol invasion of Europe

In the winter of 1241, the Mongol armies found themselves in Europe. The immediate reason was their pursuit of the Cumans, a nomadic people whom the Mongols regarded as their subjects. The Cumans had left their regular grazing lands north of the Black Sea and sought refuge in Hungary. The Mongols had insisted that the Hungarian king return them, and when he refused the Mongols came looking for them.

The Mongol armies had no problems operating during the winter months. Indeed, this was when rivers were frozen and easier for their horses to cross, but winter warfare was not common in medieval Europe. Moreover, the Mongols operated with two separate armies — one in Hungary and one in Poland. Eventually, they came as far as the walls of Vienna and they also reached several towns under the control of the Hanseatic League. On March 24, 1241, they sacked Krakow in today's Poland.

After the initial confusion, the Europeans eventually put together a common defense. The Mongols were met by a collection of Polish, Czech and German forces, together with a contingent of chivalric knights sent by the pope. Two battles ensued — at Legnica, Poland, on April 9, 1241, and, in a far larger confrontation, at Mohi, Hungary, two days later. The Europeans were defeated on both occasions. In fact, the European armies seem to have been more or less obliterated. As a result, in the summer of 1241, Europe was defenseless against further attacks. But the Mongols did not invade. When news reached them of the death of Ögedei Khan, the Mongol commanders decided to return home. Although they conducted new raids in Poland in 1259, 1286 and 1287, the Mongols never again bothered with a large-scale invasion.

Read more online: https://hdl.handle.net/20.500.12434/6e99ab32

The Mongols continued swiftly across eastern Europe and into the lands of the Holy Roman Empire; meanwhile the scouts who preceded them came right up to the city walls of Vienna. This, however, was when news reached them from Mongolia that Ögedei Khan had died and that a *kurultai* was to be assembled to elect a new leader. Since Ögedei's brothers had all recently died too — either in battle or under some distinctly suspicious circumstances — it was clear that the title of *khagan* this time would be given to one of Genghis Khan's grandchildren. Since several of the potential candidates for the job were engaged in the European wars, they had to return home to fight for the position. Despite the brilliantly executed campaign and their decisive victories, the Mongols never invaded Europe.

Kalmykia, Europe's only Buddhist republic

Kalmykia is a republic in the Russian Federation, located between the Black and the Caspian Seas. The Kalmykian republic, with some 300,000 inhabitants, is the only place in Europe where a majority of the population is Buddhist. The Kalmyks were nomads who originally arrived here from today's Xinjiang, in the seventeenth century, most probably in search of better pasture for their animals. Read more: *Khotan to the Khotanese!* at p. 32. In their new location the Kalmyks became nominally the subjects of the czar. They were supposed to protect Russia's southern borders, but in practice, Kalmykia constituted its own independent khanate. The Kalmyks kept in close contact with their kinsmen in Xinjiang and also with the Dalai Lama, the Buddhist leader in Tibet.

In the eighteenth century, the Russian Empire asserted itself in Central Asia. Russian farmers settled here and Moscow tried to control the Kalmyks. In a desperate move, a large portion of them decided to return to Xinjiang, but many died on the way. In the civil war which followed the Russian Revolution in 1917, the Kalmyks sided with the opposition. This too turned out to be a disastrous mistake. After the Bolshevik victory, many were forced to flee. Some Kalmyks went to Belgrade in Serbia where they established Europe's first Buddhist temple in 1929.

But their troubles were not over. In the 1930s the Kalmyks were forced to join the collective farms set up by the Soviet regime and many Buddhist monasteries were closed. During the Second World War, Kalmykia was invaded by the Germans. In 1943 Stalin declared the Kalmyk people collectively guilty of cooperation with the enemy and they were deported to various locations in Siberia and Central Asia. In 1957, after the death of Stalin, they were allowed to return home but in many cases only to find that their land had been taken over by Russians. Badly planned and badly executed attempts by the Soviet authorities to irrigate the steppe turned their grazing lands into deserts.

Today some 60 percent of Kalmykia's population are ethnic Kalmyks, while 30 percent are Russian. The proportion of Russians has been going down since the fall of Communism, primarily because the Kalmyks have higher birthrates. Although very few Kalmyks live as nomads on the steppe, many still practise their religion. In 1991 the Dalai Lama visited the republic.

Read more online: https://hdl.handle.net/20.500.12434/6e7f45c3

Yet the Mongols stayed on in Russia. Here they maintained a presence in the new capital they built for themselves on the Volga, named Sarai. This was where various Russian princes showed up to pledge allegiance to the Mongols and to receive a *jarlig*, a tablet which identified them as legitimate rulers recognized by the Great Khan himself. In the latter part of the thirteenth century, this Russian part of the Mongol Empire, known as "the Golden Horde," came increasingly to assert its independence. As a result, it came into conflict not only with external enemies but also with other parts of the Mongol lands. It wasn't until 1480, however, that the Russian princes finally assembled a united army strong enough to defeat the enemy. Even then, instead of simply disappearing, the Golden Horde broke up into smaller units which took their places among the other Russian city-states. In 1556, Sarai was conquered and burned, but the successor states lived on. One particularly successful successor was the khanate on the Crimea peninsula which was annexed by the Russian state only in 1783. The last descendant of Genghis Khan to rule a country was Alim Khan, the Emir of Bukhara, who was overthrown by the Red Army of the Soviet Union in 1920.

Muhammed Alim Khan, the last Emir of Bukhara

Muhammed Alim Khan, 1911–1920, was the last Emir of Bukhara, in today's Uzbekistan. His family considered themselves the direct descendants of Genghis Khan via Nogai, Genghis's great-great-grandson. Once the Mongols had been ousted from Russia, the Nogai Horde, as it was known, retreated to two main areas, one north of the Black Sea, the other north of the Caspian Sea. From here they conducted raids on Russian territory, absconding with young boys whom they sold to the Ottomans in Constantinople as soldiers. Read more: *Janissaries and Turkish military music* at p. 94.

Little by little, however, the Nogais were pushed south and eastwards by Russian settlers and by the advancing Russian army. In the end, they came to inhabit an area in Central Asia known as Transoxania, with Bukhara and Samarkand as its two main cities. Here the family established themselves as emirs in 1785. Yet the Russians eventually caught up with them and in 1868 they occupied and annexed much of the emirate. The remainder became a Russian protectorate in which the emirs retained full power only over domestic matters.

At the age of thirteen, Muhammed Alim Khan was sent to Saint Petersburg to study government and modern military techniques. In 1910, when he succeeded his father, he tried to reform the country but soon realized that any lasting changes only were going to make his own position more precarious. He was challenged by modernizers — a movement known as "Young Bukhara" — who sought a far more radical transformation of society. After the Russian Revolution in 1917, these radicals called on the Soviet state to help them and in September 1920 the Red Army intervened. A "Bukharan People's Soviet Republic" was established. This was exactly 800 years after Genghis Khan himself first had invaded Bukhara. Muhammed Alim Khan was the last of Genghis Khan's direct descendants to rule a state.

Read more online: https://hdl.handle.net/20.500.12434/9f983a8d

Dividing it all up

Once the Mongol princes returned from Europe in 1241, a prolonged struggle ensued over the succession, which pitted Genghis Khan's grandchildren against each other and which for a while resulted in an open war among them. During the coming decade, the Mongols were too occupied by this conflict to pay much attention to their empire. It was only with the election of Möngke Khan in 1251 that the foreign conquests resumed. This time the first targets were the Muslim caliphates in the Middle East. Although Persia had been conquered already by Genghis Khan himself, the Abbasid Caliphate in Baghdad had not been subject to sustained attacks. It was Hülegü, Möngke's brother, who was in command of these armies. He began by dispatching envoys to Baghdad with a list of grievances and demands. In November 1257, after the caliph had refused to provide him with the answers he wanted, Hülegü attacked. Baghdad was besieged and, once gunpowder had been used to undermine the city walls, it surrendered. The looting lasted for a full seventeen days. In the confusion the attackers set fire to the city. The destruction of Baghdad, 1258, is remembered to this day as the event which put an end to what the Arabs remember as their "Golden Age." Read more: *Arabian Nights* at p. 79.

Their presence in the Middle East put the Mongols in contact with the Mamluks in Cairo. The Mamluks were slaves in the service of the sultans and they were soldiers who in several respects resembled the Mongols themselves. Read more: *A caliphal international system* at p. 86.

Many of them were descendants of nomadic tribes and they too were highly trained and disciplined. In September 1260, at Ain Jalut, in what today is Israel, the Mongols were defeated. Although they had lost battles before, the Mongols would always come back to avenge their losses and exact a terrible punishment on their enemies. Yet after Ain Jalut this did not happen and the Mongols never made it to Cairo. This victory, and the way Cairo was spared while Baghdad was looted, decisively transferred power within the Muslim world to the Mamluks. From the fourteenth century onward it was Cairo that was the center of Muslim civilization. After the defeat at Ain Jalut it was clear that the enormous Mongol Empire had found its westernmost frontiers. This in itself was a problem, however, since the success of the Mongol armies depended on constant expansion. There were now no more spoils of war to distribute.

Their presence in the Middle East also put the Mongols in contact with the *Faranj*, the "Franks," known in Europe as "the Crusaders." To the Europeans, the Mongols seemed at first to be heaven-sent. Any enemy of the Muslims, they argued, must be a friend of ours. According to one interpretation common at the time, the Mongol forces were those of Prester John, a legendary Christian ruler who was said to have founded a mighty kingdom somewhere in the Far East. Even once they realized their mistake, however, the Crusaders remained keen to form an alliance with the Mongols. Several diplomatic missions were dispatched both by the Mongols and the Europeans.

Yet although Hülegü's armies invaded Syria several times, they never coordinated their attacks with the Crusaders in a meaningful fashion. In the end not only the

Rabban Bar Sauma, Mongol envoy to the Pope

Rabban Bar Sauma, 1220–1294, was a Nestorian monk who became a diplomat for the Mongol khan and visited Europe. Born near present-day Beijing, and apparently of Uyghur descent, he embarked on a pilgrimage to Jerusalem, but because of the ongoing wars, he was forced to turn back. Instead, he spent several years in Baghdad, which at the time was a part of the Ilkhanate. It was from here that he was dispatched to Europe on a diplomatic mission to seek an alliance with France. The idea was that the Mongols and the Europeans should join forces against their common, Muslim, enemy.

Rabban Bar Sauma began his journey in 1287. First, he crossed the Black Sea to Constantinople where he had an audience with the Byzantine emperor. He then continued on to Italy, sailing past Sicily where he observed a spectacular eruption of Mount Etna. He arrived in Rome, but too late to meet the pope who just had died. Instead, he went to Florence, Genoa, and Paris where he spent a month as the guest of the French king. In Gascony, which at the time was an English possession, he met the king of England. Both the French and the English were enthusiastic about the idea of a military alliance, but the details were difficult to work out. Going back to Rome, Bar Sauma was received by the newly elected pope who gave him communion on Palm Sunday, 1288. From here he returned to Baghdad with gifts and messages from the various European rulers he had met. This is also where he spent the rest of his days, compiling a book in which he recounted his far-flung travels. Rabban Bar Sauma died in Baghdad in 1294. The military alliance between the Europeans and the Mongols never materialized.

Nestorian Christians, by the way, are the branch of Christianity which expanded in an eastwardly direction from antiquity, forming thriving congregations in Central Asia, India and in China during the Tang dynasty. The Nestorians were independent of Rome and worshiped according to their own rituals. They denied that Christ could simultaneously be both god and man. Today a few hundred thousand Nestorians remain, mainly in Iraq, Syria, Iran and the United States.

Read more online: https://hdl.handle.net/20.500.12434/77312d4d

---

Mongols but also the *Faranj* were defeated by the Mamluks. Read more: *Saladin and the Crusaders* at p. 88.

Soon enough the Mongol armies who had conquered and sacked Baghdad came to think of themselves as a separate political entity, and their leader, Hülegü, to think of himself not as a general or a governor working for the Great Khan in Mongolia but as a khan with a khanate of his own. This realm, made up of Persia and big chunks of Central Asia and the Middle East, came to be known as the "Ilkhanate," or "subordinate khanate." Much like the Arabs who had conquered these lands before them, the Ilkhanate khans and their courts came to be heavily influenced by the local, essentially Persian, culture. That is, in a radical transformation of their own ways of life, the Mongols got off their horses and settled down in cities. They also adopted Islam as the official religion of the state and the khans became great supporters of scholarship and the arts. The most celebrated example is the astronomical observatory at Maragheh which, in addition to astronomers, had mathematicians, philosophers and medical doctors in residence. Yet, and much as in the case of the Golden Horde in Russia, the Ilkhanate began to fall apart in the first half of the fourteenth century, and eventually it was broken up into a number of small successor states. The most famous such successor was the state which Timur, or Tamerlane, in the fourteenth century turned into a vast, if short-lived, empire.

The only neighbors which the Mongols had not yet successfully attacked were the Chinese. This is surprising given both how relatively close China was to the Mongol heartlands and how singularly wealthy the country was. Although already Genghis Khan had successfully occupied the nomadic buffer states which were located between the Mongols and the Chinese, he made no sustained attacks in Chinese history. It was only once Möngke was elected *khagan* in 1251 that China came back into focus. China at this time was ruled by the Song dynasty, 960–1279. The Song is one of the most celebrated dynasties of China. Read more: *China and East Asia* at p. 13.

Militarily, however, they were weak and the Jurchen had already forced them to relocate their capital to the southern city of Hangzhou. Although this move constituted an embarrassment, the Song continued to thrive economically, and they still controlled some 60 percent of China's population. Hangzhou, amazed visitors reported, had no fewer than 12,000 bridges across the canals of the city and the most beautiful women in the world.

Möngke Khan had picked his brother Kublai to be in charge of the invasion of China, but Kublai had no aptitude for war and besides he was too fat to ride a horse. He moved only reluctantly against the Chinese, complemented by the generals who Möngke himself had dispatched to support him. The strategy was to attack the Song court in a diversionary pattern, starting with an invasion of Sichuan to the west and Yunnan to the southwest. If the Mongols gained control of these areas, went the plan, they could attack the Song from all sides at once. Yet the death of Möngke Khan in 1259, and the subsequent struggle over the succession, meant that China once again became a less important concern. Although the wars eventually resumed, it took another twelve years before Kublai Khan could declare himself emperor of China, and another ten years after that before he had decisively defeated the last pockets of Song resistance. Eventually the last Song emperor, an eight-year-old boy, committed suicide together with his prime minister and 800 members of his family. From 1279 on it was Kublai Khan who held the Mandate of Heaven as the leader of a new dynasty, the Yuan.

While the attacks on China were taking place, the Mongols successfully invaded the Korean peninsula where the kings agreed to pay regular tributes. Kublai Khan also tried to invade Japan. He assembled an army of some 100,000 men for the purpose, but the ships which they constructed were not quite seaworthy and besides the invaders were unlucky with the weather.

The first invasion in 1274 had to be aborted and the second invasion in 1281 failed miserably. Japan, as a result, was never occupied. Cut off from China by the presence of the Mongols, Japan had to depend on its own resources. Kublai Khan also tried to

Kamikaze

The Mongols tried to invade Japan twice. Late in the autumn of 1274, a Mongol fleet of some 300 ships and 20,000 soldiers reached the Japanese island of Kyushu. At the ensuing battle, the inexperienced and badly equipped Japanese army was defeated, yet an impending storm convinced the Mongol generals to set out to sea so as not to become marooned on the shore. The fleet was destroyed and the few ships that remained in the harbor were easy for the Japanese to deal with. In the summer of 1281, the Mongols attempted another invasion. Again, however, a large typhoon appeared and wiped out their fleet. The Mongols, clearly, were not very experienced seamen and the flat-bottomed boats they had built for the passage to Japan were not well suited to the task. After these experiences, the Mongols gave up their attempts to invade the country.

Given that they twice had been saved by miraculous typhoons, the Japanese began to believe that their country enjoyed divine protection — that the winds, *kaze*, were sent by the gods, the *kami*. The *Kamikaze* was also the name given to the Special Attack Units of the Japanese air force established towards the end of the Second World War. The unit sent pilots on suicide missions with the goal of dropping their planes, themselves and their explosive cargo on important enemy targets — on American airplane carriers in particular. The pilots were all volunteers — young recruits without much training whom the military authorities considered expendable. In fact, there were many more volunteers than airplanes. At least 47 Allied ships were sunk by means of these suicide pilots, some 300 ships were damaged and altogether 3,860 pilots were killed. However, the term "kamikaze pilot" was not used in Japan during the war. It is instead an American term which was imported into Japan after 1945, together with many other features of American culture.

Read more online: https://hdl.handle.net/20.500.12434/28e35742

invade Java, in today's Indonesia, and his armies conducted campaigns in Vietnam, Thailand and Burma. Due to the hot and humid weather, however, these expeditions were hampered by disease, in a land which was in any case unsuitable for soldiers on horseback due to its tropical terrain and thick jungles.

Kublai Khan's favorite wife died in 1281; his favorite son and chosen successor died in 1285. After that, he grew increasingly despondent and withdrew from the daily business of government. He fell ill in 1293 and died in 1294. The last years of the Yuan dynasty were characterized by famines and distress among ordinary people. The reigns of the later emperors were short and marked by intrigues and rivalries. Uninterested in administration, they were separated both from the army and from people at large. The Yuan dynasty was eventually defeated by the Ming, a native Chinese dynasty, which replaced them in 1368. The Mongols retreated to Mongolia, forming what is known as the "Northern Yuan dynasty," but they never rescinded their claims to the Chinese throne. They ruled Mongolia until 1635 when they were deposed by the Manchus, descendants of the Jurchen tribes which Genghis Khan had defeated so easily four hundred years earlier.

An international system of khanates

In the first part of the thirteenth century, the Mongols invaded almost the entirety of the Eurasian landmass, yet already by mid-century their empire began to fall apart. As long as Genghis Khan's descendants could agree on the election of a *khagan*, the empire could be described as united, but after the death of Möngke Khan in 1259 no such consensus could be reached. Möngke's brothers — Hülegü, Kublai and Ariq Böke — began fighting with each other and the conflict soon escalated into a civil war — the Toluid Civil War, named after Tolui, their father — which resulted in four separate Mongol khanates being established: the Golden Horde in Russia, led by Batu Khan; the Ilkhanate in Persia, led by Hülegü Khan; the Chagatai khanate, comprising the traditional heartland of the Mongols, led by Chagatai Khan; and the Yuan dynasty in China, led by Kublai Khan. As we saw, these entities had asserted their independence for some time already, and the outcome of the Toluid War only confirmed the situation on the ground. And yet, throughout these conflicts a number of commonalities remained. If nothing else, they were united by personal ties and a shared commitment to a Mongol identity. The result is an international system with quite distinct characteristics. Perhaps we could talk about "the international system of the Mongol khanates."

One distinct feature was the fact that Genghis Khan's descendants had strong economic interests in the countries they ruled. The 10 percent share they received of all loot soon came to constitute considerable economic assets. What they owned was not just treasure but productive resources — men, animals, fields, factories, and ships. Before long they developed an extensive personal stake in the economic activities and the economic well-being of the entirety of the Eurasian landmass. The khans, from this perspective, were more like leaders of a multinational corporation than leaders of armies or states. Yet this particular multinational cooperation was also a family business. When the empire came to be divided into four separate realms, the economic stakes were impossible to divide in the same fashion since all khans maintained large assets — known as *khubi*, "shares" — in each other's territories. Thus Hülegü in the Ilkhanate owned 25,000 households of silk workers in China which were ruled by his brother Kublai, but he also owned entire valleys in Tibet and had claims on furs and falcons from the steppes of the Golden Horde. Such cross-cutting ownership was duplicated in the case of the other khans and their families, creating an intricate pattern of economic interdependence.

Although the khanates became ever more rooted in the societies they ruled, they did maintain a distinct Mongolian identity. Or at least, they made considerable efforts to do so.

Tuvan throat singing

Tuva is an autonomous region of the Russian republic, located just north of today's Mongolia, right in the geographical center of Asia. For some 500 years, Tuva was a part of the Mongol Empire; in the nineteenth century it was dominated by China;

from 1921 it was an independent country, and in 1944 Stalin made it a part of the Soviet Union. Protected by heavy forest, by the Altai mountains and by Soviet restrictions that kept outsiders out, traditional Tuvan culture has remained strong. A large proportion of the 300,000 inhabitants are still pastoralists — tending sheep, goats, horses and reindeer — or they are hunters and fishermen.

What more than anything has made Tuva famous is its tradition of throat singing. Throat singing, overtone or polytonal singing, is a technique that allows you to sing several notes at once. The trick is not only to employ the vocal cords but also other parts of the respiratory tract. In normal song, these other organs are vibrating too, creating what we think of as "timbre," but the throat singers have found a way of increasing the level of the sound produced in this way. In Tuva there are at least five different versions of the technique, varying depending on which part of the human anatomy is emphasized. The main style, *khoomei,* is also the Tuvan name for throat singing in general.

Throat singing is common among Mongols too, and Tibetans, and it is widely practiced among people of the arctic north, including by Inuits in North America. In Tuva, they think of throat singing as a way of imitating the sounds made by rivers, animals, and mountains. This way of singing is a means of communicating with nature. The singers often accompany themselves on the igil, the horse-head fiddle, or on large drums. The technique plays a role in shamanic practices too. Today several artists combine throat singing with other musical genres, including jazz and hip hop.

Read more online: https://hdl.handle.net/20.500.12434/814e9772

This awareness of their shared descent helped unite the khanates even as they increasingly asserted their independence. For example, they insisted on using Mongolian in communications with officials and adopted a version of the Uyghur alphabet in order to use the language in their official correspondence. Meanwhile, knowledge of Mongolian was forbidden to non-Mongols — although the princes of Muscovy must have ignored the ban since speaking Mongolian became popular at their court. When Kublai Khan moved his capital to Beijing in 1264, he reserved a large area in the center of the city — corresponding roughly to what today is known as the "Forbidden Palace" — where he and his court set up their *ger*, their tents, which they continued to prefer to regular buildings. There were hills in this enclosure too, and animals which members of the court could hunt in the traditional Mongolian fashion.

How to make kumis

Fermented mare's milk, milk from female horses, is the traditional drink of choice for people on the steppes of Central Asia, including the Mongols. The Mongols call it *airag* but it is commonly known as "kumis" from *kımız*, its Turkish name. *Kumis* is a slightly alcoholic beverage, but not very much so — only 2–3 percent. Traditionally, the milk was fermented in bags made from horse-hide which were strapped to a saddle and jogged around in order to prevent coagulation. After a day on horseback, the milk was ready to drink. In industrial production today, the drink ferments at 27 degrees Celsius and it is ready to drink in about five hours. The fermentation process is caused by a combination of lactic acid bacteria and yeast.

The Greek historian Herodotus, fifth century BCE, described mare-milking among the Scythians, a nomadic people living on the steppes of Central Asia, and the friar William of Rubruck who visited the Mongols in the thirteenth century gave an account of *kumis* drinking. "It is pungent," he reported, "and when a man has finished drinking, it leaves a taste of milk of almonds on the tongue, and it makes the inner man most joyful and also intoxicates weak heads, and greatly provokes urine." Milking a horse is more difficult than a cow and it yields far less milk. Moreover, mares cannot be milked continuously but only for a few months after the foals are born. A mare typically produces between 1,000 and 1,200 liters of milk during a season.

Kumis drinking caught on as a health fad in the decades before the First World War, in particular in Russia. The Russian composer Alexander Scriabin and authors Leo Tolstoy and Anton Chekhov all tried the "*kumis* cure." The Kyrgyz capital Bishkek is named after the paddle used to churn the mare's milk during the process of fermentation.

Read more online: https://hdl.handle.net/20.500.12434/0bc34d87

The key aspect of this identity was the experiences that all Mongols shared as nomads on the steppes of Central Asia. The logic of nomadic societies differs from the logic of sedentary societies in crucial respects. According to the Confucian rhetoric, farmers were considered the most important social class since they produced the food which fed everyone else. Merchants, by contrast, were the least important since their labor contributed nothing which did not already exist. To the Mongols, however, this made no sense. As their own example clearly demonstrated, the farmers' way of life was nowhere near as important as the Confucians assumed. It was obviously possible to feed a nation that did not put stakes into the ground. Thus the Mongols demoted farmers to one of the lowest ranks in society, below prostitutes but above beggars.

They also thought of land quite differently. The Mongols were interested in booty but not really in territorial acquisitions. They would take what they could get their hands on and then move on. As a result, the Mongols never had to defend a fixed position. To them there was no military difference between attack and retreat; they were as happy to defeat an enemy who pursued them as one they themselves pursued. This is also why their empire left no monuments or buildings. During Genghis Khan's reign the Mongols did not even have a proper capital. Instead, Genghis would take his court and his advisers with him in a *ger* mounted on a cart which was pulled by a set of strong horses. He toured the country and the world accompanied by his capital. It was only during Ögedei's reign, in 1235, that Karakorum became more than a collection of tents, but even then the city was used mainly for storing the treasures that the soldiers brought home. The Mongols left a very light footprint on the land they occupied, we might say. Even a once-large city such as Sarai in the Golden Horde has only left traces which you have to be an archaeologist in order to appreciate.

The only thing the Mongols built were bridges. Bridges were crucial in order to move armies and to give merchants free passage. The Mongols built them whenever they were needed. They were also experts at breaching walls. They recruited Chinese engineers who taught them how to construct siege engines. Before long they were building their own catapults, trebuchets and battering rams — siege warfare being the only area in which they made technological advances. Before the thirteenth century the defenders had usually had the advantage during a siege, but after the Mongol invasions this was no longer the case.

The Mongols also built bridges and breached walls metaphorically speaking and thereby helped facilitate interaction between all the corners of their far-flung empire. It was during the *Pax Mongolica* that Europeans first acquired a taste for Asian luxury goods and Chinese inventions first reached Europe. The most obvious part of this trade-friendly infrastructure was physical. Although the various routes which made up the "Silk Road" had been in place for a long time already, the Mongols radically improved them, making travel easier, safer and quicker. They referred to the system as *örtöö*, a network of interconnected relay stations where travelers could stop to rest and replenish their supplies, change horses, engage in trade or swap information and gossip. The relay stations, or *caravanserai*, were set approximately thirty kilometers apart. Staffing and maintaining these stations was a way to pay one's taxes and twenty-five families were responsible for each one. The network was used for government officials too and for communicating with generals and administrators throughout the empire. Important travelers would carry an imperial seal, known as a *paiza* — a small tablet made from gold, silver or wood — which assured them protection, accommodation, and transportation but also exemption from local duties. The *paiza* worked as a combination of passport and credit card. Read more: *Sogdian letters* at p. 20.

In addition to the physical infrastructure, the Mongols provided legal and institutional infrastructure. One example is the standardization of weights and measures. By making sure that goods were weighed and measured in the same fashion throughout the empire, the Mongol authorities made it easy to compare prices. Money was standardized too. In 1253 Möngke Khan created a department of monetary affairs that issued paper money of fixed denominations. This made it possible to pay taxes in cash instead of in kind. This vastly improved the state's finances. Even time itself was standardized, or at least the days and months of the year. At observatories in both the Ilkhanate and in Mongol-run China, calendars were produced which showed the same astronomical data.

However, it was not only people and goods that traveled along the *örtöö* network, but also disease.

The Black Death

The trade routes of Central Asia did not only disseminate goods and ideas but also diseases such as the bubonic plague, known as the "Black Death." The contagion first hit the Mongols, then the Arabic world and Europe. The first wave came in the 1340s and later waves in the 1360s and 70s. In 1347, the story has it, the Mongols had laid a siege on the prosperous Genoese city of Caffa on the Crimean peninsula, yet their army was already seriously weakened by the disease. In an act of what would come to count as biological warfare, the Mongols catapulted the corpses of their dead across the city walls, thereby infecting the inhabitants. In October the same year a Genoese ship fleeing the city anchored in the harbor of Messina, Sicily. By the time they arrived, it was clear that its crew too carried the disease. From Messina the plague spread quickly along Europe's trade routes, reaching southern England the following year. It is estimated that some 75 million people died from the plague worldwide and 20 million people in Europe alone — perhaps as many as half of the continent's population. Read more: *The Columbian exchange* at p. 156. Although it was obvious to everyone that the disease was spread through contagion, no one understood the biological mechanisms involved. Initially, it was rats that had become infected, then the rats were bitten by fleas which in turn bit humans. The disease causes the lymph nodes to become sore and to swell to the size of apples. In about 80 percent of the cases, death would follow within two days.

Everyone looked for an explanation for the great calamity. Weak and marginal groups were often identified as culprits — Catalans, Jews, beggars and the poor — but the weak and the marginal were dying too and could not, in the long run, serve as scapegoats. A religious explanation made more sense. The outbreak, various firebrand preachers explained, was God's punishment for the sins of mankind. Throughout Europe, the deaths led to labor shortages which made it easier for serfs to renegotiate their contracts with their lords or to simply run away and settle on their own land. As a result, the medieval feudal economic system was more difficult to maintain. The Black Death helped pave the way for economic markets and thereby for capitalism.

Read more online: https://hdl.handle.net/20.500.12434/34b81cb0

In the latter part of the fourteenth century, the bubonic plague hit first China, then the Mongols, the Arabic world and finally Europe in a series of successive waves. It is estimated that some 75 million people died worldwide and that China lost between one-half and two-thirds of its population, and Europe perhaps half. The disease had a profound and immediate impact on commerce and on the Mongol Empire itself. Although contemporaries had no notion of epidemiology, they understood that the disease was spread through contagion and that people who suddenly appeared in their midst from infected lands were potential carriers. As a result, people became suspicious of travelers, merchants, foreigners and mendicant monks. With a sharp reduction in trade, the *örtöö* network temporarily collapsed.

The Mongols have had a singularly bad press. They are known as bloodthirsty barbarians who annihilated entire cities, killing all inhabitants together with their cats and dogs. And the Mongols did indeed use terror as a means of defeating their enemies, but it is not clear that their way of making war was substantially more destructive than that of other people at the time — or, indeed, more destructive than wars fought today. Another question concerns their long-term impact on the societies they invaded. In China, Russia and the Middle East, the Mongols have often been blamed for causing economic and cultural stagnation. Arab scholars have pointed to the destruction of Baghdad as the pivotal event that ended their "Golden Age" — right at the time when the revival of learning was making Europe increasingly dynamic. Chinese scholars have similarly faulted the Mongols for ending the Song dynasty — during which China came tantalizingly close to embarking on an industrial revolution of its own. Some Russian scholars, meanwhile, have blamed the Golden Horde for the fact that Russia never managed to keep up when the rest of Europe was modernizing. Yet apart from the direct destruction they wrought, it is not at all clear that the impact of the Mongols, on the whole, was negative. Indeed the opposite case can be made — that the Mongols encouraged commerce and innovation by transmitting goods, services, and new ideas to every corner of the enormous Eurasian landmass. The exchange facilitated in this fashion had a civilizing impact even as it undermined or irrevocably destroyed the local culture.

Lev Gumilev and Eurasianism

Lev Nikolayevich Gumilev, 1912–1992, was a Soviet historian, anthropologist and translator, and the son of two celebrated poets, Nikolay Gumilev and Anna Akhmatova. His father was shot when Lev was only seven years old and he spent most of his youth in Soviet labor camps. His mother, who had always been critical of Stalin, even wrote paeans of the regime in an attempted to help her son, but to no avail: Gumilev was released only after Stalin's death. Upon his release he began working at the Hermitage Museum in Moscow where he studied the history of the Khazars and other people of the Central Asian steppes. Gumilev was a neo-Eurasianist who believed Russian identity to be closer to the identity of the peoples of Central Asia than to Europeans.

The Eurasianist movement originally arose among the Russian diaspora in Western Europe in the 1920s. Although the Eurasianists were staunchly anti-Communist, they defended the October Revolution of 1917 as a way to protect Russia against European capitalism and its materialistic values. Yet when their main organization in 1929 turned out to be sponsored by the Soviet regime, the Eurasianists lost credibility. In today's Russia, Eurasianist arguments are used to defend the notion of a "Greater Russia," a Russia which is based on Asian rather than European values, and which once again incorporates Central Asian states within its territory. A Eurasian Economic Community was established in October 2000, with Russia, Belarus, Kazakhstan, Kyrgyzstan, Tajikistan and Uzbekistan as members.

Some observers regard the organization as a way of recreating a Soviet-style empire or perhaps a twenty-first-century version of the Golden Horde.

Gumilev's most notorious argument was that the Mongol invasion never happened. Rather, he said, the small Russian principalities concluded a defensive alliance with the Mongols in order to repel the European forces which had attacked them from the west. Read more: *The Mongol invasion of Europe* at p. 109. Gumilev supported the nationalist movements of Tatars, Kazakhs, and other Turkic peoples, as well as of Mongolia, but his ideas were rejected by the Soviet authorities and he, much like his parents, was unable to publish anything he wrote. This changed when the Soviet Union disintegrated in the 1980s. Then Gumilev came to be widely read by nationalists in both Russia and in the former Soviet republics of Central Asia.

Read more online: https://hdl.handle.net/20.500.12434/e7685392

Further reading

Allsen, Thomas T. *Culture and Conquest in Mongol Eurasia*. Cambridge: Cambridge University Press, 2004.

Barfield, Thomas J. *The Perilous Frontier: Nomadic Empires and China 221 BC to AD 1757*. Oxford: Wiley-Blackwell, 1992.

Golden, Peter B. *Central Asia in World History*. Oxford: Oxford University Press, 2011.

Halperin, Charles J. *Russia and the Golden Horde: The Mongol Impact on Medieval Russian History*. Bloomington: Indiana University Press, 1985.

Khazanov, Anatoly. *Nomads and the Outside World*. Madison: University of Wisconsin Press, 1994.

Ostrowski, Donald. *Muscovy and the Mongols: Cross-Cultural Influences on the Steppe Frontier, 1304–1589*. Cambridge: Cambridge University Press, 2002.

Rossabi, Morris. *China Among Equals: The Middle Kingdom and its Neighbors, 10th–14th Centuries*. Berkeley: University of California Press, 1983.

Turnbull, Stephen R. *Genghis Khan and the Mongol Conquests, 1190–1400*. London: Routledge, 2003.

Vernadsky, George. *The Mongols and Russia: A History of Russia*. New Haven: Yale University Press, 1970.

Weatherford, Jack. *Genghis Khan and the Making of the Modern World*. New York: Broadway Books, 2005.

Timeline

1206	Temüjin is elected khagan. Takes the name "Genghis Khan."
1220	Genghis Khan enters Bukhara. Sacks the city and kills the inhabitants.
1227	Death of Genghis Khan. His son Ögedei succeeds him.
1236	Invasion of Russia begins.
1241	The Mongols defeat the European armies at the battles of Legnica and Mohi, but return to Mongolia. Their invasion of Europe never takes place.
1258	Baghdad is sacked. The caliph is rolled up in a carpet and trampled to death by horses. End of the Arab "Golden Age."
1260–1264	The Toluid wars, fought between Genghis Khan's grandchildren. Led to the division of the empire into four separate khanates.
1260	The Mongol armies are defeated at Ain Jalut, in today's Israel.
1274	First attempt to invade Japan. The Japanese saved by kamikaze.
1279	Kublai Khan establishes the Yuan dynasty in China.
1347	The Genoese city of Caffa in the Crimea is infected with the bubonic plague.
1368	The Yuan dynasty falls.
1556	Sarai, the capital of the Golden Horde, is conquered and burned.
1635	The last remnant of the Mongol empire — the Northern Yuan — is conquered by the Manchus.
1920	Muhammed Alim Khan, the Emir of Bukhara, and the last direct descendant of Genghis Khan to rule a country, is deposed by the Soviet Red Army.

Short dictionary

caravanserai, Persian	Relay station in the *örtöö* network.
faranj, Arabic	Literally, "Frank." Name given to the waves of armies from Europe who invaded the Middle East from the eleventh to the thirteenth century.
ger, Mongolian	"Tent." What the Turks refer to as *yurt*.
jarlig, Mongolian	A document given by the Mongol khagan to Russian princes to authorize their rule.
kamikaze, Japanese	The "wind of the gods" which was thought to have protected Japan from a Mongol invasion.
khagan, Turkish	The "khan of khans," equal to emperor. The title given to the leader of the Mongol Empire, but also to other rulers in Central Asia.
khubi, Mongolian	"Share." Share of economic assets held by members of the Mongol elite.
kurultai, Mongolian	The assembly of Mongol leaders. Responsible for electing *khagan* and for making decisions regarding foreign conquests.
örtöö, Mongolian	*Yam* in Russian. Systems of roads and relay stations that covered much of the Mongol empire.
paiza, Mongolian	A tablet that gave the bearers right of passage and exempted them from taxes when traveling along the *örtöö* network.
pax mongolica, Latin	"Mongol peace." A period in the thirteenth and fourteenth centuries when the Mongol presence throughout Eurasia facilitated commerce and travel.
yassa, Mongolian	"Order" or "decree." The legal code of the Mongol empire which regulated many aspects of social and economic life.

Think about

From Temüjin to Genghis Khan
- Describe the social relation in the traditional societies of the Asian steppe.
- What explains Temüjin's success as a military leader?
- What is a kurultai?

A nomadic state
- Which administrative reforms did Genghis Khan undertake?
- What are the challenges of creating a nomadic empire?
- Why was the Mongol victory over the Khwarazmian Empire a pivotal event?

How to conquer the world
- How was the Mongol army organized? What made it so successful?
- Describe some of the battlefield tactics employed by the Mongols.
- Why did the Mongols never invade Europe?

Dividing it all up
- How did the Mongol empire come to be divided? Give a brief description of its constituent parts.
- How did the Mongols eventually come to occupy China? Which challenges did the Mongols face when ruling the country?
- Why did the Mongol invasion of Japan fail?

An international system of khanates
- Describe the road network maintained by the Mongols.
- What was the "Black Death" and what impact did it have?
- How should we assess the long-term impact of the Mongol invasions?

Map of Africa from Abraham Ortelius, *Theatrum orbis terrarum* (Antverpiae: Apud Aegid. Coppenium Diesth, 1570), p. 35, https://archive.org/details/theatrumorbister00orte

6. Africa

All human beings are Africans. It was in today's Ethiopia, some 200,000 years ago, that the first settlements of *homo sapiens* were established. From this origin we gradually came to migrate to every corner of the planet. Africa is an enormous continent, occupying a fifth of the world's landmass. It includes a number of radically different climates and environments, from dense jungles to extensive grasslands, and it includes the Sahara, a desert the size of Europe. Africa is actually larger than we think since the Mercator projection used for most world maps under-represents the true size of territories around the equator — and Africa straddles the equator. Africa has at least a thousand languages and many more ethnic groups. In order to talk sensibly about this diversity, we have to divide the continent into regions. The most commonly-made distinction is between "North Africa" and "Sub-Saharan Africa," with the Saharan desert dividing the two.

North Africa has a coastline along the Mediterranean Sea and from the very beginning people here have interacted with people in the Middle East and Europe. Pharaonic Egypt, one of the world's oldest civilizations, dating back to 3000 BCE, is located in North Africa and so is Carthage, in today's Tunisia, which for hundreds of years was Rome's main adversary.

Black Athena

Black Athena: The Afroasiatic Roots of Classical Civilization is the name of a book by the historian Martin Bernal, which gave rise to a major controversy when it first appeared in 1987. Bernal's thesis was that much of Greek culture had been imported from Greece's African and Asian neighbors, especially from the Phoenicians and Pharaonic Egypt. His interpretation was controversial since ancient Greece often has been identified as the origin of everything we think of as "European." If it turns out that the Greeks had borrowed most, or much, of their culture from Africa and the Middle East, the Europeans would no longer be able to be who they think they are.

Bernal himself was a scholar of contemporary China, not Greece, and it was easy for specialists to point to mistakes in his analysis. For that reason, the Black Athena thesis has often been rejected. However, ancient Greece really did borrow heavily from its neighbors, from Egypt in particular. The ancient Greeks themselves readily admitted as much. More generally, it might be a mistake to think of "Greece"

© 2019 Erik Ringmar, CC BY 4.0

https://doi.org/10.11647/OBP.0074.06

> as a discrete civilization which can be easily distinguished from the societies that surrounded it. For one thing, the people we think of as Greeks were seafarers who interacted closely with everyone else around the eastern Mediterranean. Greek and non-Greek societies were not as distinct as we often believe.
>
> It was only in the nineteenth century that German scholars, in particular, started thinking of Greece as the origin of their own society. And the choice of Greece was, at least in part, a consequence of the fact that the French — Germany's enemies in a series of wars — often retraced their own history to the Romans. In fact, the Black Athena debate may say more about us than it does about the ancients. The 1980s and 90s were a time when various "culture wars" were fought on American university campuses. Members of minority groups often complained that the academic canon contained too many "dead white males." Calling Athena "black" was a way to turn the tables on the academic establishment.
>
> *Read more online:* https://hdl.handle.net/20.500.12434/8271bfd2

Northern Africa was one of the first parts of the world to convert to Christianity, with an important center of scholarship being Alexandria, in Egypt. The kings of today's Ethiopia converted to Christianity in the fourth century. Later, in the seventh century, North Africa was overrun by Muslim armies. In the eleventh century, two Berber kingdoms, located in today's Morocco, invaded Spain.

South of the Sahara — in Sub-Saharan or "Black" Africa — most people speak Bantu languages. The Bantu speakers originated in western and central parts of the continent but started moving east and southward in the first millennium BCE, spreading their language, cultural practices and crafts. The political organization of Sub-Saharan Africa has been strongly influenced by nature and by the climate. Along much of the coast of Sub-Saharan African there are rainforests that can stretch up to 300 kilometers inland, and around the equator — in today's Congo — there is a continuous band of jungle. In the rainforest the climate is hot and humid, vegetation is dense and light is often blocked by trees that can grow to be up to 50 meters tall. The jungle is a generous environment that provides for its inhabitants, despite the presence of scourges such as the tsetse fly, an insect that carries disease. But the communities created here were small and they had little by way of political institutions.

Away from the coastal regions and the jungles around the equator, there is savanna, less dense woodlands and in eastern Africa also high mountains. The savanna with its grass is an ideal environment in which to raise animals and often it was possible to plant crops. Far larger societies could be established here than in the rainforest. These societies had a more elaborate division of labor, meaning that people could take up specialized tasks and professions. States on the savanna grew rich from trade and manufacturing; they taxed the people subject to them, and they built flourishing capitals administered by public bureaucracies and ruled by laws. In many cases, the savanna-states expanded their power over their neighbors, either by outright occupation or by tying them together into networks of allies and tribute bearers. In this way a number of powerful states were created — including Nubia in today's Sudan; Benin, Mali, Songhai and the Asante in western Africa; Ethiopia, Bunyoro and Buganda in eastern Africa; and Zimbabwe in the south.

The Nile River Valley

The Nile is the longest river in the world. It takes the rain that falls in the jungles of tropical Africa northward, passing through eleven countries and the deserts of the Sahara, before it eventually flows into the Mediterranean. Despite the harsh climate, the Nile made it possible to make a living here from the earliest times. Since the water of the Nile periodically flooded the river banks, thereby irrigating and fertilizing the surrounding fields, the valley provided an excellent environment for agriculture. The Nile River Valley is one of the first places in the world where human beings took up farming.

It was here that Pharaonic Egypt emerged around 3000 BCE, quickly growing into one of the mightiest kingdoms of the ancient world. The Pharaohs built pyramids and temples and elaborate irrigation systems; they developed a writing system too, and are famous for their funeral rites, not least for their embalmed mummies. The pyramids at Giza, built in the middle of the third millennium BCE, with their iconic sphinx, were considered by the Greeks as one of the "seven wonders of the world." Indeed, the Greeks were much impressed with everything Egyptian. This ancient African civilization had a profound influence on the subsequent development of Greek culture. Read more: *Black Athena* at p. 127.

If we had followed the Nile southward in Pharaonic times we would have arrived in the kingdom of Nubia in today's Sudan. From ancient times there were important cities here — Dongola, Nabta Playa, Napata, Meroë and others. There are engravings in rocks in the Nubian desert, dating from 5000 BCE, which show cattle, indicating that the people living here were pastoralists, possibly with the cow playing a part in their religious rites. At roughly the same time, the people living at Nabta Playa built stone constructions which may have served as astronomical observatories. It is not clear exactly how they were used, but archeo-astronomers have argued that the stones line up with particular stars. Perhaps they indicated the time of the summer and winter solstice.

Around 3500 BCE the Kingdom of Nubia was established here. The Nubians made money by selling goods from tropical Africa to the Egyptians, gold and ivory in particular. Their culture had much in common with Pharaonic Egypt, but Nubia was an independent kingdom with its own pyramids and system of writing. The Nubians were periodically invaded by the Egyptians who tried to control the lucrative trade, but the Nubians also invaded Egypt. Around one thousand years BCE there was a Pharaonic dynasty run by Nubians. The Nubians were later conquered by the Romans and by the sands of the Saharan desert. Today there are still monumental walls to be seen in their former capitals and the remnants of elaborate irrigation systems with tunnels that transported water deep under the desert.

In Khartoum, the capital of today's Sudan, the Nile divides into two separate rivers — known as the Blue and the White Nile. The Blue Nile takes you further south into the jungles of Central Africa and to the source of the river in Lake Victoria. The White Nile, on the other hand, takes you into the mountains of Ethiopia. Today Ethiopia is a landlocked country which has suffered badly both from droughts and political instability, but two thousand years ago there was a powerful kingdom here, with Aksum as its capital. The Aksumite Kingdom, 100–940, had close connections with Yemen in the Arabian Peninsula, across the Red Sea. Yemen at the time was dominated by Jewish culture and Jewish culture spread to Ethiopia too. Indeed, Ethiopians insist that the Queen of Sheba came from here.

Jews of Ethiopia

Beta Israel, the "House of Israel," is the name of the community of Jews which existed in some 500 separate villages scattered throughout the former Kingdom of Aksum, in today's Ethiopia. This community is African, yet it has been Jewish since biblical times. Before Christianity and Islam came to be established, much of the Arabian peninsula was Jewish. There was, for example, a strong Jewish community in Yemen. They, in turn, traded with people on the other side of the Red Sea and this is how Jewish culture came to spread to Africa. Read more: *Coffee and croissants* at p. 95. The Jews of Ethiopia insist that they are the descendants of King Solomon and the Queen of Sheba. After the rise of Christianity and Islam, Ethiopian Jews were cut off from other Jewish communities, but their culture and religion survived.

After the establishment of Israel in 1948, the Jews of Ethiopia obtained the right to immigrate there — a right which some took advantage of during the famines and wars of the 1980s. The Israeli government, with American support, organized two rescue operations — "Operation Moses" in 1984 and "Operation Solomon" in 1991 — in which tens of thousands of people were airlifted to Israel. At the time, some Israelis questioned their Jewishness, and the very notion of a "black Jew," while others identified them as one of the "lost tribes of Israel." Today there are 120,000 people in Israel who claim Ethiopian descent. Some of them complain that Israeli society is racist; many in the older generation have little education and find life in Israel difficult. A majority cannot read and write Hebrew and unemployment rates are high. But not many have decided to return. It is estimated that there are still some 8,000 people of Jewish descent living in Ethiopia. The Israeli government is officially committed to bringing them to Israel.

Read more online: https://hdl.handle.net/20.500.12434/3da5cc6b

What is more certain is that the Aksumite Kingdom was heavily involved in trade both with the Arabian Peninsula and with the world beyond. The Aksumites were famous exporters of frankincense and myrrh, which together with gold were the presents said to have been given to Jesus after his birth. The Aksumites were trading across the Indian Ocean too. They are referred to as ivory merchants in *Periplus of the Erythraean Sea*, a Greek merchant's manual dating from the first century of the Common Era. Located at the intersection of these shipping lanes, the Aksumite Kingdom became a major player in the trade which connected India and the Roman Empire. The Aksumite kings minted their own coins in order to facilitate trade, and they erected steles, enormous stone slabs, on which they commemorated their achievements. Many of the steles are preserved to this day.

The Aksumite king converted to Christianity in 325 — after Armenia, in the Caucasus, but a hundred years before the Roman emperors — and from this time onward the symbol of the cross appears on their coins. Today at least half of the population of Ethiopia are Christians. The Ethiopian church follows the Coptic liturgy, first developed in Alexandria in Egypt in the first century CE. Yet links to the Arabian Peninsula have remained strong. In the sixteenth century, Ethiopia exported coffee to Yemen from where it was sent on to fashionable coffee shops all over the Ottoman Empire. Read more: *Coffee and croissants* at p. 95.

Ethiopia was never colonized by a European power and when the country was invaded by Italy in the 1930s, the emperor, Haile Selassie, made a personal appearance at the League of Nations in Geneva, Switzerland, asking for help. Read more: *Countries that were never colonized* at p. 196.

This established his reputation worldwide and many black people in the Americas, in particular, were amazed to hear about this African emperor who claimed to be the descendant of King Solomon and the Queen of Sheba. In Jamaica, of all places, Haile Selassie became something of a God in the Rastafari religion practiced by some of the locals. Read more: *The Ark of the Covenant* at p. 54.

North Africa

In the seventh century, North Africa was overrun by the armies of the expanding Umayyad Caliphate. Read more: *The Umayyads and the Abbasids* at p. 78.

In 640 the Arabs conquered Egypt and continued westward. The North African terrain was easy to move across since the population was sparse and there were few proper towns. Yet the people the Arabs ran into here were in many respects similar to themselves. A majority were Berbers, and many of them were nomads too, including the Tuaregs of the Saharan desert. Instead of putting up a fight, the nomads of the desert simply moved away from the path of the invaders, while the Berbers who lived along the Mediterranean coast gradually came to be assimilated into the new elite. To this day we tend to think of the people of North Africa as Arabs but many of them would prefer to be known as Berbers. At least some still regard the Arabs as invaders and dream of establishing an independent country.

> ### Independence for Azawad
>
> The Berbers are an ethnic group indigenous to North Africa who live in and around the Saharan desert. The Berbers are semi-nomadic, combining the tending of goats and sheep with farming and commerce. Two of the kingdoms that ruled Spain were run by Berbers; and the last of the four original caliphates, the Fatimid Caliphate, 909–1171, was initially dominated by Berbers. Read more: *The Muslim caliphates* at p. 73. The Tuaregs, the "blue men of the desert" — named after the color of their headgear — are Berber too. For hundreds of years, the Tuaregs were in charge of the caravans that traded with Timbuktu in the Kingdom of Mali and beyond.
>
> Today there are between 25 and 30 million people who speak the Berber language; most are Muslims, but some are Christian and a small minority are Jews. For the past couple of decades, there has been a strong revival of Berber culture. Berber arts and crafts are taught to younger generations, together with the Berber language, and festivals such as equestrian shows attract large audiences. Berber-style rock music has received worldwide attention.
>
> There are also demands for political rights. Some Berbers want independence for their homeland which they regard as occupied, and mismanaged, by Arabs in the north and by black Africans in the south. The political instability of countries such as Algeria and Libya has provided opportunities to realize these aims. The overthrow of the Gaddafi regime in Libya in the fall of 2011 allowed some Tuaregs to escape with their weapons to Mali where they began a guerrilla war against the government. In April 2012, the guerrilla movement, the MNLA, declared independence for a country they called "Azawad," with Gao and Timbuktu as its main cities Read more: *The libraries of Timbuktu* at p. 135. In 2013, Timbuktu was recaptured by the Malian government, supported by international troops. The dream of an independent Azawad has been once again postponed.
>
> *Read more online:* https://hdl.handle.net/20.500.12434/c6f7fead

The Berbers would soon reassert themselves. In the early eighth century, when the Arab armies continued their expansion into the Iberian peninsula, many Berbers went with them. Together they established a capital in Córdoba in the province they were to call al-Andalus. Read more: *The Arabs in Spain* at p. 81.

Some groups of Berbers also went southward on a mission to convert pagans living in what today is Mauritania and Ghana. In general, the Berbers seem to have taken Islam very seriously. In the eleventh and twelfth centuries two revivalist movements arose among them led by leaders who declared themselves disgusted by the lack of religious zeal among their fellow Muslims. The first of these movements, the Almoravids, was made up of Saharan tribes who left the desert and built a capital for themselves in the city of Marrakesh, on the northern side of the Atlas Mountains. They proceeded to create an empire which included all of today's Morocco, but also vast areas of the deserts to the south and a broad strip of land along the Mediterranean coast. The Almoravids imposed sharia laws on the territories they occupied, banning the sale of alcohol and pork and, unusually for Muslim rulers, tried to convert the members of other religions by force.

Before long the Berbers had occupied Spain too. By the middle of the eleventh century, the political power of the Caliphate of Córdoba had disintegrated and a number of smaller Muslim kingdoms, known as the *taifa*, had made themselves independent of any central power. Read more: *The Arabs in Spain* at p. 81.

The *taifa* kingdoms were often at war with each other and with the Christian kingdoms in the north of the peninsula. In 1086, as a way to restore peace and unity, the Almoravids were invited to al-Andalus by the *taifa* kings. This is how they came to expand their African empire into Europe. Much as in North Africa, the Almoravids were appalled by the low standard of morality among the local elites and before long they had imposed strict Islamic laws in Spain too. Yet the Almoravids were unable to maintain the purity of their faith. When the original leaders died, they were replaced by rulers who had far less interest in religious matters. With the help of architects imported from Muslim Spain, the Almoravids turned Marrakesh into a fortified city filled with sumptuous palaces and mosques.

This was when the second revivalist movement, the Almohads, began gathering in opposition to them. The Almohads were not from the desert but from the high Atlas Mountains of Morocco, yet they were if anything even more serious about their religion than the Almoravids had originally been. From their mountain stronghold they undertook increasingly successful military campaigns and in 1147 they captured Marrakesh. In 1159 they had conquered all of North Africa and in 1172 all of al-Andalus. They made Sevilla into their second capital, although they regarded Spain as little more than an outpost of their empire. In addition, the Almohads proceeded to impose strict Islamic laws on the people they had conquered. This had severe consequences for the cosmopolitan culture of cities like Córdoba. Many Christians fled northwards, and many Jews fled eastwards to Cairo. Read more: *Mosheh ben Maimon* at p. 85.

Yet the Almohads also mellowed with time, and they too became more interested in architectural projects than in imperial expansion. This was when the city of Fez was turned into a center of religious learning and scholarship. The medina of Fez — the market quarters of the city — was particularly famous. What sometimes is regarded as the oldest university in the world, the University of Al Quaraouiyine, was founded by a woman, Fatima al-Fihri, in Fez in 859. Read more: *Nalanda, a very old university* at p. 56.

In addition, the Almohads turned the city of Rabat, on the Atlantic coast, into a major port and a fortified naval base. Yet their empire began crumbling as early as the first part of the thirteenth century. In 1212, only forty years after the initial occupation, they were defeated in Spain by an alliance of Christian rulers and by 1269 it was all over for the Almohads.

The kingdoms of West Africa

The Saharan desert is certainly a harsh environment, but nomadic peoples have made a living here since the earliest times. In some ways the desert served more like a bridge that connected different parts of Africa than as a wall which separated them. This is why the division commonly made between "North Africa" and "Sub-Saharan Africa" should be questioned. The Berbers were one of the peoples who traded across the Sahara. Their partners on the other side were often located in the empire of Mali. Since much of Mali, then as now, consists of sand, agriculture should really have been impossible here and we would not expect to find many settled communities. Yet the presence of the Niger River changes that calculation. Much of the rain that falls in the highlands of today's Guinea, a country on Africa's Atlantic coast, flows not westward into the Atlantic but instead north and eastward, straight into the Sahara. Here the water runs through today's Mali and Niger, and eventually into the Atlantic in Nigeria, where it forms a vast delta. Yet, the Niger River forms another delta too — an inland delta, right in the deserts of Mali. Here there has been enough water to make settled agriculture possible.

This is where we find cities like Timbuktu, Gao and Djenné. It was primarily with these cities that the Berbers conducted their trade. Two commodities — gold and salt — were more important than all others, although ivory, copper and slaves were traded too. Salt was used for preserving food and it was almost as valuable as gold. Much of it was hacked out of the rocks at Targhaza, a desolate salt mine in the middle of the Saharan desert. As far as gold was concerned, it was traded by a rather mysterious guild of merchants known as the Wangarans. Although the Wangarans were reluctant to reveal the exact source of their supply, it is clear that it originated in the south, in the region of today's Ghana. This was the gold which, thanks to the trans-Saharan trade, eventually ended up in the Middle East and Europe. During this time, in the late Middle Ages, something like half of all gold in the world came from Africa.

As one would expect, the rulers of Mali were quick to take their cut of this lucrative trade. Indeed, in the first part of the thirteenth century, a powerful empire was established here, funded above all by taxes on trade. The Mali Empire had a well-trained army, comprising some 100,000 soldiers staffed and supplied by the emperor's subjects. Before long the rulers of Mali had conquered a large area stretching from the Niger River westward to the Atlantic Ocean. The founder of the empire, Sundiata Keita, was not only a ruthless military leader but also by all accounts a wise politician. In 1235, at a meeting of notables, a constitution was adopted, known as the *Kouroukan fouga*, which gave the empire a legal system and a decentralized, federal political structure. Guilds of craftsmen were granted monopolies on crafts such as the smelting of metals, woodworking, and tanning; women were protected by law and given a role in politics.

The origin of writing

In order to learn about the past, we need primary sources. Many of these are texts. In the case of Africa, however, there are relatively few texts available from the time before the Europeans arrived. Instead, historians are forced to rely on archaeological evidence or on oral traditions. The lack of writing systems has been presented as evidence of how "primitive" people in Africa are. Yet, as so often, it is all a matter of politics. Systems of writing first developed in agricultural societies with powerful states. The state needs writing in order to keep track of tax revenue, to communicate with its officials and to lay down the law. Besides, kings like their achievements to be remembered — how much land they conquered and how many enemies they killed. From this perspective, writing is a means for the state to exercise power. People are subject to writing much as they are subject to other state-run institutions. It is consequently not surprising to find written records in parts of Africa — such as Egypt and Ethiopia — where there were powerful, agriculturally-based states.

For people who do not live in agricultural societies, and who are not subject to states, oral traditions often serve better. After all, what we need to know in order to live successful lives is above all what people like ourselves did when faced with similar situations to our own. This information does not have to be written down. Ordinary people do not need a written history as much as they need myths. Myths are taught by the elders and kept alive by the community itself. To live subject to a myth is to live subject to a shared memory of which each person is the custodian. This is not to say, of course, that writing is not a useful technology. In small, non-state, societies people can communicate directly with each other, but in large societies, people communicate by means of written texts.

Read more online: https://hdl.handle.net/20.500.12434/f950db17

The trade in gold and salt made the emperors of Mali enormously wealthy. The most famous among them was Mansa Musa. After having conquered some twenty-four cities and expanded the empire to three times its original size, the story has it, Mansa Musa went on a *hajj* to Mecca in 1324. People in the Arab world were astonished to see his procession which included camels, elephants and no fewer than 60,000 men and some 12,000 slaves carrying gold bars. Along the way, gold nuggets were handed out to local dignitaries and gold dust to beggars. In Cairo, Mansa Musa's lavish gifts were sufficient to cause an inflation which was said to have lasted for twelve years. When he returned to Mali, Mansa Musa rebuilt Timbuktu and established the city as a center of Muslim scholarship and learning. It was more than anything as a result of his largess and his subsequent building program that Timbuktu became known as a city of exotic wonders.

The libraries of Timbuktu

Timbuktu was established as a center of Islamic learning during the Mali Empire in the thirteenth century and the town continued to flourish well into the seventeenth century. Scholars, teachers, and students assembled at the *madrasa* — the religious school — at the Sankore mosque. In addition, Timbuktu was at the center of the book trade across the Sahara and many of the town's inhabitants were avid book collectors. The books were written in Arabic, but also in a number of indigenous languages, using Arabic script. The inhabitants of Timbuktu have remained book lovers to this day. It has been estimated that Timbuktu has some 700,000 books. However, since the manuscripts are fragile and often in poor condition, the owners have been encouraged to deposit them in libraries where they can be better preserved and also digitized and put on the Internet.

In April 2012, Timbuktu was captured by Tuareg rebels in collaboration with Al-Qaeda forces who declared the town a part of the independent country of Azawad. Read more: *Independence for Azawad* at p. 132. They outlawed music and football and destroyed a number of shrines dedicated to Sufi saints. They also began destroying ancient books. By then, however, the vast majority of the books had already been saved thanks to the heroic efforts of a few librarians.

The preservation and digitization project is proceeding apace, funded by South Africa and various international organizations. However, many families are understandably reluctant to part with their treasures. So far only a fraction of the texts have been digitized. It is only when this work is completed that we can properly begin to understand the intellectual world of medieval West Africa.

Read more online: https://hdl.handle.net/20.500.12434/9030fd44

Yet it was during the rulers of the Songhai Empire in the fifteenth and sixteenth centuries that Timbuktu really thrived. Also, Songhai had the inland delta of the Niger River as its center, and Gao, in today's Mali, was its capital. Much as the kings of Mali before them, the Songhai rulers grew rich from the gold trade and they emulated Mansa Musa's example in going on ostentatious pilgrimages. The armies of the Songhai Empire had a cavalry of horsemen and a navy made up of canoes. Gao and other towns had guilds of craftsmen, and slave labor played a prominent role in the economy. In addition to gold, the Songhai exported kola nuts and slaves and they imported textiles, horses, salt and assorted luxury goods. A traveler from Muslim Spain, Leo Africanus, who visited Gao in the early sixteenth century, was amazed at the poverty of the lower classes but also at the great wealth of its rulers. The position of Songhai came to an end in 1591 when the Moroccans invaded.

The other delta of the Niger River, where the water runs into the Atlantic Ocean, is today the center of the Nigerian petroleum industry. This is where the Yoruba people live, which together with the Igbo and the Hausa is the largest of Nigeria's more than 500 ethnic groups. It was here, some 900 years ago, that a number of flourishing city-states came to be established. There were at least sixteen such cities — including Ife, Ijebu, Katunga and Ibadan — and many smaller ones besides. Between the twelfth and the eighteenth centuries this was one of the most highly urbanized parts of the world. The largest cities among them may have had some 100,000 inhabitants. The Yoruba city-states were all organized in much the same fashion. They were built like fortresses, with high walls surrounded by moats and gates that could be closed to visitors or to approaching armies. In the case of the larger city-states, these walls could become very extensive indeed, reaching several thousands of kilometers in length.

> ### Walls and bronzes of Benin
>
> The Kingdom of Benin was one of the city-states in the delta created by the Niger River in today's Nigeria. The people of Benin grew rich from trade, not least in slaves, which they were happy to sell to the Europeans who began arriving in the sixteenth century. The state of Benin was surrounded by an enormous set of walls and moats, known as *iya*, constructed between the ninth and the fifteenth centuries. The walls could be as high as 10 meters and the moats just as deep. They had a combined length of some 16,000 kilometers, making this one of the largest construction projects on earth. Archaeologists have compared the walls of Benin to the Great Wall of China and complained that the former construction has received none of the attention lavished on the latter. *Read more: The Great Wall of China does not exist at p. 26.* It is not quite clear why the walls and moats were built. A project of this scale is difficult to explain as purely a military arrangement. Perhaps it was rather a question of politics — of demonstrating the extent of the *oba*'s power.
>
> The opulent lifestyle of the rulers of Benin is vividly portrayed in a remarkable collection of bronze sculptures and plaques which were cast from the thirteenth century onward. The metal was imported from Europe, but the artworks were made by local craftsmen using local techniques. Occasionally the plaques portray European merchants too — they appear as small figures in the background, wearing odd-looking hats. The bronzes were looted by the British when they occupied Benin in 1897. Many of them are now on display in the British Museum.
>
> *Read more online:* https://hdl.handle.net/20.500.12434/e96d8419

All Yoruba city-states had an elaborate structure of professional guilds and there were many social clubs, religious sects and secret societies. Each city-state had a leader, the *oba*, who lived in a large palace in the center of the city with a marketplace in front of it. The *oba*s were elected from the often quite extensive pool of royal princes. Some of the *oba*s ended up as autocratic rulers but others were restrained by the power of their councilors. Some city-states were in effect more like republics.

In the fifteenth century the *oba*s of Benin grew particularly rich and powerful. During the rule of Ewuare the Great, 1440–1473, Benin expanded to become a fully-fledged empire. Ewuare taxed trade and established a military force that included a navy made up of canoes. The Benin army was also skilled in the art of siege warfare, which was crucial in this world of fortified cities. The enemies captured in these wars were turned into slaves who were employed in various construction projects, of which the very extensive system of moats and walls was the most remarkable. The court of the *Oba* of Benin is vividly depicted in a series of plaques and statues, known as the "Benin bronzes." *Read more: Walls and bronzes of Benin at p. 137.*

Further west, in what today is Ghana and the Ivory Coast, we find the Akan people. The Akans lived in the rainforest which they, through painstaking labor, managed to control. In order to cut down the enormous trees they relied on slave labor and the slaves were bought in gold. Akan territory was gold country, and thereby the ultimate source of much of the wealth of all of West Africa. Yet gold did not only pay for slaves, but also for soldiers, and in the year 1701, the Akan established an empire of their own, known as the Asante. The Asante was a confederacy of assorted rivaling groups skillfully unified by Osei Tutu, 1675–1717. The Asante confederacy had Kumasi, in today's Ghana, as its capital. Yet the alliance was more than anything held together by symbolic means. Osei Tutu took a stool made of gold as a symbol of the unity of the confederation. The occupant of the golden stool was to be the ruler of them all.

Golden Stool of the Asante

The Golden Stool of the Asante is the throne of the ruler of the Asante Kingdom and the ultimate symbol of power in Asante society. As legend has it, the stool descended from the sky and landed on the lap of Osei Tutu, the first Asante king. Thrones are symbols of authority in many societies; they allow the ruler to sit while his subjects are forced to kneel or bow. Yet the Golden Stool of the Asante has particular powers. It embodies the spirit of the Asante — the living members, the dead and the yet to be born. As a sacred object, it may never touch the ground and must always be placed on a blanket. It can only be handled by the ruler himself. On particularly solemn occasions the throne is itself seated on a throne.

As one would expect, the Golden Stool has been the cause of numerous conflicts. In the year 1900, when the English governor of the newly occupied colony of the Gold Coast insisted that he be allowed to sit on it, it suddenly mysteriously disappeared. It was later recovered and has been used in royal ceremonies after Ghana's independence. The power of the stool is intact and today no one but the current Asante king and his closest advisers know its whereabouts. On ritual occasions, copies of the stool are often used. Tourists can buy cheap replicas of their own in the market of Kumasi, the Asante capital.

Read more online: https://hdl.handle.net/20.500.12434/eed5f046

In general the Asante kings surrounded themselves with much pomp and circumstance and they were often carried around in public procession wearing their gilded paraphernalia. A bit less symbolically, the empire was held together by drums. Although drums are common all over Africa, the drumming of the Asante is particularly famous. Asante drums were talking drums. They were not only beating out a rhythm but conveying entire messages which, with their help, were quickly transmitted from one part of the empire to the other. In the rainforest, where mobility is blocked and visibility is limited, nothing travels as quickly as sound.

As we have seen, both Benin and the Asante confederacy owned and traded in slaves. Indeed slaves, together with gold, were the main sources of wealth for both empires. Land, by contrast, was not considered as a form of private property. Land had little value since there quite simply was too much of it. Instead, it was what the land produced, and those who could be forced to work on it, which were valuable. Thus a man would count his wealth in the number of slaves he owned, and throughout West Africa taxes were levied on slaves and paid in terms of slaves. Slaves were also given as tributary gifts by a subordinate state or by a neighboring state which sought to avoid occupation. In general, there was a strong connection between warfare and slavery, and prisoners of war were usually enslaved. The revenue derived from the transcontinental slave trade across the Atlantic Ocean, which began in the sixteenth century, was more than anything what helped make both Benin and the Asante rich and powerful.

Dancing kings and female warriors of Dahomey

When the kings of Dahomey received visitors they would always put on an ostentatious display. A large contingent of soldiers would show up, brandishing their weapons and waving flag-staves decorated with human skulls and with the jawbones of their enemies. In addition, the kings of Dahomey would dance before the visitors, accompanied by drums and by singing soldiers. Afterward, the soldiers would fire their guns in a salute and the king would approach the visitors and shake hands with them.

The kings of Dahomey had an elite guard made up entirely of women, known as the *mino*. They were established in the seventeenth century, initially as a group of elephant hunters, but later they became the king's bodyguard, equipped with muskets and regular uniforms. They also participated in slave raids. The *mino* underwent rigorous physical exercises and learned survival skills, how to storm defenses and to execute prisoners. They were not allowed to have children or to marry. By the mid-nineteenth century, there were between 1,000 and 6,000 of these female warriors, making up about a third of the Dahomeyan army.

The *mino* participated in the wars against France at the end of the nineteenth century. Initially, the French soldiers found it difficult to fight female adversaries, but eventually, they overcame their scruples. In a major battle in 1890, the *mino* were slaughtered. The female battalion was disbanded after Dahomey became a French colony in 1894. Interviews with former female soldiers conducted in the 1930s indicated that many of them had problems adapting to civilian life. The *mino* guard has recently been discovered by Hollywood and popular culture in the United States. There is no doubt that they provide an image of female empowerment. Whether they really are appropriate role models for young black women today can be discussed.

Read more online: https://hdl.handle.net/20.500.12434/d87f3953

East Africa and the Indian Ocean

It is the Bantu migration which will take us from West Africa to the other side of the continent. The Bantu migration is the name given to a massive movement of peoples which took place some time in the first millennium BCE. Leaving a region in what is today eastern Nigeria and Cameroon, people speaking Bantu languages began moving south and eastward, eventually settling in much of central and southern Africa. The migration was a spontaneous movement, not an invasion, but exactly why it took place is not clear. Some scholars suggest that it was due to overpopulation while others cite disease or changes in the climate. The Bantu people knew how to work iron and this allowed them to make better tools and more deadly weapons. The iron tools, in turn, made it possible to cut down trees and open up new fields. The original populations of these parts of Africa were hunters and gatherers, not farmers, and they were either assimilated into the Bantu population or forced to eke out a living in more remote places.

People of the forest

Before human beings took up agriculture, we all gathered our food or we hunted it. There are small groups of hunters and gatherers throughout the world to this day — and many of them live in Africa. This includes some 900,000 Pygmies in the jungles of Central Africa, but also groups such as the San people of the Kalahari desert and the Hadza of Tanzania. The people of the forest are the remnants of the original inhabitants of Central Africa who were displaced when the Bantu people arrived. There is still a lot of tension between the two groups. The Pygmies of Congo often live in close proximity to a village of farmers, but as soon as new sources of food supply become available they disappear into the forest. The Bantu farmers often think of them as unreliable. The Pygmies, for their part, often think of the Bantu farmers as overbearing and rather gullible.

Sedentary people always look down on people who move around in order to make a living, but they also romanticize their lives. One example is the "paleolithic diet" which has recently become fashionable in Europe and North America. People who follow a paleolithic diet stay away from agricultural products like cereal and milk and eat only the kind of food that can be hunted or gathered. The presumption is that our bodies are better adjusted to the kind of food that we consumed during 95 percent of human history. Apparently, "paleolithic diet" is Google's most popular search term in the category of weight-loss methods.

Another group of people who romanticize the lives of hunters and gatherers is a brand of political activists known as "anarcho-primitivists." Agriculture, they argue, was a mistake, and so was the state and the very notion of civilization. Some anarcho-primitivists predict that a catastrophe of some kind one day will occur — perhaps as the result of a war or an environmental collapse. After that cataclysmic event, the few humans who survive will have to return to Africa and to the only form of human life which is sustainable in the long run. The societies of hunters and gatherers who live there today are thus not the remnants of some remote past but rather models of our future.

Read more online: **https://hdl.handle.net/20.500.12434/197e9c14**

The Bantu migration explains why many people in Africa speak related languages. There are today some 450 Bantu languages and Bantu speakers make up a third of Africa's population. All Bantu people share a belief in a supreme God who is usually associated with the sky. The world was not created, they say, but it is eternal. The spirits of people who have died linger on in this world and can influence the lives of the living, at least as long as the dead are still remembered. Many Bantu folktales feature speaking animals — cunning hares, sneaky hyenas and powerful lions. "Ubuntu" is a shared political principle which African politicians still occasionally invoke in their rhetoric. It is usually translated as "humanity," or the notion that "I am because we are."

When the Bantu-speaking migrants eventually arrived on the shores of the Indian Ocean, they came across people and influences from entirely different parts of the world — the Arabian Peninsula, Persia, India and beyond. Arab traders had traveled up and down this coast at least since the first millennium of the Common Era and they had established themselves in places like Lamu, Mombasa and Zanzibar. Merchants from Oman played an important role in this trade too. They transported their goods on ships, known as *dhows*. Read more: *A giraffe in Beijing* at p. 25.

This is not to say that the trading ports on the coast were Arabic. Rather, they were cosmopolitan hubs with a culture, and a way of life, which was uniquely their own. The main language spoken here today is Swahili, which is a Bantu language mixed with loan-words from Arabic, Hindi and assorted European languages. In fact, Swahili was not originally anyone's native tongue but was instead a lingua franca used by merchants. In the tenth century, a sultanate was established in Kilwa Kisiwani, in today's Tanzania.

Kilwa Kisiwani

Kilwa Kisiwani, just off the southern coast of today's Tanzania, was one of many trading ports along Africa's east coast, and for a while, it was the most powerful among them. In the tenth century, a Muslim sultanate was founded here by a group of explorers coming from the city of Shiraz in today's Iran. They established themselves as a ruling class and imposed their own culture and values on the community. Kilwa Kisiwani was famous for its fort which served as a residence for the sultan, but also as a place of trade. The residence had over one hundred individual rooms, reception halls, wide staircases, and an octagonal swimming pool. Kilwa's other main attraction was its mosque, constructed entirely out of coral stone. Ibn Battuta, who came here in 1331, was highly impressed with the way the city was laid out and with the generosity and religiosity of its ruler. Read more: *Ibn Battuta, the greatest traveler of all time* at p. 142. He also describes how the sultan went on raids to capture slaves in the interior of Africa.

By the time of Ibn Battuta's visit, Kilwa had already been engaged in commerce for some thousand years. The *Periplus of the Erythraean Sea*, a Greek manual for merchants compiled in the first century CE, mentions the ports along the eastern coast of Africa as excellent places to buy ivory and tortoiseshell. Coins minted in Kilwa have been found in Great Zimbabwe, Oman, and even in Australia. Read more: *Great Zimbabwe* at p. 127. During excavations in the sultan's palace, a small flask from the Yuan dynasty was discovered together with many shards of Chinese pottery. Read more: *Dividing it all up* at p. 112. Today only ruins are left of the once-powerful sultanate.

Read more online: https://hdl.handle.net/20.500.12434/f8256e9b

Ibn Battuta, the greatest traveler of all time

Ibn Battuta, 1304–1369, was a Moroccan explorer of Berber descent. He is a good candidate for the title of the greatest traveler of all time. His journeys began in 1325 when he set off on a *hajj* to Mecca. However, once his religious obligations were completed, he did not go home but continued instead to the Mongol Ilkhanate in Persia. He visited Baghdad in 1327 and went to Mecca for a second *hajj*, but again he refused to go home. Instead, he continued southward to Yemen, Aden, and Somalia. He then went for a third *hajj*, and this time he stayed in Mecca for a year. He then decided to seek employment with the sultan of Delhi. He traveled to India via Constantinople, the Black Sea and the trade routes of the Golden Horde. He visited Astrakan and Samarkand, and via Afghanistan and the Hindu Kush he eventually made it to Delhi. Here he worked as a judge for six years before he was dispatched as the sultan's ambassador to the Yuan dynasty in China.

On his journey to China Ibn Battuta's ship was attacked, and he ended up in the Maldive Islands where he stayed for nine months and married into the royal family. Continuing his original assignment, he set off for Sri Lanka, Bangla Desh, Malacca, Vietnam and eventually he arrived in the Fujian province of China. In Beijing, he introduced himself as the long-lost ambassador from India and was kindly received by the emperor. Only then did he decide to return to Morocco. Traveling along the caravan routes of Central Asia he saw the first signs of the contagious disease, the Bubonic plague, which was to kill millions of people. Read more: *The Black Death* at p. 120. Coming home in 1349, he discovered that his father and mother were dead. Restless, he decided to go on a trip to southern Spain. He then went to Timbuktu where he gives an account of an encounter with a hippopotamus.

Scholars are uncertain whether Ibn Battuta really visited all the places he describes, and in some cases, he may be recounting tales he heard from other travelers. However, Ibn Battuta himself was confident regarding his achievements. "I have indeed — praise be to God — attained my desire in this world, which was to travel through the earth, and I have attained this honor, which no ordinary person has attained."

On the beaches of Kilwa one can still find shards of pottery originating in India and China.

A state which benefited greatly from the trade conducted across the Indian Ocean was the Kingdom of Zimbabwe, 1220–1450. Although its capital, Great Zimbabwe, was located inland, on the savanna, it was connected to the sea through well-traveled trade routes and also by the Limpopo River which flows from today's Botswana to Mozambique.

Read more online: https://hdl.handle.net/20.500.12434/3075aa43

Great Zimbabwe

Great Zimbabwe is called "great" in order to distinguish it from the many smaller zimbabwes, over 200 of them, which are scattered in an area from today's country of Zimbabwe to Mozambique on the East African coast. A "zimbabwe" is a fortress built of stone which served as protection against military attacks but also as a residence for the ruling class. The zimbabwes were connected to each other as nodes in a network, and trade tied the network together. Great Zimbabwe was the greatest of them all. It was the center of a commercial network that connected inner Africa to trading communities all around the Indian Ocean. The people of Great Zimbabwe were selling all kinds of products, but mainly ivory and gold. They even traded with China. Read more: *Kilwa Kisiwani* at p. 141.

Great Zimbabwe was a strongly hierarchical society with a rigid separation between ordinary people and the ruling elite. The king lived in a fortress on top of a hill surrounded by enormous stone walls, and in the city, at the foot of the hill, lived an estimated 25,000 inhabitants. Yet we actually know very little about the people who once lived here and how the buildings were used. It seems the construction began in the eleventh century, but that it was abandoned at the end of the fourteenth century. We do not know why. Perhaps the land could not sustain such a large population, or perhaps the gold mines no longer yielded as much wealth.

When Europeans in the nineteenth century first came across Great Zimbabwe they failed to accept that it could have been constructed by Africans. The Phoenicians must have done it, they concluded, or the Egyptians or perhaps the Arabs. Between 1965 and 1980, when Zimbabwe was run by a small group of renegade white farmers, they even commissioned archaeological research designed to prove that no Africans were involved in its construction. Not surprisingly, when Zimbabwe became democratic in 1980, Great Zimbabwe quickly became a symbol of the achievements of its people. The country itself was named after the monument and it was depicted on stamps and banknotes.

Read more online: https://hdl.handle.net/20.500.12434/69127b74

There are some two hundred trading-posts — smaller "zimbabwes" — scattered between Great Zimbabwe and the coast. Not all that much is known about the Zimbabwe Kingdom, but the ruins of the capital leave no doubt regarding its power and wealth. Here too there are abundant indications of a connection to lands all around the Indian Ocean. Archaeologists have found Chinese ceramics in the ruins of Great Zimbabwe, but also coins from Arabia and glass beads from India.

Further north, in the mountains of what today is Uganda, we find Bunyoro and Buganda, two kingdoms that were rivals from the thirteenth century well into the nineteenth. The traditional economy here revolved around big game hunting but they were making money from trade too. And just as in West Africa, salt was a key commodity. To this day both Bunyoro and Buganda have royal families which take court ceremony very seriously indeed.

Bunyoro and Buganda

Bunyoro and Buganda are two ancient kingdoms in the region of the Great Lakes in eastern Africa. The two were rivals from the thirteenth well into the nineteenth century. Bunyoro's present ruler is Rukirabasaija Agutamba Solomon Gafabusa Iguru I. The kingdom has 800,000 inhabitants, some three-fourths of whom are subsistence farmers. Only about half of the population is literate. The traditional economy in this part of Africa revolved around the hunting of big game — elephants, lions, rhinos and crocodiles — the various parts of which were exported, first to the East African coast and then across the Indian Ocean. Salt was another key commodity, produced at Kibiro, on the banks of Lake Albert, controlled by Bunyoro. Today a majority of the land is still virgin forest and there are plenty of large animals.

As for the people of Buganda, they were mainly farmers, but they also had blacksmiths who were famous for producing high-quality tools and lethal weapons. Buganda eclipsed Bunyoro in the eighteenth century when it gained control of the salt trade. Nineteenth century visitors to Buganda were amazed at the wealth of the country and the elaborate ceremonies conducted at its court. The present king of Buganda is Kabaka Muwenda Mutebi II. During the period of dictatorship in Uganda — prior to 1993 — he lived in exile in England where he went to university. The king of Bunyoro maintains an active Facebook account and you can follow the Kingdom of Buganda on Twitter.

Today Bunyoro and Buganda are constituent parts of Uganda. However, since the country is a republic, neither monarch has formal powers. Their mandate, according to the country's constitution, is restricted to "cultural and development advocacy matters." Yet they also engage in various projects aimed at promoting information technology and sustainable development. Both royal houses are still greatly admired by the descendants of their former subjects.

Read more online: https://hdl.handle.net/20.500.12434/529e7b43

An African international system?

The question is whether it is possible to talk about a distinct African international system and, if so, what its characteristics might be. There are good reasons to conclude that there is no such system. After all, in many parts of Africa, geography and the climate have put up obstacles to the formation of the kinds of political structures which we think of as states. In the rainforest, the vegetation was usually too dense to clear and no large communities could be formed, and further inland people were often pastoralists and not that easy to organize politically. And if there are no states, there can be no inter-state system. Yet one's ecological niche is not one's fate, and Africa has been full of mighty empires, elaborate political structures and unimaginably wealthy kings. Even the most remote locations have been connected to international trading networks.

Two separate waves of expansions have served to unite the African continent — the Arab invasion and the Bantu migration. The Arab invasion connected North Africa to the caliphates in the Middle East and thereby to prosperous centers of civilization. Moreover, Islam united people behind one God and one set of religious practices. Likewise, the Bantu migration spread kindred languages throughout the continent together with cultural practices and technical know-how. Yet it was trade which more than anything brought the continent together. The trade in gold, salt and slaves was particularly brisk and it was the profits derived from these key commodities that convinced Berber merchants to cross the Sahara, and that took Arab *dhows* down the Swahili coast. This is also what eventually brought European explorers and merchants to Africa. It was by taxing this trade that city-states grew rich and expanded into kingdoms and empires. It was also trade which more than anything allowed people to escape their ecological niches. Trade made cities spring up in the desert and gave the people of the jungles the resources they needed to cut down even the tallest of trees.

But relations were not always peaceful. The groups of people living in the rainforest often conducted raids on each other, and the states on the savanna relied on powerful armies which could subjugate and enslave their enemies. Yet wars in Africa were different from many wars fought elsewhere. Since land was an abundant resource, it was not worth fighting over; and while a salt or a gold mine would constitute a precious catch, there was little point in territorial expansion as such. The only proper exceptions to this rule are the Yoruba city-states in the Niger Delta which were very concerned indeed about territorial boundaries. For the most part, however, political leaders were content to raze the capital of the enemies they had defeated, humiliate them and include them as a subordinate partner in an alliance. That is, diplomacy would soon come to replace overt acts of warfare. By means of diplomacy the subordinate state would become a tribute bearer who brought gifts to the suzerain state. This is how the empires of Africa were created.

Often these political relations were expressed in the language of kinship. The powerful state was the "father," while the subordinate states were "children" or other, more distant, relatives. By tracing their genealogy back to a common ancestor, the unity of the alliance was strengthened. This was also how the empires expanded. If a group of people established a community at a new location, they would link their ancestry back to the original state. Thus, even while the original state was broken up, the result was an expanding alliance of related states. Alternatively, states which shared no political genealogy might make one up in order to cement their common bonds. Similar ties helped protect the trading routes. In Central Africa long-distance traders often declared each other "brothers" and insisted on the right of safe passage and on political protection. States that traded with each other could be declared friends and relatives too and thereby exempt from acts of warfare.

But this does not amount to one, all-encompassing African international system. The continent is too vast and relations between its assorted regions not nearly strong enough to be described as integrated. Although trade connected west and east with north and south, no political relations were equally extensive. Besides, the trade routes did not only link various African locations with each other, but Africa with the rest of the world. Northern Africa had close links to the Middle East and Europe; Eastern and Southern Africa traded across the Indian Ocean; and West Africa, from the sixteenth century onward, was a partner in the trade across the Atlantic Ocean.

Further reading

Davidson, Basil. *West Africa Before the Colonial Era: A History to 1850*. London: Routledge, 1998.

Diop, Cheikh Anta. *The African Origin of Civilization: Myth or Reality*. Chicago: Chicago Review Press, 1989.

Kane, Ousmane Oumar. *Beyond Timbuktu: An Intellectual History of Muslim West Africa*. Cambridge: Harvard University Press, 2016.

Kusimba, Chapurukha M. *The Rise and Fall of Swahili States*. Walnut Creek: AltaMira Press, 1999.

McCaskie, T. C. *State and Society in Pre-Colonial Asante*. Cambridge: Cambridge University Press, 1995.

Mudimbe, V. Y. *The Idea of Africa*. Bloomington: Indiana University Press, 1994.

Oliver, Roland and Anthony Atmore. *Medieval Africa, 1250–1800*. Cambridge: Cambridge University Press, 2001.

Pella, John A. *Africa and the Expansion of International Society: Surrendering the Savannah*. London: Routledge, 2016.

Pikirayi, Innocent. *The Zimbabwe Culture: Origins and Decline in Southern Zambezian States*. Walnut Creek: AltaMira Press, 2001.

Smith, Robert S. *Warfare and Diplomacy in Pre-Colonial West Africa*. Madison: University of Wisconsin Press, 1989.

Timeline

3500 BCE	The Kingdom of Nubia is established.
3000 BCE	Pharaonic Egypt is established in the Nile River Valley.
1000 BCE	Beginnings of the Bantu migration.
325	The king of the Axsumite kingdom converts to Christianity.
859	Al Quaraouiyine, a university, is founded in Fez by Fatima al-Fihri.
960	The Kilwa Sultanate is founded by settlers from Shiraz, Persia.
1054	The Almoravids capture Sijilmasa.
1086	The Almoravids are invited into Spain by the *taifa* kings.
1172	The Almohads conquer al-Andalus.
1220–1450	The Kingdom of Zimbabwe.
1235	The emperor of Mali, Sundiata Keita, calls a meeting that establishes a constitution for the empire.
1324	Mansa Musa, the richest man in the world, goes on a *hajj* to Mecca.
1440	Ewuare the Great comes to power in Benin and greatly expands the empire.
1591	Moroccan troops invade the Songhai Empire.
1675	Osei Tutu unites the Asante Confederacy, with Kumasi as its capital.

Short dictionary

dhow, Arabic	Generic name for sailing vessels, especially those used in the Red Sea and Indian Ocean.
hajj, Arabic	Pilgrimage to Mecca. A religious duty for all Muslims.
iya, Edo language	"Wall." Used for the earthwork constructions making up the walls of Benin.
lingua franca, Latin	Literally, "the Frankish tongue." A third language, such as Swahili, used for communication between people who do not share a native language.
madrasa, Arabic	"Educational institution," traditionally school teaching the Quran, theology and Islamic law.
medina, Arabic	A walled part of a city in the Arab world, with markets and many narrow streets.
mino, Fon language	Literally "our mothers." The all female body-guard of the king of Dahomey who also served as soldiers in the army.
oba, Edo language	"Ruler." Title of the rulers of the Yoruba city-states in the Niger delta of today's Nigeria.
taifa, Arabic	The small, Muslim, kingdoms that were formed all over southern Spain after the fall of the Caliphate of Córdoba in 1031.

Think about

The Nile River Valley
- Which ancient states can be found along the Nile River Valley?
- What explains the power of the Aksumite kingdom?
- Why was Ethiopia one of the first countries to convert to Christianity?

North Africa
- Who are the Berbers?
- Contrast and compare the Almoravids and the Almohads.
- Who are the Tuaregs?

The kingdoms of West Africa
- What explains the wealth of the Mali kingdom?
- Explain the importance of the Niger river.
- Give an account of the political relations of the Yoruba city-states.

East Africa and the Indian Ocean
- What was the Bantu migration?
- Describe the societies that developed on Africa's eastern coast.
- What made Great Zimbabwe great?

An African international system?
- What unites Africa? What separates it?
- What role has territory played in relations between African states?
- What role did slavery play in traditional African society?

Map of the Americas from Abraham Ortelius, *Theatrum orbis terrarum* (Antverpiae: Apud Aegid. Coppenium Diesth, 1570), p. 26, https://archive.org/details/theatrumorbister00orte

7. The Americas

Taken together the Americas, North and South, cover an enormous geographical area which runs from one polar region to the other, comprising all kinds of climates and ecological environments, including rainforests, deserts, prairies and some of the highest mountains in the world. Human beings began settling here some 20,000 years ago. Scholars are convinced that the first Americans wandered across the land bridge which at the time connected Asia and North America — across today's Bering Strait, between Siberia and Alaska — but there is an abundance of other, far more fanciful theories. From this time onward, although they had some contact with each other, the peoples of the Americas had no connection with the rest of the world. As a result, their societies developed entirely according to their own logic.

The social and political diversity of the two continents is at least as great. Many very different political entities have been located here, and at least three major empires — the Maya and the Aztecs in Central America and the Incas in South America. In North America, meanwhile, societies were smaller and more dispersed. There was no proper empire here until the nineteenth century of the Common Era. Despite the enormous distances involved, trade connected these various communities — people in North America, for example, sold turquoise to the Aztecs. Neighbors fought each other in bloody wars, made peace and forged alliances. Yet all of the Americas were not connected into one international system, and as a result, it makes the most sense to discuss the Maya, the Aztecs, and the Incas separately.

It is at the same time true that societies in the Americas resemble each other in distinct ways. For one thing, compared with the rest of the world they were all quite limited in terms of the technologies at their disposal. For example, although elaborate works of art were produced in both gold and silver, there were no iron ores and hence neither tools nor weapons made from iron could be made. Furthermore no cereals like wheat or rice existed, corn and maize being the main crops in the region. Moreover, in the Americas there were no horses or cows and no domesticated sheep or goats. While the Incas used llamas for carrying things, these animals were never ridden. And no one in the Americas invented the wheel. Or rather, there were wheels on children's toys in Mexico, but not on carts. But then again wagons would have been quite useless in

© 2019 Erik Ringmar, CC BY 4.0 https://doi.org/10.11647/OBP.0074.07

the dense jungles of the Mayan Empire or in the vertical terrain of the Andes. Yet, the empires of the Americas were sophisticated in other ways. The Maya had their own system of writing — an elaborate and playful set of hieroglyphics — and a system of mathematics which included use of the number zero. And all three empires engaged in massive building works — irrigation systems, road networks and enormous public buildings in stone, of which the flat-top pyramids are the most famous.

There were many political similarities too. For one thing, the empires of the Americas had societies that were as hierarchical as their pyramids. At the top of society there was an aristocracy, a priestly class and a king who was associated with the sun and treated as a deity. Ordinary people had few rights and many obligations but they were at the same time subjects of the benevolent care of the state. This was most obvious among the Incas where there were no economic markets and no money, and where the government instead provided all the goods, including foodstuffs, which people could not produce themselves.

Moreover, each empire was held together by a strong sense of shared political values which were fostered by performances staged in public places such as squares and on the top of pyramids. The most notorious examples of such performances were the public rituals which included sacrifices of human beings. The aim of the rituals was religious — to convince the sun to rise in the sky, to keep away sickness, and to ensure another year of plentiful harvests. However the aim was also political: human sacrifices were a means of instilling terror both in the emperor's enemies and in his own subjects. Human sacrifices were public displays of power.

Many of the people sacrificed were prisoners of war. War in the Americas was not a matter of killing adversaries as much as of impressing them with one's might. In general, most military battles were ceremonial occasions, governed by a chivalric code in which elaborately dressed warriors engaged each other in combat. Yet it was always far better if one's enemies could be subdued without a fight, and often they were. Although the Incas in particular would send diplomatic missions, carrying lavish gifts, to other states asking for an alliance, more rational arguments were also used. The Incas would calmly explain to their neighbors why their way of life was superior and why it was a great privilege to become one of their subjects. Engaging in similar carrot and stick practices, first the Maya and then the Aztecs created large federations which included a multitude of various ethnic groups.

The Maya

People speaking Mayan languages first appeared in the first millennium BCE, but it was between 250 and 900 CE that the Mayan civilization came to dominate Central America, including what today is Mexico's Yucatán Peninsula, Guatemala, Honduras and Belize. There had been other powerful societies in this part of the world before: the Olmecs, for example, who today are most famous for the colossal stone heads they carved of their rulers.

Big heads of the Olmecs

The Olmecs was the first major kingdom to emerge in Mexico, around 1800 BCE. The center of their society was the basin of the Coatzacoalcos River in the tropical lowlands of southern Mexico. That is, it was a state similar to, and appearing at the same time as, the far more famous states of Mesopotamia, the Nile, and the Indus. The Olmecs lived in cities, built pyramids, carried out human sacrifices and engaged in ritual bloodletting. Read more: *Royal bloodletting rituals* at p. 154. They also invented a system of writing, created a calendar with 365 days in a year and recorded their histories in books made of fig tree bark. They were the first to play games with large balls made of rubber. The many achievements of the Olmecs were built on by all Central American societies that came after them, including the Maya and the Aztecs.

What they also created, and what they are known for today, is their artwork. Using jade, clay, basalt, and greenstone, they made figurines of remarkable expressiveness and individuality. Often they show babies with chubby bodies, jowly faces, down-turned mouths, and puffy eyes. The babies have holes in their earlobes and probably wore earrings. They may also have worn clothes. Why babies were depicted, and which role the figurines played in Olmec society, we do not know.

The most famous Olmec artworks are the colossal heads they created in stone. Many of these statues are more than 2 meters tall, and the tallest is 3.4 meters, weighing an estimated 50 tons. Perhaps they were kings, but judging by the helmet-like headgear they are wearing, they may also have been famous ballplayers. Read more: *Pitz, the first team sport* at p. 155. The stone used for the statues was transported from far away. How this was done, in a society that had no beasts of burden and no carts with wheels, is difficult to explain. There are seventeen of these gigantic heads in existence today, all in Mexico, while the Olmec figurines can be found in museums around the world. Some have decided that the colossal heads have African features, and argued that this proves that the Olmecs were settlers from Africa. No serious scholar of ancient Mexico holds that view.

Read more online: **https://hdl.handle.net/20.500.12434/09244c27**

Mayan civilization inherited features from their predecessors. The Olmecs had a written language, which the Maya adopted and perfected; the Olmec kings practiced various gruesome rituals, a tradition which the Maya made even more horrendous. The Maya built large cities, yet since they were constructed in dense rainforest, they had none of the urban feel we associate with cities elsewhere in the world. More than anything the Maya cities resembled sprawling gardens in which large public buildings were located, including the large flat-top pyramids, administrative buildings and plazas. People lived here too of course, and they kept animals and cultivated the earth. The overall layout and enormous size of these garden cities have only recently been properly understood thanks to aerial laser photography. Read more: *Angkor Wat* at p. 61.

Mayan society was made up of distinct social classes. The state was ruled by a king and by a royal house that acted as mediators between ordinary human beings and the supernatural realm. It was the job of the king to keep society orderly and to convince the Gods to grant plentiful harvests and success in wars. The king ruled the political, administrative and judicial systems but was also expected to lead the army in battles. In addition, the king mobilized both the aristocracy and ordinary subjects in carrying out huge infrastructure projects, such as the building of the pyramids. The aristocracy comprised perhaps 15 percent of the population and it included both artisans and craftsmen. The position of the Mayan rulers rested heavily on the public displays of power in which they engaged. One highly theatrical occasion was the enthronement of a new king, but the kings would also dance beforehand together with their subjects. The most spectacular of all were the bloodletting ceremonies to which members of the royal family subjected themselves. Kings and queens were pierced and cut and the pain that they suffered was supposed to put them in contact with transcendental realms. The ability to achieve such transcendence was a sign of their power.

Royal bloodletting rituals

The empires of the Americas are notorious for practicing human sacrifice, but what is less well known is that the rulers also practiced a form of sacrifice on themselves. They cut themselves using sharp objects such as obsidian, stingray spines or shark's teeth. Any soft part of the body could be cut, but it was usually the tongue or the genitals. The scattered blood was then collected on paper made from bark and burned. The smoke conveyed messages to the gods.

Blood, to the Maya, was the very force of life and at the beginning of time the gods had sacrificed their own blood in order for the world to come into existence. Ever since humans have owed blood to the gods and the sacrifices were a way to repay this debt. Interestingly, the best blood was that of noblemen and, for that reason, enemy noblemen were a prized catch in wars. The Maya would maintain "farms" of foreign noblemen who could be sacrificed on ceremonial occasions.

Leaders who claimed political authority for themselves would have to go through these ceremonies. This included the kings and members of the royal family. A particularly gruesome scene from a Mayan relief shows a queen with her tongue pierced. A thread with thorns was then pulled through a hole in the tongue. The agony which the queen experienced must have been perfectly mind-altering. And that, indeed, seems to have been the point. The pain that the royals suffered put them in contact with transcendental realms, and made clear to everyone else that they possessed unique spiritual powers. To make the point as effectively as possible, self-harm was performed in front of large gatherings of people — in a plaza or on the top of a pyramid. That the leaders of a country had to sacrifice themselves in these tangible ways surely meant that they were far more careful in embarking on risky ventures. If today's political leaders were required to mutilate their genitals in public before going to war, wars would be less common.

Read more online: https://hdl.handle.net/20.500.12434/f9c26946

Somewhat less gruesome were the ball games in which the Maya engaged. These are the first team sports known in human history. Here too, however, human sacrifices would occasionally take place.

Pitz, the first team sport

The first team sport was a ball game played by the Olmecs in the first millennium BCE. It was later adopted by other Mexican societies, and it was particularly popular among the Maya. It was known as *pitz* among the Maya and as *ōllamaliztli* among the Aztecs. Although the exact rules are unclear, the game was played by two teams with two to four players each. The object was to keep a large rubber ball in motion by means of the hips. The games were played in large ball courts with enthusiastic crowds betting on the outcome and cheering on their favorite teams. Successful ballplayers were celebrities in Mayan society, adored by women and favored by the gods. Occasionally ball games would serve as a substitute for war. Instead of fighting it out on a battlefield, two kings would confront each other in a ball court. It was also a way for noblemen to resolve conflicts.

The game had religious connotations too and features in the creation myths of the Maya. According to a legend which often was depicted on the walls of the ball courts themselves, two twins, Hun Hunaphu and Xbalanque, made so much noise playing ball that the gods of the underworld became annoyed and challenged them to a match. The game ended with one of the brothers being decapitated and his head used as a ball. From his decapitated trunk blood squirted out which fertilized the earth. Ordinary ball games made references to this myth, but in addition, commemorative games were occasionally held in which bloodlettings took place and human beings were sacrificed. Read more: *Royal bloodletting rituals* at p. 154. Yet ordinary games could be quite brutal too. The large rubber ball would bounce around in an unpredictable fashion and could hit the players to devastating effect. To protect themselves they used belts and helmets.

There are still many ball courts left in Central America. In the Chiapas region of Mexico alone there are some 300, and there is a ball court as far north as the U.S. state of Arizona. In fact, the game is still played in parts of Mexico. Today the rules are similar to those of volleyball, but played without a net.

Read more online: https://hdl.handle.net/20.500.12434/4e69605c

Everyone else in Mayan society was a farmer, yet farming in Central America did not look like farming elsewhere in the world. For one thing, there were no large grazing animals — no cows, goats or sheep. For that reason there was no need to clear the jungle in order to provide grassland. In addition, there were no cereals — no wheat, barley or rice — which required extensive fields for their cultivation. Instead the Maya kept smaller animals, like guinea-pigs, and they cultivated corn. Indeed corn was not only the main staple of their diet, but also their god — the Corn God was a central figure in their religious pantheon. Corn was even regarded as the very stuff of which both human beings and the gods were made. In addition, the Maya grew beans, squash and chili peppers which helped to give flavor to the rather bland corn diet.

Chocolate and chilies

Chocolate and chilies are both species native to Central America, meaning that before 1492 they were completely unknown in the rest of the world. Read more: *The Columbian exchange* below. Chocolate is made from the roasted and ground seeds of the cocoa tree, yet the beans themselves have a bitter taste and must be fermented in order to develop the right chocolatey flavor. Already the Olmecs consumed chocolate, and it was popular with both the Maya and the Aztecs. Read more: *Big heads of the Olmecs* at p. 153. Among the Aztecs, chocolate was a ritual beverage and cocoa beans were used as a means of payment. Today, two-thirds of the world's cocoa comes from West Africa, with Ivory Coast as the largest producer.

Chilies originated in Mexico but spread throughout the Americas, and after 1492 quickly throughout the world. Columbus called them "peppers" since the flavor was similar to that of black pepper. They are commonly divided into bell peppers, sweet peppers, and hot peppers. Chilies were introduced to India by the Portuguese in the 1500s. Today they are an indispensable ingredient in Indian cuisine. *Prik* is essential to all Thai cooking, just as no Indonesian food is possible without *sambal*, a mixture which includes chilies, shrimp paste, fish sauce, garlic, ginger, spring onion, and lime juice. *Berbere* and *mitmita* are similar chili-based spice mixes popular in Ethiopia whereas Tunisians use *harissa*. In Hungary, *paprika* is the national vegetable.

Capsaicin, the compound responsible for the fiery flavor, has medical properties and it releases endorphins in the brain. Since it can be used to relieve pain, capsaicin is a banned substance in equestrian sports. Moreover, chili spray is an effective means of crowd control since it produces pain when in contact with skin, eyes and mucous membranes. Today China is the largest producer of fresh chilies, responsible for half of the world's output.

Read more online: https://hdl.handle.net/20.500.12434/b10e249f

To wash it all down they drank chocolate, the cocoa bean being native to Central America.

The Columbian exchange

"The Columbian exchange" is the name given to the transfer of plants, animals, peoples, and microbes which took place between the Americas and the rest of the world after the year 1492. The Columbian exchange had a profound impact on nutrition, population growth, food culture and the prevalence of diseases. For example, today chilies are essential to the food of India and Southeast Asia, yet prior to 1492, they were unknown in these parts of the world. Before Columbus, Indian curries were made with black pepper, not chilies. Read more: *Chocolate and chilies* above. It is equally difficult to imagine that Italian food was made without tomatoes, that there was no coffee in Brazil, no bananas in Central America and no sugarcane in Cuba, or that the native peoples of North America had no horses.

Species that did not exist outside of the Americas before 1492 include: corn, potatoes, tomatoes, tobacco, cassava, sweet potatoes, turkey, peanut, manioc, chocolate, vanilla, pineapple, avocado, cashew, squash, rubber, and strawberry. Species that did not exist in the Americas include coffee, wheat, and barley, sugarcane, banana, rice, horse, donkey, mule, pig, cow, sheep, goat, chicken, large dogs, cats, and honeybees. The potato had a particularly important impact on the level of nutrition in Europe, yet it was slow to be adopted. Often the production had to be officially promoted. In Sweden, the potato only caught on once it was discovered that it could be used to make *invincibly* or vodka. The nutritional content of the potato was one reason for Europe's rapid population growth between the years 1700 and 1900.

Diseases were also exchanged, and with devastating effect. Some 80 percent of the native population of the Americas died as a result of measles and smallpox epidemics caused by interaction with Europeans who carried these diseases. In some places, like the island of Hispaniola where Columbus first landed, all of the natives died. In return the Europeans got syphilis. The first known European case of the venereal disease dates from 1493. The first great outbreak of syphilis occurred in Italy the following year.

Read more online: **https://hdl.handle.net/20.500.12434/9efb82cf**

All in all, theirs was an abundant environment; their world was rich and the gods were good at providing for their people, at least in a normal year. There is evidence that ordinary people ate meat on a regular basis — an unthinkable diet in farming societies in much of the rest of the world.

In addition, the Maya were business people who engaged in long-distance trade across Central America and beyond. Kings and the aristocracy imported objects made from gold from today's Colombia and Panama, and turquoise and obsidian — a volcanic rock which resembles glass — from New Mexico. In addition, there was a flourishing trade in everyday items across Mayan territory, such as salt from Yucatán. The cities that became prominent, and were most successful in wars, were the ones that controlled access to the trading routes by means of which these goods were exchanged.

The Maya had a written script that combined pictographs and alphabetic letters. It was long believed that these pictures merely held artistic significance, but in the 1950s scholars realized that they constituted texts which could be read.

Cracking the Mayan code

The consensus among scholars used to be that the Maya had no script. The images that decorate their artifacts are wonderfully creative but they are works of art, not ways to communicate information. However, in the 1940s, a linguist called Yuri Knorozov began to question this conclusion. The only problem was that he lived in the Soviet Union, had little access to books and no chance to travel to Mexico. During the Second World War, Knorozov was among the soldiers in the Soviet Army that captured Berlin. Here, as luck would have it, he managed to get his hands on copies of Mayan manuscripts as well as a book, *Relación de las cosas de Yucatán*, written by a Spanish conquistador, Diego de Landa, in 1566. There are twenty-seven letters in the Mayan alphabet, de Landa had insisted. Although it was easy to prove that de Landa was wrong, Knorozov was now able to pursue his research. He published an article on the subject in 1952. The writing system of the Maya, he explained, is not an alphabet; it has characters for sounds but also for entire words.

However, as Knorozov's article was published in Russian in the Soviet Union, it took a long time for scholars elsewhere to find out about it, and even once they did, Knorozov's argument was summarily dismissed. It was only in 1973, at a conference in the old Mayan city of Palenque, that the consensus shifted. "That evening," a scholar who was present recalled, "we were able to decipher the names of seven Maya rulers." The writing system of the Maya, it turns out, has around 800 characters and today we can read some 75 percent of their texts. The Maya wrote about history, astronomy, and mathematics, but also the histories of their rulers and their reigns. Unfortunately, many Mayan texts were destroyed by the Spanish. Since the books only contained "lies of the devil," Diego de Landa recalled, "we burned them all." The Mayan people, he added, "regretted this to an amazing degree."

Read more online: https://hdl.handle.net/20.500.12434/db3a5cbd

A few Mayan texts, known as codices, have been preserved. They tell stories of kings, their reigns, honorific names and their greatest achievements.

Books from ancient Mexico

A *codex*, in the context of the history of the Americas, refers to a book put together before or right at the time of the European conquest. Both Maya and Aztecs had a tradition of making such books. They describe their customs and rituals, the history of the respective empires, but also the encounters between them and the Europeans. Today there are at least 500 codices in existence in libraries around the world. They are our best source of information about life in pre-Columbian Mexico.

The most important example is the *Dresden Codex*, a work consisting of seventy-eight pages, dating from the thirteenth or the fourteenth century. It was lost for many years, but eventually rediscovered in a library in Germany, hence its name. The *Dresden Codex* was of great importance for scholars trying to decipher the Mayan script. *Read more: Cracking the Mayan code* at p. 157. It contains astronomical information as well as the schedules for rituals such as the celebration of the Mayan new year. The book suffered serious water damage during the Allied bombings of the Second World War.

The *Florentine Codex* is the most important of the Aztec codices. It was compiled by a Spanish priest, Bernardino de Sahagún, with the help of his native students.

The work runs to 2,400 pages and has more than 2,000 images, organized into twelve books. It describes the culture of the Aztecs, their cosmology and rituals, but also social and economic conditions and the history of the Aztec people. Sahagún's aim was to facilitate the conversion of the Aztecs to Christianity. We need information about the Aztecs, he argued, just as a doctor needs information about the illnesses of patients in order to cure them. The *Florentine Codex* was written in Nahuatl, the language of the Aztecs, but has been translated into Spanish and English. It is today available online.

The Incas did not compile similar books, but an important primary source for their society and culture is the work of Inca Garcilaso de la Vega, 1539–1616. He was the son of a Spanish conquistador and an Inca noblewoman. His account was written when Garcilaso de la Vega had retired to Spain, but it provides a history of the Incas from a native point of view.

Read more online: https://hdl.handle.net/20.500.12434/b02ba153

In addition, the Maya were skilled mathematicians and astronomers. Their number line included a zero which allowed for sophisticated calculations to be performed. They also constructed an elaborate calendar by which they organized time. Read more: *Indian mathematics* at p. 48.

The Maya never created a centralized state, but what we have come to call their "empire" consisted instead of a rather loose federation of related cities, including Palenque, Calakmul, Caracol, Mayapan and Tikal. Relations between these assorted centers were always unstable and alliances shifted; a city-state that traditionally had been the subject of another city-state could suddenly find itself on top. The kings formed alliances, exchanged daughters in marriage, gave each other tributary gifts, and engaged in plenty of ritual feasting. In addition, they made war on each other as well as on outsiders. Yet the point of a battle was typically not to kill enemies but instead to capture them and to take them back to one's capital where they could be ritually slaughtered on top of a pyramid. Reliefs show pictures of kings who were defeated, captured, tortured and sacrificed.

Incidents of warfare increased in the tenth century. This was also when several of the large Mayan cities began to decline. Some scholars, and documentaries on YouTube, discuss the "mystery of the disappearance of the Mayan civilization." Yet the Maya did not disappear. There are to this day some 10 million people who speak the Mayan language and they are fiercely proud of their heritage. Indeed, today's Maya has been crucial in providing information which has allowed scholars to decipher their inscriptions. Several of these scholars are themselves of Mayan descent. In 1994, an armed rebellion against the Mexican government was started by the so-called Zapatista movement in the southern Mexican province of Chiapas. The Zapatistas want autonomy and better living conditions, and rely on an ideology that combines libertarian socialism with traditional Mayan beliefs. Today the military uprising is over, but the Maya continue their struggle by means of public campaigns and civil disobedience. The Maya have not gone away.

The Aztecs

In the center of Mexico — in the region where we today find Ciudad de México — is the Valley of Mexico, a fertile highland plateau located some 2,000 meters above sea level. People have lived here for some 12,000 years, and it has always been one of the most densely populated regions in the world. Today the urban sprawl which is the Mexico City Metropolitan Area has an estimated 21.3 million inhabitants. Two thousand years ago, it was the city of Teotihuacán which dominated the valley. With its estimated 150,000 people it was the largest city in the Americas at the time. Indeed, it was so crowded that some of the inhabitants had to live in multistory apartment buildings. Teotihuacán was a cosmopolitan city, but it was not the center of an empire. It was looted and destroyed in 550 CE. Today Teotihuacán is the most visited archaeological site in Mexico, famous for the large pyramids located along the so-called "Avenue of the Dead." The Pyramid of the Sun was both the political and the religious center of the city.

Once Teotihuacán had lost its position, power shifted to Tula, the capital of the Toltec Empire, 674–1122, a bit further to the northwest. In Tula too we find impressive pyramids. Ceramics from Tula have been found all over Central America, and its cultural influences spread at least as wide. This was when the cult of the Feathered Serpent, a god associated with the city of Tula, became a common object of worship. Subsequent kingdoms that rose to prominence in the Valley of Mexico, including the Aztecs, would always bolster their claim to power by tracing their heritage to the Toltecs. The Feathered Serpent, known to the Aztecs as Quetzalcoatl, symbolized this lineage.

The power of Tula also lasted for about 500 years, but instead of being replaced by another large empire, it was replaced by a system of smaller states. After the year 1000, a number of city-states, known as *altepetl*, sprung up in the Valley of Mexico. In the sixteenth century, there were as many as fifty of them. Each city-state was led by a king, known as a *tlatoani*, who controlled all land and acted as the political, military and religious leader. The *tlatoani* spoke in the name of the people — he was the source of law and wisdom — and the one who interpreted and carried out the will of the gods. In return, he had the right to collect taxes. Each city-state was rigidly hierarchical. Under the king, there was a class of noblemen, and under them a class of warriors whose rank varied depending on their achievements on the battlefield. The political system was reflected in the layout of each city. The royal palace was at the center, together with the main temple pyramid and the main market square. Around this center lived the nobility while the commoners lived in the outskirts. The noblemen too were regarded as chosen by the gods, and this gave them wide-ranging powers. Yet, the Mexican city-states were not dictatorships. The power of the *tlatoani* was balanced by the power of a royal council, and by judges who acted to protect the rights of ordinary people.

Relations between the Mexican city-states ranged from friendly to openly hostile. Many joined together in alliances and some attached themselves as tribute bearers to more powerful neighbors. No state dominated all the others, and none of them was sufficient unto itself. Wars were common, but they tended to be small-scale affairs and rarely upset the balance of power. It was only by trading with each other that the city-states could survive. Socially and culturally too they were closely interconnected. Shoppers would visit a neighboring city looking for bargains and members of the nobility of different states participated in each other's ceremonies, festivals, and funerals. The families of the various *tlatoani* were often related to each other by marriage. Indeed marriages were an important means of establishing political alliances and maintaining peace. A lower-ranking *tlatoani* would always try to marry off his daughter to a *tlatoani* of a more powerful state.

It was into this city-state system that the Mexica arrived in the thirteenth century. Read more: *Independence for Aztlán* below.

The Mexica were Nahuatl-speaking people who had started moving south from their legendary homeland of Aztlán, located somewhere in northern Mexico, some two hundred years previously.

Independence for Aztlán

Aztlán is, according to the legend of Nahuatl-speaking peoples, the land from which they began the migration which eventually took them to the Valley of Mexico, some time in the eleventh century. There were seven different tribes that migrated, of which the Mexica were one. It is clear that Aztlán was located somewhere to the north, but exactly where is less certain. Guesses point to northwestern Mexico or to somewhere in the southwestern parts of the United States.

References to Aztlán have been important among members of the Chicano movement in the United States. "Chicano" is the name given to Mexicans who have emigrated to the U.S., originally as seasonal labor in the agricultural industry. In response to mistreatment by employers and U.S. authorities they began organizing themselves politically in the 1960s. According to some Chicano activists, today's Americans are aggressors who have invaded the land which originally belonged to them, and to which they have a right of return.

Prior to 1848, all of the southwestern United States was a part of Mexico. In 1835, Texas declared itself an independent republic, something which the Mexican government refused to accept. When Texas was annexed by the United States in 1845, Mexico declared war. Yet the Mexican government was weak, its troops badly equipped and trained, and they were easily defeated. As a result, Mexico lost about half of its territory — corresponding to the present-day states of California, Nevada, and Utah, most of New Mexico, Arizona and Colorado, and parts of Texas, Oklahoma, Kansas, and Wyoming.

There are activists who hope for a new, independent Aztlán. According to one version of the project, Mexicans on both sides of the border should create one country, sometimes referred to as "la República del Norte." Others have talked about the need for a "reconquista" of the parts of the United States which were parts of Mexico until the Mexican-American War. The Chicano movement lost much of its political momentum in the 1970s, but the problems they reacted to have not gone away. Their most lasting legacy might be the departments of "Chicano studies" that have been established at various American universities. If a wall is built between the United States and Mexico, it would be regarded as a provocation by Aztlán activists.

Read more online: https://hdl.handle.net/20.500.12434/229ddbf5

Stopping in various places along the way but never settling for more than a couple of decades in each place, they eventually arrived in the Valley of Mexico. As outsiders without a city-state of their own, the Mexica began by hiring themselves out as soldiers and tried to gain a foothold in the system by making alliances with established rulers. The first such alliance was with the city of Culhuacán whose *tlatoani* allowed them to settle on his territory. When the arrangement with the Culhuacán king broke down in the 1320s, the Mexica were once again looking for a home. Next they allied themselves with the Tepanec state. The Tepanecs too were Nahuatl-speaking migrants who originated in the north. Again they began by working as soldiers and in return they were given the right to build a city, Tenochtitlan, established in 1325. The location, on an island in the middle of the swampy Texcoco lake, was hardly prime real estate, but it provided excellent protection from attackers and the shores of the lake provided good agricultural land. In 1372, the Mexica appointed the first *tlatoani* of their own.

In 1426 the Tepanec king died and shortly afterwards the king of the Mexica was murdered. This provided an opportunity for new political alignments. A new group of people came to power in Tenochtitlan who broke off the alliance with Tepanec and instead allied themselves with the city-states of Texcoco and Tlacopan. Together these three states formed a triple alliance, which was to become known as the Aztec Empire, 1428–1521. The alliance covered political, military and economic matters. The three states agreed not to fight each other but instead to cooperate in wars of conquest against other city-states. All spoils of war were to be divided equally between them, as would be all the taxes they collected from the cities they conquered.

Yet warfare was not always the best way to subdue enemies. Often threats of force were enough, or perhaps lavish gifts were given, or offers of friendship or membership of a military alliance made. As a result, the practices of diplomacy and of warfare blended into each other. Much as for the Maya, war for the Aztecs was a highly ritualistic affair. Instead of massive peasant armies colliding with each other, which was common elsewhere in the world, warfare was often understood as one-on-one combat between noblemen. Once defeated, the enemy was not killed but instead, and again much as among the Maya, taken back home and ritually sacrificed in a public ceremony.

In the course of the fifteenth century, the Aztecs created a large empire covering the entire Valley of Mexico and much of Central America besides. King Moctezuma I, 1398–1469, who was Mexica, was the person responsible for much of this expansion. During his reign, taxes were levied directly on the subdued city-states and a number of extensive building projects were embarked on, including new pyramids. Trade continued to flourish. In fact, the Aztec Empire could be described as a series of related marketplaces where you could buy everything from precious metals and construction materials to weapons, fruits, vegetables and herbs. There were also markets that specialized in products such as dog meat. Vendors were organized into guilds, and depending on their wares they were allocated to different streets. A new legal code, established under Moctezuma, laid down the rules for how Aztec society was to be organized. The state had a firm grip on society: only great noblemen and successful soldiers were allowed to build two-story houses; commoners could not wear cotton clothing; adulterers were to be stoned and thrown into rivers; thieves would be sold off for the price of their theft, and so on.

The Incas

The Inca Empire, 1438–1533, was almost the exact contemporary of the Aztecs but it was located in the Andes of South America. In the Andes the highest mountain peaks approach 7,000 meters, and much of the area consists of a highland plateau located some 4,000 meters above sea level. This is an inhospitable environment to say the least, in particular since the high mountains block most rain clouds coming from the Atlantic. As a result, the western slopes of the Andes are mainly desert. Some weather stations in the Atacama desert, in today's Chile, have never recorded any rain at all. Before the establishment of the Inca Empire there were many other kingdoms and empires here.

Kingdoms of Peru

Everybody has heard of the Incas, but next to no one has heard of the many diverse societies that preceded them. Yet there were many cultures, kingdoms, and empires in the highlands of the Andes, on the narrow coastal plain of the Pacific Ocean and in the Amazonian jungle. These are a few examples:

- The Nazca culture, 100 BCE–800 CE, flourished in the river valleys of southern Peru. They produced complex textiles and ceramics and are famous for their geoglyphs: line drawings of animals and humans which are best viewed from the sky. Read more: *Huacas, ceque and Nazca lines* at p. 168.

- The Tiwanaku Empire, 300–1150, was located on the shores of Lake Titicaca. Tiwanaku was a city which at the height of its power may have had some 100,000 inhabitants. The Tiwanakus kept llamas, caught fish in Lake Titicaca and used its water to irrigate their fields. They traded widely across their empire which gave them access to a varied diet.

- The Muisca Confederation, 1450–1550, was a loose alliance of rulers in the mountains of today's Colombia. Unusually, they did not build large temples or pyramids, but they developed an elaborate calendar, created artifacts in gold and drank *chicha*, an alcoholic beverage, in large quantities. Their most prominent members were mummified after their deaths, and placed in temples or carried along by advancing armies in order to impress their enemies.
- The Chachapoya society, 750–1500, was located in the Peruvian part of the Amazon. The Chachapoya are famous for their vertical burial sites. They placed their dead in tiny houses worked into the walls at the highest point of a precipice. As a result, they have not been excavated until recently.
- The Chimú, 900–1470, was located in the Moche Valley of today's Peru. Their work in precious metals was very intricate and they created black ceramics. Since they were conquered late by the Incas, there were still people alive who could tell the Spaniards about life as it originally had existed in Chimú society.

The society that the Incas assembled, and transformed into an empire, was a patchwork of peoples such as these. Some of them greeted the arrival of the Europeans as a liberation.

Read more online: https://hdl.handle.net/20.500.12434/4dc6710a

The vertical nature of life in the Andes meant that large states were difficult to establish and instead there was a jumble of small political entities, all with a specific culture which had developed more or less on its own. One exception was the Tiwanaku, who created a large empire in the first millennium of the CE, and then the Incas who did the same thing in the fifteenth century.

Inca means "lord" in Quechua, the Inca language, and it was originally a term that applied only to the ruling elite. The Incas themselves referred to their land as Tawantinsuyu, "the four regions," an alliance of four states, but the name also referred to the cardinal points of the compass. Cuzco, in today's Peru, was the capital of the empire. It was here that the Sapa Inca, the ruler, resided and where the main temples and government buildings were located. From Cuzco the Incas controlled a vast area, some 5,000 kilometers in length, which included most of the Andes but also the narrow strip of lowland along the Pacific coast and parts of the Amazon rainforest. The Inca Empire was the largest empire in the world at the time — larger than the Ottomans and the Ming dynasty in China.

The Sapa Inca was an autocratic ruler who wielded enormous power. He ruled for life and was not only the head of state but also in charge of military and religious affairs. The Incas worshiped Inti, the sun god, and the Sapa Inca was considered as Inti's living representative on earth. Indeed, the Sapa Inca was considered so holy that ordinary people were not allowed to even look at him. Everything he touched was burned in order to prevent witchcraft being performed against him. The rituals carried out at the Temple of the Sun in Cuzco, with the Sapa Inca in attendance, were great religious occasions but also a source of political identity for the empire and its subjects. When a Sapa Inca died, a period of mourning ensued which lasted for up to a year. And yet the Sapa Inca would continue to exercise power even after his death — by means of his mummified corpse which continued to make an appearances on various state occasions.

The government of the Inca Empire was centralized and hierarchically organized. Below the Sapa Inca was his relative, the high priest of the Temple of the Sun, who in addition to his religious duties also served as commander of the army. Below him, in turn, we find the nobility of Cuzco, made up of various distant relatives of the ruler. The leading members of the nobility constituted a council which advised the Sapa Inca, but they were also responsible for choosing his successor. Although each Sapa Inca was to be succeeded by a son, there were often many sons to choose from, and conflicts regarding succession often split the ruling elite and undermined the power of the empire. Below the nobility we find the leading members of ethnic groups who had been present in the region before the Incas rose to power. It was these people who staffed the imperial bureaucracy. They levied taxes, conducted censuses of the population and were in charge of irrigation works, road building, and other infrastructural projects. At the bottom of the social hierarchy we find the peasants who made up some 98 percent of the population. Exactly how many people lived in the empire is less clear. The Incas kept excellent data on the population but the records were kept by means of *quipu*, a rope-based language which so far has not been deciphered.

Reading knots

The Incas, much like the Maya, had a system of writing. At least if we by writing mean "a medium of human communication by means of signs." Yet the Incas did not write their signs down, instead, they used ropes. They called it *quipu*, meaning "knot" in Quechua, the Incan language. A *quipu* consisted of a set of colored strings, perhaps as many as 2,000, usually made of cotton. On each string, there were knots tied at various distances from each other. The color of the string, its length, the number of knots and their distance from each other, all conveyed information. The Incas had *quipu* experts, trained to read these messages.

Economic relations in Incan society were organized by the state. For this reason, a lot of statistical information was needed. State officials needed to know how much food was produced, how much taxes they received, which products the government-run warehouses contained, and data on births and deaths. All this information was conveyed by the *quipu* which could easily be dispatched by a courier from a provincial governor to the bureaucrats in Cusco.

Since the *quipu* was made of cotton, many have perished. Many were also destroyed by the Spanish conquistadors. There are today some thousand *quipus* in existence. In contrast to the hieroglyphs of the Maya, the *quipu* has not been deciphered. Read more: *Cracking the Mayan code* at p. 157. Code-breakers and historians are still working on it. An international database project is responsible for collecting data and coordinating the research. If scholars one day manage to

> read the *quipu*, the chances are we will obtain far better data concerning life in the Incan Empire.
>
> *Read more online:* https://hdl.handle.net/20.500.12434/59673078

Current estimates of the size of the population vary widely — from 4 million to almost ten times as many — but a commonly cited figure is 12 million inhabitants.

The economic basis for the Incas' success lay, more than anything, in their ability to master the climate and geography of the land. They built enormous systems of terraces that provided irrigation, harnessed and reused water, but also helped to stop soil erosion. In addition, the terraces created micro-climates in which a range of different plants could be grown. Here as elsewhere in the Americas, corn was the main staple. It is estimated that more land was under cultivation during the Incas than is the case today. Although the Incas kept animals — llamas and alpacas — which provided both meat and wool, they could also get food from far further away. Communities high up in the Andes would often have contacts with people living along the Pacific Ocean. In the river valleys along the coast it was possible to grow beans, squash, and cotton, and from the sea came fish and shellfish.

Whatever surplus was left over once the peasants had had enough to survive was gathered together by the Inca authorities and stored in enormous warehouses. Many other goods — clothing, ceramics, weapons, tools — were stored there too. In times of need, these items were distributed to the people. There were no public markets and there was no currency. Instead whenever a particular item was required, it had to be requested and was then dispatched by the bureaucracy. In addition, the Inca authorities organized feasts in the public squares throughout the empire in which the common supplies were consumed.

Much of the agricultural labor was organized by community groups known as *ayllu*. The *ayllu* took the household as its basic unit but it expanded through neighbors and family networks to include entire villages. Members of the *ayllu* worked the land together, sharing what the earth produced — from all according to ability, to all according to need. The *ayllu*, in combination with the welfare programs of the Inca state, provided a safety net and an insurance scheme that protected all inhabitants of the empire. Aspects of the *ayllu* system have remained to this day, and it has often been referred to in the political manifestos of various left-wing organizations.

Túpac Amaru

Túpac Amaru, 1545–1572, was the last Sapa Inca. He was the ruler of the Incan state which survived in Vilcabamba, in a remote part of Peru, once Cusco itself had fallen to the Spanish invaders. In 1572, the Spaniards attacked the new capital too, but Túpac Amaru fled into the jungle where, after a month-long pursuit, he was arrested and executed.

In 1780, a peasant uprising started against Spanish rule, led by a certain José Gabriel Condorcanqui who called himself "Túpac Amaru II" and claimed to be a direct descendant of the last Sapa Inca. Túpac Amaru II gathered many indigenous people behind him and organized an army that comprised some 60,000 followers. However, after he failed to take Cusco, he was captured and killed. After his death, Túpac Amaru II became a mythical figure in the struggle for indigenous rights, as well as an inspiration to various left-wing causes in Spanish America and beyond.

In Uruguay, in the 1960s and 70s, an urban guerrilla movement — the "Tupamaros" — committed a number of bank robberies and kidnappings. They also stole food which they distributed to the poor. The military junta which ruled Uruguay at the time began an unofficial war against them and against other left-wing organizations. The Tupamaros collapsed in 1972 when the leading members were assassinated by paramilitaries working for the government. Democracy was re-established in Uruguay in 1984, and in 2010 a former member of the Tupamaros, José Mujica, was elected president of the country.

In Peru, a Marxist guerrilla group, the Túpac Amaru Revolutionary Movement, was founded in the early 1980s. They wanted to turn Peru into a socialist state and to fight imperialism. They too robbed banks and organized kidnappings. In December 1996, fourteen members of the movement occupied the Japanese embassy in Lima and held seventy-two people hostage for more than four months. The hostages were eventually freed and the hostage-takers killed.

The American rapper, Tupac Amaru Shakur, 1971–1996, was named after Túpac Amaru II. His parents were both members of the Black Panther Party, a revolutionary organization in the United States fighting for the rights of black people. Tupac Shakur was killed in a gang-related shooting in Las Vegas.

Read more online: https://hdl.handle.net/20.500.12434/13ed10e2

Although the Incas had lived in Cuzco since the thirteenth century, it was only in the middle of the fifteenth century that their imperial conquests began. The first Sapa Inca, Pachacuti, 1438–1471, began by attacking people living in the Ecuadorian lowlands and in the rainforests of what today is Bolivia and Peru. However, his most famous victory was against the Chimor, the powerful kingdom to the north of Cuzco. Read more: *Túpac Amaru* above.

Despite attempts to reach an amicable settlement, the Chimorese king refused to surrender, a decision he was to regret bitterly. When Pachacuti died, shortly after this victory, he was succeeded by his son, Tupac Inca Yupanqui, 1471–1493, who had already served as commander of the army. During his reign the conquests continued, first against the Kingdom of Quito to the north and then against a number of smaller kingdoms, including several located in the extreme south, in what today is Argentina. Here, however, the Incas met with considerable resistance. It was clear that the empire had found its southernmost limits.

Despite these bloody conflicts, warfare was not in fact the chief means by which the conquests were made. The Incas much preferred their enemies to surrender voluntarily and to this end they, much as the Aztecs, relied on a mixture of kindness and cunning. Combining lavish gifts with assurances of protection, they made offers that their enemies could not refuse, and often a marriage alliance with a daughter from the Sapa Inca's extended family was thrown into the bargain. Other tactics included ostentatious displays of power and spectacular acts of cruelty, which both overwhelmed and terrified their enemies. The Incas used rational arguments too. We, they explained, represent a higher civilization and a better way of organizing social and political life. No one else can guarantee peace and a constant food supply, even during droughts and other calamities.

Once a kingdom had joined the empire, the Incas put one of their governors in charge of the province in question. Auditors made regular visits to ensure that the local administration was running smoothly and in line with Cuzco's demands. At the same time the imperial authorities were concerned with preserving a measure of local autonomy. Provinces were administered by local people and traditional local elites often mixed socially with the new rulers. Although the cult of Inti, the sun god, was enforced throughout the empire, local religions were respected and supported too. Local administrators who had proven themselves to be loyal were rewarded with yearly trips to Cuzco where they exchanged gifts with the Sapa Inca and were wined and dined. In addition, the large building projects in which the imperial authorities engaged were thought of both as a way of improving the living conditions of their new subjects and a means of connecting them more firmly to the authorities in Cuzco. But clearly, these efforts did not always work. There were rebellions in the Ecuadorian lowlands, in the jungles of Bolivia and Peru and in many other places.

The power of the Incas rested more than anything on their ability to build things — roads, dams, terraces, and irrigation canals. For these purposes, they employed conscript labor and the work crews were clothed, fed and housed by the state. The road network may be the most stunning of these achievements. There was a main road that ran the entire length of the empire from the north to the south, and many branch roads too that ran in an east-west direction. The Incas carved out paths along the sides of the most precipitous cliffs, across the highest of mountain passes, and they bridged the deepest gorges. At regular intervals there were relay stations — in total some 2,000 of them — where travelers could stop on their journeys and where the authorities would store food, weapons, and garrison soldiers. Travelers would walk on these trails and an official team of mail carriers would run. Taken together the road network covered some 40,000 kilometers — almost exactly equivalent to the circumference of the earth.

The empire was held together by spiritual means too. In addition to the sun god, the Incas worshiped *huacas*, the Quechua name for unusual rock formations or other peculiar features of the landscape.

Huacas, ceque and Nazca lines

Huaca is the Quechua word for "revered object." In Incan society, it referred to a monument or a feature of nature where energy of some kind had gathered, perhaps a cosmic force or an emanation of the divine. In order to harness that energy and placate the gods, people would conduct ceremonies at the *huacas*, making offerings and saying prayers. Members of a particular family would often have the task of looking after a specific location. *Huacas* existed in pre-Incan societies and they exist to this day all over Peru. Indeed, downtown Lima has been built around them.

Different *huacas* were joined together in pathways known as *ceques*. The *ceques* would run throughout the landscape conducting spiritual energy from one place to another. Together they formed a pattern that radiated from the capital of Cusco to every part of the empire. When children were dispatched to various places of sacrifice, they were located according to the *ceque* system. Read more: *Children of the mountain* below. Together these lines formed a spiritual grid in which all imperial subjects could find their respective places, and through which they all were connected. By conducting the required rituals at a *huaca*, each conquered people could show that they accepted the power of the Inca rulers. In this way, the *ceque* brought a sense of unity to a geographically very dispersed set of subjects.

Nazca lines are enormous geoglyphs, "earth engravings," created by the Nazca people sometime between 500 BCE and 500. Read more: *Kingdoms of Peru* at p. 163. They consist of trenches, 10 to 15 centimeters deep, which create a line-drawing in the landscape. And they are enormous — up to 1 kilometer long. Popular motifs are animals or humanoid forms. Why the Nazca lines were created is unclear. Perhaps they were a part of an irrigation system or perhaps they played some role in an astronomical calendar. Curiously, many of them are best viewed from the sky, leading to speculations that they were a way for the Nazca people to communicate with extraterrestrials. Nazca lines are a favorite subject of late-night documentaries on less reputable TV channels.

Read more online: https://hdl.handle.net/20.500.12434/5dac553a

According to Inca belief, the *huacas* were connected to each other in lines of spiritual energy that radiated out from the center of the empire. The spiritual connections reached even the remotest of places and the Incas built temples and held religious ceremonies even on the highest peaks of the Andes. Many of these religious sites have only recently been discovered and many sites, no doubt, remain unknown to this day.

Children of the mountain

In 1999, a horrible discovery was made by a team of researchers near the summit of Llullaillaco, a 6,700-meter-high volcano on the border between Argentina and Chile. Three small children were found dead in a pit. The researchers knew right away that these were not recent casualties. The children of the mountain were the sacrificial victims of an Incan ceremony conducted some 500 years ago. Subsequent analysis showed that the three — two girls, fifteen and six years old, and a boy of seven — had been fattened up and drugged with alcohol and coca before they died. They had most likely fallen asleep in their tomb and then frozen to death. Their mummified bodies have been extraordinarily well preserved in the cold and very dry environment. The internal organs are intact, individual hairs are preserved, and they look more or less as they must have looked the day they died.

Child sacrifice was an important part of the religion of the Incas. It was a way to commemorate important events, such as the death of a Sapa Inca, or else such sacrifices could be offerings to the gods in times of famine or war. It was considered a great honor to die as a sacrifice, and only the most physically perfect children were selected, often of noble families. First, they were taken to Cusco where they underwent various purification rituals, and from there they were dispatched to mountaintops throughout the empire. The fifteen-year-old girl was most likely a "Sun Virgin," chosen at the age of ten to live with other girls who would become royal wives, priestesses, and sacrifices. According to Incan beliefs, the children who were sacrificed did not actually die but watched over the surrounding landscape from atop their mountaintop perches.

Today a museum has been built for the children. At the Museum of High Altitude Archaeology in Salta, Argentina, they have recreated the exact conditions of the mountain where they were found. Yet some indigenous groups object to what they regard as "their children" being put on display in this fashion. Meanwhile, other groups strongly approve of any research that can help spread knowledge of their ancestors. It is estimated that there are some forty similar burial sites in the region, but for now, at least, no more mummies will be removed from the mountains.

Read more online: https://hdl.handle.net/20.500.12434/0b061074

North America

We rarely think of the North American continent, prior to the arrival of the Europeans, in political terms, and we never think of it as an international system in its own right. In our imagination the people living here — the "Indians" — spent all of their time chasing buffaloes and engaging in various forms of savage warfare. Since their societies lacked fixed territorial boundaries, they had no political or administrative institutions. Indeed, the very notion of history is inapplicable to societies such as these. Yet, as it turns out, none of these descriptions is true. In North America too there were plenty of sedentary societies, agriculturally-based kingdoms and large states which grew rich from trade conducted in far-flung networks that spanned the entirety of the continent. There are still many impressive monuments to be seen which testify to these achievements. The fact that we know little about these societies is our fault, not theirs.

The first societies identified by historians are those which belong to the so-called "Woodland period," which comprises the two millennia from 1000 BCE to about the year 1000 of the Common Era. These societies can be found in a geographical area which stretches from what now is eastern Canada down along the eastern United States to the Gulf of Mexico. The people of the Woodland period were hunters and gatherers and they used spears, bows and blowguns in order to catch deer, moose, turkey, grouse, beavers and raccoons. They did not, however, hunt buffaloes. There were indeed enormous herds of buffaloes grazing further out west, but since there were no horses in the Americas, these large animals were difficult to kill. Read more: *The Columbian exchange* at p. 156.

In addition, the people of the Woodland period collected nuts, acorns, mushrooms and wild berries; some rivers provided a continuous supply of fish and shellfish which made it possible to establish settled communities. In communities that controlled particularly rich fishing grounds, differentiated social classes developed. In addition, the people of the Woodland period worked leather, made tools and used pottery.

After the Woodland period, archaeologists have identified a number of separate cultures, distinguished above all by their artwork and their funeral rites. The Adena culture is the name given to a number of societies in today's Ohio, Indiana and West Virginia. Here archaeologists have found conical mounds that were used as burial sites and perhaps also for various ceremonial purposes. The dead were buried together with various goods, including copper bracelets, beads and cups. The people of the Adena culture produced ritual objects used by shamans who sought to transform themselves into birds, wolves, bears and deer. These societies were gradually replaced by the so-called Hopewell societies, 200–500, located further inland, in today's Ohio and Illinois. The Hopewell societies continued to build conical mounds and they engaged in trade. Historians have talked about the "Hopewell exchange system," which, judging by the many exotic products discovered here, must have connected much of the North American continent. In Hopewell societies, archaeologists have found shells from Florida, obsidian from the Rocky Mountains and mica — a mineral used for making pots — from Tennessee.

Although Hopewell societies began to decline around the year 500 CE, the mound-building tradition continued in the societies that flourished in the Mississippi River valley between 800 and 1600. The people of the Mississippian culture created large urban settlements, of which the city of Cahokia, in today's Illinois, was the largest. The mound built at Cahokia reminds us of the pyramids that were built in Mexico at the same time. On top of the mound, wooden structures were erected which served as temples, burial sites and centers for political administration. Cahokia was a chiefdom with sharp social distinctions. Here political and religious power was in the hands of a small elite. Ordinary people were farmers, growing corn, the staple food, but there were many craftsmen too. Again, trade was important. The Cahokians traded with a number of satellite cities, but also with people as far west as the Rocky Mountains. They worshiped the sun, moon and stars, but above all the Great Serpent — again there may be a connection to Mexico here. Cahokians used to wear amulets in the form of a falcon, perhaps to protect a warrior against the arrows of his enemy or to assure health and many children.

Mound builders of the Mississippi

For the longest time, Europeans refused to believe that the enormous mounds they had discovered in the valley of the Mississippi River were constructed by native people. The sheer size of the monuments was just too impressive. The "Indians," the Europeans had decided, were hunters and gatherers, but the people of the Mississippi valley lived in large cities and grew crops. The construction of the mounds must have required years of dedicated labor, and only a highly organized society could have managed that task. Perhaps it was the Vikings who had built the mounds, or the Chinese, or perhaps the ancient Egyptians?

Europeans should have known better. There were still mound-builders in North America as late as in the eighteenth century. In 1682, French explorers visited the Natchez, a tribe in the valley of the Mississippi River. They were astonished to be greeted by their leader, known as the "Great Sun," who lived in a large house on the top of a platform mound. The Great Sun was treated as a living god by his people and was carried in a litter wherever he went. His mother, known as "White Woman," was his principal adviser and lived in a house on top of another mound. The Natchez were defeated in a war with French settlers in the 1730s. As a result, some were sold into slavery in the Caribbean while others were forced to take refuge with other tribes. Today the Natchez nation has only some 6,000 members. It is led by a chief, still known as "Great Sun," and by four "Clan Mothers." The last fluent speaker of the Natchez language died in 1957.

Read more online: https://hdl.handle.net/20.500.12434/29a90ddf

Further west, in today's New Mexico and Arizona, in the southwestern parts of the United States, we find the so-called "Pueblo cultures." *Pueblo* means "village" in Spanish and the village-like structure of the settlements was the first thing that struck the Europeans when they arrived in the sixteenth century. The houses consisted of apartments made in adobe and stone, with numerous rooms and courtyards built very close together and even on top of each other, sometimes creating apartment-style buildings four or five stories high. The pueblos not only made for a closely connected community, but also provided a defense against robbers and roving bands. The most elaborate pueblo settlement was that of Chaco Canyon in today's New Mexico.

The kivas of Chaco Canyon

A *kiva* is a pit in the ground constructed by the peoples of the Pueblo culture living in today's southwestern parts of the United States. The *kivas* were used for living in, for various social purposes, but above all for religious ceremonies. There are *kivas* of different sizes. Most are only big enough to fit one person but some are enormous. In Chaco Canyon, in today's New Mexico, there is a *kiva* which is as big as any mosque or temple elsewhere in the world. It was the largest building in North America until the nineteenth century.

Chaco Canyon was the center of the Pueblo culture, and hundreds of buildings were constructed here between 900 and 1150, organized into fifteen major complexes. Pueblo Bonito is the most studied. In addition to its great *kiva*, it contained a structure in four stories that had as many as 650 rooms. There were many smaller houses too which all faced a common plaza. In addition, there were many smaller *kivas* — roughly one for every twenty-nine rooms. And yet the resident population at Chaco Canyon appears to have been quite low. It seems that people instead traveled here from outlying villages in order to participate in annual ceremonial occasions.

Why Chaco Canyon was abandoned we do not know, but it is easy to suspect environmental changes, possibly drought. Members of the indigenous Hopi nation, who now live in Arizona, are still telling stories of their migration from Chaco Canyon. In fact, the Hopi are still using *kivas* in their ceremonies. During the eight days of the annual Wuwuchim festival, the rituals are all performed in *kivas*. They are said to represent the world below from whence human beings once emerged. They are also symbolic of the womb.

In 1680 the Pueblo people joined together to fight the Spanish colonizers. Uniting around their shared religion, they pushed both conquistadors and missionaries off their land for some twenty years. The Spaniards eventually returned, but never to the land of the Hopi. Indeed, the Hopi have retained a high degree of self-governance to this day. Today all Pueblo peoples are heavily dependent on royalties from the extraction of natural resources, in particular of coal. The Hopi have repeatedly voted against casinos, but in 2017 they concluded an agreement with the state of Arizona to allow gambling to take place on their reservation.

Read more online: https://hdl.handle.net/20.500.12434/a5d18db4

There are today some 5 million people in the United States who count themselves as "Native Americans," corresponding to less than 2 percent of the population of the country. In addition, there may be some 1.5 million Native Americans in Canada. There are 562 federally recognized tribal governments in the U.S. These "reservations" govern and police themselves and collect their own taxes. Many have recently opened casinos where they offer visitors Las Vegas-style gambling. Today only about a fifth of Native Americans live on reservations. There are twenty-one surviving inhabited pueblos in the southwestern United States. They are the oldest continuously inhabited communities in North America.

Kingdom of Hawai'i

Before it was occupied by the United States in 1893, Hawai'i was a sovereign country with its own royal house, foreign policy, bank notes and stamps. In fact, it had been recognized as independent by European countries for close to one hundred years. The last ruler of independent Hawai'i was a woman, Queen Lili'uokalani, 1838–1917. She was an accomplished author and the composer of "Aloha 'Oe," the most famous of all Hawai'ian songs. She represented her country at Queen Victoria's Golden Jubilee in London in 1887. Queen Lili'uokalani is still revered by indigenous Hawai'ians.

By the 1890s, the European occupation of all of North America was secure and the U.S. government continued its expansion across the Pacific. In 1898, they proceeded to annex the islands, the same year that they occupied the Philippines. Hawai'i became a U.S. state in 1959, following a referendum in which 93 percent of voters approved of statehood. As a result, the islands were removed from the United

Nations list of territories subject to decolonization. In 1993, the U.S. Congress issued an apology in which they admitted that "the overthrow of the Kingdom of Hawai'i occurred with the active participation of agents and citizens of the United States" and that "the Native Hawai'ian people never directly relinquished to the United States their claims to their inherent sovereignty as a people over their national lands."

There are today some 150,000 Hawai'ians of pure indigenous ancestry and another 400,000 people who claim partial indigenous ancestry. Together they constitute about a third of the population of the islands. Native Hawai'ians are over-represented among the homeless and unemployed. Although there is an active independence movement, it has limited support. A more popular proposal is that the islands should be given a semi-sovereign status within the United States and that native Hawai'ians should be recognized as an indigenous American tribe. Queen Lili'uokalani still has descendants who claim a right to the vacant throne. There are today some 42,000 U.S. soldiers stationed on the islands.

Read more online: http://hdl.handle.net/20.500.12434/ae962e90

Further reading

Besom, Thomas. *Inka Human Sacrifice and Mountain Worship: Strategies for Empire Unification*. Albuquerque: University of New Mexico Press, 2013.

Bremmer, Jan N. *The Strange World of Human Sacrifice*. Leuven: Peeters, 2007.

Clendinnen, Inga. *Aztecs: An Interpretation*. Cambridge: Cambridge University Press, 1991.

Mann, Charles C. *1491: New Revelations of the Americas Before Columbus*. New York: Vintage Books, 2006.

Pauketat, Timothy R. and Thomas E. Emerson, eds. *Cahokia: Domination and Ideology in the Mississippian World*. Lincoln: University of Nebraska Press, 2000.

Read, Kay Almere. *Time and Sacrifice in the Aztec Cosmos*. Bloomington: Indiana University Press, 1998.

Salomon, Frank. *The Cord Keepers: Khipus and Cultural Life in a Peruvian Village*. Durham: Duke University Press, 2004.

Sharer, Robert J. *Daily Life in Maya Civilization*. Westport: Greenwood Press, 2009.

Sugiyama, Saburo. *Human Sacrifice, Militarism, and Rulership: Materialization of State Ideology at the Feathered Serpent Pyramid, Teotihuacan*. Cambridge: Cambridge University Press, 2005.

Urton, Gary. *Inca Myths*. London: British Museum Press, 1999.

Timeline

20,000 BCE	The Americas are populated by migrants coming across the Berling land bridge.
1800 BCE	Olmec civilization in Central America. Famous for figurines of babies and enormous statues of heads.
550	Teotihuacán is looted and destroyed. Its pyramids are Mexico's most visited tourist attractions today.
250	Mayan Empire in today's southern Mexico and Central America. Flat-top pyramids and garden cities in the jungle.
674–1122	The Toltec Empire, with Tula as its capital. Important cultural influences on the Aztecs.
900	Chaco Canyon is established as a major center for the Pueblo culture. Construction of the great *kiva*.
950	Mayan cities are abandoned.
1050	The city of Cahokia is founded in the Mississippi Valley. Mound builders.
1200	Various nomadic peoples from the north, including the Mexica, arrive in the Valley of Mexico.
1325	Tenochtitlan is founded in the Lake Texcoco.
1428	An alliance between Tenochtitlan, Texcoco and Tlacopan. The triple alliance is known as the Aztec Empire.
1438–1533	The Inca Empire is established in Cusco, with Pachacuti Inca as the first leader.
1463	Túpac Inca Yupanqui greatly expands the Inca empire.
1521	The Aztec Empire is defeated by an alliance of Spanish conquistadors and subjects of the empire.
1572	The last Inca stronghold in Vilcabamba falls to the Spanish.

Short dictionary

atepetl, Nahuatl	"City-state" of the Valley of Mexico. Prominent before the emergence of the Aztec empire.
ayllu, Quechua	A traditional form of social organization among people of the Andes. Emphasizing social solidarity and mutual self-help.
ceque, Quechua	System of ritual pathways conducting spiritual energy from Cusco, the Inca capital, to all parts of the empire.
chicha, possibly Taino language	An alcoholic beverage made from corn, grain or fruit.
codex, Latin	"Book." Name for manuscripts describing the cultures of the Maya and the Aztecs before the arrival of the European.
huaca, Quechua	Revered object among the peoples of the Andes. Often a natural feature such a large rock.
kiva, Hopi	A subterranean room used by the Pueblo peoples for religious purposes.
nazca lines	Enormous geoglyphs created by the Nazca people of today's Peru. Best viewed from outer space.
pueblo, Spanish	"Village." Name given to the societies of the south-western parts of North America.
quipu, Quechua	"Knot." Rope-based language used for record-keeping by the Incas.
Tawantinsuyu, Quechua	Literally, "the four regions." Inca name for the Inca Empire.
tlatoani, Nahuatl	The ruler of the *atepetl* city-state.

Think about

The Maya
- How was Mayan society organized?
- What role did human sacrifices and blood-letting ceremonies play in Mayan society?
- Describe some of the cultural achievements of the Maya.

The Aztecs
- Briefly describe some of the societies which preceded the Aztecs in the Valley of Mexico.
- Give an account of the history of the Mexica people.
- How did the Aztecs conduct wars?

The Incas
- Describe the economic system of the Inca empire.
- Who was the Sapa Inca?
- How was the Inca empire held together?

North America
- Why are the most common images of the indigenous people of North America incorrect?
- Describe life in Cahokia.
- What was going on in Chaco Canyon?

Map of the world from Abraham Ortelius, *Theatrum orbis terrarum* (Antverpiae: Apud Aegid. Coppenium Diesth, 1570). p. 26, https://archive.org/details/theatrumorbister00orte

8. European Expansion

A study of comparative international systems is by definition a historical study. There are no separate international systems to compare anymore. There is only one system — the system which first made its appearance in Europe in the late Renaissance, and which later came to spread to every corner of the globe. But "spread" is not the right word. This was not a matter of a process of passive diffusion. Rather, the eventual victory of the European international system was a result of the way the Europeans first came to "discover" and later to occupy and take possession of most non-European lands. This is a story of imperialism and colonialism. In this, the final chapter of the book, we will tell the story of how Europe for a while at the turn of the twentieth century came to rule the world.

For most of its history Europe had quite a peripheral position in relation to everyone else. Europe was an international system turned in on itself, confident in its own culture and largely uninterested in what was going on elsewhere. Moreover, outsiders made only occasional forays into Europe — like the Berber kingdoms in the eleventh and twelfth centuries and the Mongols in the thirteenth century. What these outsiders found were a few impressive cathedrals, the occasional castle, but also a lot of desperately poor people, serfs without much food and without education. Before the year 1500, no European city was a match for the splendors of Baghdad, Xi'an, Kyoto or Tenochtitlan.

Yet Europe eventually did become rich, powerful and important, and it came to have a profound impact on the rest of the world. In the first half of the fifteenth century, Europeans began to embark on sea voyages which took them down the western coast of Africa, and eventually far further afield. Here they discovered a number of commodities which found a ready market back home. Before long the Europeans began looking for new goods and for opportunities to trade. The commercial activities transformed Europe's economy and enormously strengthened the institutional structure of the state. It was at this point that the Europeans established their first permanent colonies overseas. In some areas, such as in the Americas, Europeans settled permanently, but in Asia they mainly established small trading posts.

Beginning at the end of the eighteenth century, the development of an industrial economy based on mechanical production in factories radically changed European societies, making them "modern." Modernization entailed changes in almost all aspects of social, economic and political life — often analyzed as a question of

© 2019 Erik Ringmar, CC BY 4.0 https://doi.org/10.11647/OBP.0074.08

"urbanization," "industrialization," "democratization," etc. As far as the rest of the world was concerned, the modernization of Europe had a number of far-reaching consequences. The Europeans needed raw materials for the goods they were producing and often these resources could be found outside of Europe itself. Moreover, European producers needed to find more people who were prepared to buy all the things their factories were spewing out. The hope was that these consumers could be found in India, for example, or in China. And as people outside of Europe were to discover, the industrial revolution had given the Europeans access to far more lethal weapons than ever before. Armed with these new incentives, and these new guns, the Europeans set out to conquer the world.

A sea route to India

Europe's isolation came to an end in the thirteenth century when the first sustained contacts were established with East Asia. During the *Pax Mongolica*, the "Mongol peace," European merchants and the occasional missionary traveled as far eastward as China. Read more: *Dividing it all up* at p. 112.

The Europeans were amazed at the wealth of the countries they discovered here, the power of their rulers and all the curious objects which no one in Europe knew anything about. Returning home they would tell tales of their wondrous adventures. The objects they brought with them — spices, tea, precious stones, china, silk and so on — embodied these mysteries and for that reason alone they were highly sought after. This was not least the case for members of the elite who derived power and prestige from buying and displaying these exotic objects. There was, European merchants discovered, a lot of money to be made for those who could satisfy this market. It was the Italians who took the lead — the Venetians and Genovese in particular. Marco Polo, the most famous among them, was a Venetian.

Did Marco Polo go to China?

In 1271, the merchants Niccolò and Maffeo Polo left their native city of Venice and set sail for the east. The two brothers had already done business in Constantinople and in the Crimea, and they had visited the lands of the Mongols. When they had returned to Europe in 1269, they carried a message from Kublai Khan to the Pope in Rome. Having delivered the letter, they were now on their way back to Asia. They had a *paiza* with them, a small tablet in gold, which gave them free passage, lodgings, and horses throughout Mongol lands. With them, as they left Venice, was Niccolò's son Marco, who was seventeen years old at the time.

Marco Polo was to find particular favor with the Great Khan who made him an official at his court. He learned to speak Mongolian together with several other languages and he traveled around the vast empire visiting lands which no European had previously seen. His account of the splendors of the khan's palace is particularly famous, together with his description of Kinsay, today's Hangzhou. The Polos came back to Venice as wealthy men and the many stories Marco told about his adventures amazed everyone who heard them. The stories of his travels were collected in *Il Milione*, a title that either derived from Polo's nickname, "Emilione," or from the millions of marvellous tales the book contained.

Yet it may be that Marco Polo never actually visited China. It is striking, for example, that he never mentions Chinese customs such as foot-binding or tea-drinking, and it is strange that place-names are consistently given in Persian rather than in Mongol or Chinese. This is not, however, a reason to dismiss the text. Despite its omissions and mistakes, the account of Polo's travels contains many details which we know from other sources to be correct. Marco Polo's book — or the book associated with a person by that name — had a tremendous impact on European readers, stirring up elaborate fantasies of the exotic East. The most famous reader was Christopher Columbus, who had his own copy of the book on which he had scribbled extensive notes in the margins.

Read more online: https://hdl.handle.net/20.500.12434/943e5744

Yet trade with the East was a perilous business. Goods traveled slowly on camelback across the caravan routes of Central Asia, where there were a number of things that could go wrong — robbers could attack, officials could interfere, and then there was the inclement weather and the turn of the seasons. As long as the Mongol Empire lasted it was possible to deal with these challenges, and the profits remained high. The Mongol khanates had not always been at peace with each other, but they understood the value of commerce and they did what they could to encourage it. Yet, with the end of the *Pax Mongolica* in the fourteenth century, both the risks and the costs associated with the caravan trade rose dramatically. The new rulers who appeared about halfway between Europe and East Asia wanted their cut of the profits. Both the Ottomans and Mamluk Egypt put up customs and tariffs which made it far more expensive to trade.

In response, the Europeans began looking for alternative ways to reach East Asia. They tried their luck by ship. One idea was to go down the west coast of Africa and find a passage to India that way. Once these attempts proved successful, trade moved away from the Mediterranean, away from Italy, and to the countries along Europe's Atlantic coast. Here Portugal took the lead, soon followed by Spain, although the Spanish, at least to begin with, continued to rely on the services of Italian sea captains. The most famous of these, Cristoforo Colombo, "Christopher Columbus," had the idea that it should be possible to travel to India by going westward, straight into the Atlantic Ocean. He did not find India this way, but he found a new world — a *Mundus novus* — of which no one in the old world had had any previous knowledge. Eventually the new world came to be known as "America," named after Amerigo Vespucci, another Italian sea captain.

Prior to the Middle Ages, Europeans had not shown much interest in the world outside of their continent, as we said before, but there were two exceptions. First of all there were the Vikings of Scandinavia. The Vikings traveled far and wide. Vikings from what today is known as Sweden went eastward along the large rivers of Russia until they came into contact with the Byzantine Empire and the Abbasid Caliphate. Read more: *A Viking funeral on the Volga* at p. 89. Meanwhile Vikings from what today is Denmark and Norway went westward, exploring first Iceland, then Greenland and finally what they called *Vinland*, that is today's "North America." Columbus was not the first European to set foot in the Americas.

The second exception concerns the military campaigns known as the "Crusades." To some Europeans — notably a few militant Popes — it was unacceptable that lands mentioned in their religious scriptures, and which before the Arab expansion had been predominantly Christian, now were in Muslim hands. The idea was to equip a pan-European army which could win them back. Altogether seven major Crusades were organized between 1096 and 1254, in which hundreds of thousands of Europeans took part. For a while the Crusaders were quite successful. They conquered Jerusalem in 1099 and managed to establish small kingdoms throughout the eastern Mediterranean. Yet at the Battle of Hattie in 1187, the Crusaders were decisively defeated by the armies of the Fatimids, the caliphate with its base in Cairo. Read more: *Saladin and the Crusaders* at p. 88. Although the Europeans gathered their forces for several more Crusades, they never achieved their ends.

Wars on behalf of the Christian religion continued on the fringes of Europe, both in Eastern Europe and in Spain. Lithuania was converted to Christianity in 1386 by means of armies consisting of so-called "Teutonic knights," a military but also a religious order. In Spain, a project — the *Reconquista* — was undertaken to invade al-Andalus. Read more: *The Arabs in Spain* at p. 81.

In 1212, the Christian coalition won an important battle at Las Navas de Tolosa, yet it would take another 250 years before the Iberian Peninsula was fully under Christian occupation. The last Muslim ruler — Muhammad XII of Granada, known to the Spaniards as "Boabdil" — was expelled in 1492, the same year that Columbus made his first journey across the Atlantic. The Christian victory severed seven-hundred-year-old links between southern Spain and the centers of civilization in the East. They also forced both Muslims and Jews to convert to Christianity on pain of death or expulsion.

Europeans in the "New World"

This was when the Europeans came to divide the world between them. Or rather, when it was divided by the Pope in Rome and given to Portugal and Spain.

Treaty of Tordesillas, 1494

In 1494, representatives of the crowns of Portugal and Spain met to divide the world between them. At the Treaty of Tordesillas, Portugal was given everything west of a meridian running between the Cape Verde Islands in the mid-Atlantic and the new lands which Columbus had discovered. The other, eastern, side of the world was divided by the Treaty of Zaragoza in 1529, along a meridian that mirrored the one agreed on in Tordesillas. On both occasions, the pope in Rome was involved. It was God who had given the earth to mankind, after all, and only his representative had the authority to approve of a division of it. The treaty is one of the first examples of how a science invented in Europe — cartography — could be used as a means of controlling the world.

From now on what amounted to the center of the world belonged to Portugal and the peripheries belonged to Spain. Thus, Africa, the Indian Ocean, and Brazil fell to the Portuguese, whereas Spain received the remainder of the Americas but also, for example, the Philippines. This is why people to this day speak Portuguese in Brazil, but Spanish in Mexico and Peru. Spain and Portugal respected this agreement fairly conscientiously; other European countries, however, did not. When the Dutch Republic and England took over much of world trade in the seventeenth century, the Treaty of Tordesillas became irrelevant.

The Treaty of Tordesillas was the first time that European powers met to divide the world between them in an orderly and civilized fashion. In the nineteenth century, Africa and China were divided in much the same way. Read more: *The Berlin Conference* at p. 195. At the end of the Second World War, the United States and the Soviet Union met to determine each other's respective "spheres of influence." On none of these occasions were the inhabitants of the partitioned territories asked for their opinion.

Read more online: https://hdl.handle.net/20.500.12434/f28aa9c7

For many Spaniards — the soldiers known as *conquistadors* — the wars in the Americas were simply an extension of the wars which they already had fought in Spain. Neither Arabs nor "Indians" were Christian and just like the Arabs, the Indians were enemies to be defeated. Hernán Cortés and his men marched into Tenochtitlan in 1519, and Francisco Pizarro's army captured Cuzco in 1533. Despite their awesome power, both the Aztecs and the Incas turned out to be surprisingly easy to conquer, and in both cases, the Spaniards took control by means of only a few hundred men. In fact, both empires consisted of loose coalitions made up of many different political entities, and some of these subjects were quite happy to side with the Europeans. Although the Incas eventually regrouped and organized a military resistance, it was far too little, too late. Their last stronghold fell in 1572.

What the Europeans more than anything were looking for in the New World was gold. Columbus's own descriptions of his discoveries contained endless references to how much gold the new continent contained. This, he knew, was the best way to get European kings to back more voyages of exploration. Although the Europeans indeed did find some gold, they found even more silver. In fact, there was a mountain — Potosí in Peru — which was said to be made entirely of silver.

In the end, the European occupation of the Americas resulted in genocide. Some indigenous people were killed in military confrontations, many were worked to death in mines or on plantations, but the vast majority of people died as a result of deliberate

A mountain of silver

In a remote, dry and cold part of the high Andes, in today's Bolivia, there is a mountain which the Incas knew as Sumaq Urqu, "beautiful mountain," and the Spaniards called Cerro Rico, "rich mountain." As the Incas had already discovered, the mountain was enormously rich in silver, the richest in the world. When the Spaniards began extracting the ore in 1545, a town, Potosí, was established there. By the seventeenth century, it had grown to include some 200,000 inhabitants, over thirty churches, and many palaces, theaters and boulevards. This was where the crown of Spain minted its money. Yet the mines relied on slave labor and the working conditions were atrocious. Hundreds of thousands of miners died of exhaustion and disease.

It was the silver from Potosí which paid all of Spain's debts, financed its armies and churches in Europe and allowed the country to go on "shopping sprees" in Asia. First, the silver was transported by llamas to the Pacific coast, then shipped to Acapulco in Mexico, and from there on to Europe. Before long the Spaniards began shipping silver across the Pacific too, to Manila in the Philippines, where it was used to pay off their Chinese creditors. It was silver from Potosí which more than anything provided the means of payment that enabled the creation of a world market. Spanish coins — the famous *peso de ocho*, "pieces of eight" — were a universal currency accepted everywhere in the world. The symbol stamped on the coin — "$," the dollar sign — has come to symbolize money ever since.

However, the windfall had disastrous long-term consequences for the Spanish economy. Since the silver from Potosí allowed them to buy whatever they wanted, Spain failed to develop a domestic industry. And when the silver boom was over and the colonies declared independence, Spain had nothing left. The country was now poor because it once had been so rich. There is still some silver left in Sumaq Urqu and today it is mined by collectives of miners. Yet the working conditions have hardly improved since the sixteenth century. It is dirty, dangerous work, and few of the miners live beyond the age of forty-five.

Read more online: https://hdl.handle.net/20.500.12434/eba42922

---

exposure to European diseases like smallpox and measles. These illnesses had long existed in Europe, and the Europeans had adapted to them, but to the people of the Americas they were deadly. It is estimated that perhaps 80 percent of the indigenous population of South, Central and North America perished as a result. This was equal to tens of millions of people. The impact on the population of the Americas was consequently far worse than the impact of the Black Death on Asia and Europe. Read more: *The Black Death* at p. 120.

As a result of the genocide, there were not enough indigenous people who could do the physical labor involved in exploiting the natural wealth of the continent. In response, the Europeans began importing slaves from Africa, often sold to them by West African kingdoms. Read more: *Dancing kings and female warriors of Dahomey* at p. 139.

From the sixteenth century to the nineteenth some 12 million African slaves were forcibly transported across the Atlantic Ocean. Although both the U.S. and Britain officially outlawed the importation of slaves as early as 1807, the international trade in slaves was banned only in the 1830s, and slavery itself was finally abolished in the United States in 1865 and in Brazil not until 1888.

Not only were germs and human beings exchanged, however, but also a wide range of plants, fruits, and animals. Read more: *The Columbian exchange* at p. 156.

Since life on the American continent had evolved independently of the rest of the world, it had developed a wide range of unique species. There were also many species that only existed elsewhere in the world. Through global trading networks these plants, fruits and animals soon spread far and wide.

Carl von Linné names the world

Carl Linnaeus, 1707–1778, or "Carl von Linné" as Swedes call him, was the botanist who came up with the Latin names for all plants and animals. In fact, they were not only named by him but organized into a system — a *Systema naturæ*, to give the title of his most famous work, published in 1735 — in which every living thing found its proper place. In this system, all species could be related to each other, even those that had not yet been discovered. Linné's system of nature had a universal scope. In order to put names into the many empty grids, Linnaeus traveled around Sweden looking for plants, but he also dispatched his students — often referred to as his "disciples" — to find new plants in the most remote corners of the globe.

Linnaeus believed botany should serve the interests of the nation. In particular, he found it an outrage that Swedes spent their hard-earned money on tea from China. "We are sending silver to the Chinese and all we get in return are dry leaves!" Thus, when one of his disciples one day returned from China with a tea bush, Linné was very excited and devised a plan to start a tea plantation. "Imagine how rich the country would be if we never have to trade with foreigners!" Unfortunately, however, the bush died when exposed to the harsh Swedish winter.

Carl von Linné may have been a great botanist, but he, together with almost all of his contemporaries, did not understand much about political economy. The wealth of a nation, as Adam Smith was later to explain, consists of what the country can produce, and Sweden cannot produce tea. It is much better to let the Chinese produce tea and for Swedes to produce what they are comparatively better at producing — cars, for example, or flat-pack furniture. By focusing on their respective advantages, and by trading with each other, the wealth of both China and Sweden will be maximized. Smith, in the *Wealth of Nations*, published in 1776, provided the intellectual rationale for a global market in which there are no borders and no customs duties.

Read more online: https://hdl.handle.net/20.500.12434/718b8209

As far as North America is concerned, it was originally settled by the Dutch, the English, and the French, but eventually it was English settlers who came to dominate. A substantial proportion of the first settlers were members of various religious minorities — the so-called "Puritans" — who took refuge there after the English Civil

War, 1642–1651. They called it "New England." In North America too, European germs quickly wiped out entire populations. This was why the land looked empty and unoccupied when subsequent waves of Europeans arrived. The Europeans referred to it as *terra nullius*, Latin for "nobody's land." Land which did not belong to anyone, the Europeans argued, was there for the taking. It was God's will that they should take charge of the New World. And take charge they did.

The Mayflower

In 1620, a ship, the *Mayflower*, transported 102 passengers from Plymouth, England, to what was to become the Plymouth Colony in Massachusetts, New England. A majority of the people on board were Puritans, members of a strict Protestant denomination who were persecuted in Europe. Yet they arrived too late in the season to plant crops and, the story goes, they survived only because of the help they received from the natives. The following year, after their own first harvest, they held a "thanksgiving," a ritual meal that is commemorated by Americans to this day.

The reason they survived the first winter, it turns out, was not that they were given food by the natives, but rather that they stole it. One of the Puritans, William Bradford, who chronicled the event, describes how they ransacked houses and dug up native burial mounds looking for buried stashes of corn. "And sure it was God's good providence that we found this corn, for else we know not how we should have done." Far greater devastation was caused by European diseases. Thomas Morgan, another early settler, recalled that the hand of God "fell heavily upon them, with such a mortall stroake that they died on heapes as they lay in their houses." Yet this too, the settlers decided, was a result of the foresight of the Christian God who had made the land "so wondrously empty." "Why then should we stand starving here for places of habitation… and in the meantime suffer whole countries, as profitable for the use of man, to lie waste without any improvement?"

People in the United States think of the passengers on the *Mayflower* as the first Americans. Those who can claim descent from one of them consider themselves as uniquely American. There are today some 10 million people who can make that claim.

Read more online: https://hdl.handle.net/20.500.12434/c95ed1c4

A commercial world economy

In a sense the European discovery of the Americas was something of a distraction. After all, it was to East Asia that the Europeans wanted to go. From this perspective the year 1498 is more important than 1492. It was in 1498 that the Portuguese sea captain Vasco da Gama rounded the Cape of Good Hope, on the southernmost tip of Africa, and started making his way up Africa's eastern coast. Here the Europeans met traders from Oman, Yemen and Gujarat; in fact, if the Europeans only had arrived half a century earlier, they would have met Chinese traders here too. *Read more: A giraffe in Beijing* at p. 25.

Benefiting from the monsoon winds, da Gama arrived in Kerala in southern India in May 1498, and from there Portuguese ships soon started exploring other ports around the Indian Ocean. This is how the Europeans came into contact with the "spice islands," the vast archipelago in today's Malaysia and Indonesia where assorted exotic spices were grown. The Europeans soon developed a taste for nutmeg, cloves, cardamom, black pepper and mace — which all helped to bring flavor to the notoriously bland European diet. Before long European ships had continued into the Pacific Ocean too, traveling northward to China and Japan. The Portuguese established trading depots in Goa in India in 1510; Malacca in Malaysia in 1511; and in Macao in China in 1557. These were not colonies, only ports where they could trade with the locals, store goods and repair their ships.

The Portuguese were soon followed by the Spanish. In 1565, conquistadors from Mexico sailed to the Philippines where they established a colony known as the "Spanish East Indies," with Manila as its capital. The Spanish visited Taiwan too, and southern China. The Spanish economy at the time was actually quite underdeveloped, yet their discovery of silver in the Americas allowed them to ignore this fact. The silver also provided a way around a problem that had always plagued European trading relations with the East: there was so much they wanted to buy from the Asians, but next to nothing that the Asians wanted to buy from them. Once silver started flowing from the Americas, however, the Europeans could suddenly buy anything they wanted. This infusion of cash caused a boom in international trade, bringing great wealth both to China and India. Before long the Spanish did not even bother to send the silver to Europe first, but instead sent it directly across the Pacific Ocean, straight to their Asian creditors.

More than the Spanish, however, it was the Dutch who came to copy the Portuguese. The Dutch also became their greatest rivals as international merchants. The Dutch lived in a republic, and officially they had no imperial ambitions, but they were very keen on trade. It was in Holland, in 1602, that the first truly multinational company — the Vereenigde Oostindische Compagnie, the Dutch East India Company — was established. The VOC, as it was known, expanded the markets for the products which the Portuguese had discovered and connected all parts of the world into one global marketplace. Similar trading companies were soon established all over Europe. Read more: *De Vereenigde Oostindische Compagnie* at p. 34.

The European states benefited greatly from the trade with the East. The seventeenth century was a time when European rulers increasingly came to call themselves "sovereign," meaning that they had pretensions to exercise supreme authority within the territory which they took to be theirs. In order to give credence to this rather extravagant claim, the kings needed resources, and this is what the trade with East Asia supplied. For one thing, each trading company was given a monopoly on trade with a particular part of the world. Or rather, these monopolies were sold by the kings and thus constituted a good source of revenue for them. Soon the kings could also borrow money from the trading companies. Making fabulous profits, they had surplus cash which they needed to invest. The kings of France were notorious for defaulting on these loans, but the kings of England were less extravagant. This is how the Bank of

England and similar financial institutions came to be established. Eventually the City of London became the leading center of international finance.

The development of these global trading networks had a profound impact on the world economy and it was to have political implications too — involving European countries in colonization and empire building. Yet in Asia, Europe's position was nothing like their position in the Americas. The Dutch established a colony, Batavia, in Indonesia, and the Spanish occupied the Philippines, but there was no way for the Europeans to successfully wage war on the powerful kingdoms of the East. China, India, Japan, Siam, the Mughal Empire, Persia and the Ottomans were far too rich and powerful, their armies too strong, and the Europeans were far too few in numbers. Portuguese traders had established a powerful grip on commerce in the Indian Ocean, ending the tradition of free competition and free trade, but this was not something that worried the rulers of Asia. The Europeans, much as in the Middle Ages, continued to be awestruck by the wonders of the East, and the eastern empires were greatly admired for their wealth and power.

The Seven Years' War, 1756–1763, is the world war few people have heard about. It was fought in Europe — between Britain and France and their respective allies — but the war spread to other continents too. The conflict was particularly fierce in North America where both Britain and France had established communities of settlers and had strong commercial interests. The Seven Years' War was intensely fought in India too where the settlers were fewer in numbers, but the commercial interests at least as strong. In both cases the conflicts concluded with victories for Britain. One long-term consequence of the wars in Europe was that the European settlers came to make themselves more independent of their home governments. In fact, relations between the European settlers and their motherland had always been complicated. The Spanish government had, for example, tried to keep some order in the empire and sought to stop the conquistadors from mistreating the natives. Yet the conquistadors were scornful of such policies and they resented Madrid's meddling in what they regarded as their own affairs. When Spain itself was occupied during the Napoleonic Wars, 1808–1814, the settlers saw an opportunity to assert themselves. One after another, they declared their independence: Colombia in 1810, Venezuela in 1811, Argentina in 1816, Peru in 1821, Bolivia in 1825, and so on.

Something similar happened in the case of North America. In the southern parts of that continent the British had established large plantations where they grew tobacco, sugar and cotton for export. In the eighteenth century these products proved extraordinarily successful. Suddenly people everywhere around the world started smoking, eating sweets and dressing in cotton fabrics. To make up for the shortfall in cheap labor, the settlers in North America began importing African slaves. When slavery eventually was abolished in 1865, there were close to 4 million slaves in the United States. Today some 13 percent of the U.S. population — around 40 million people — identify themselves as "African-American." In British North America, there were three quite distinct groups of settlers — the plantation owners in the South, the Puritan settlers in New England, and the people who lived in fledgling cities like New York and Boston. The lifestyle, outlook, and values of these three groups were really quite different, yet they, much as the settlers in South America, shared a resentment towards any outside interference. They insisted that London had no right to tax them as long as they were not represented in the British parliament. Moreover, they wanted to continue their expansion westward, a project which London regarded as too adventurous. Thirteen settler colonies in North America declared their independence from Britain in 1776.

As a result, by the 1820s European imperialism had largely come to seem a thing of the past. People in Britain looked back wistfully on the days when they had had an empire. There was still Canada to be sure, but this territory was mainly a concern for merchants involved in the fur trade; there was India too, but India was ruled by the East India Company and was not a British colony. Other European countries had even less of an empire. As a result of the Seven Years' War, the French had lost most of their commercial outposts; the Portuguese had lost Brazil, even though they retained their trading posts in Africa and Asia; there were Dutch settlers in South Africa, but the Dutch presence in the rest of the world was motivated by commercial imperatives, not by imperialism.

An industrial world economy

And yet, one hundred years later, at the time of the First World War, next to all of Africa and much of Asia were in European hands. Colonialism had returned with a vengeance. In order to understand this turn of events, we must understand the changes that took place in Europe itself. This is more than anything the story of the industrial revolution.

At the end of the eighteenth century, new ways of manufacturing goods were invented in Europe. Things were now being made in factories and by machines, powered first by steam and later by electricity. Before long cheap, mass-produced goods were flooding European markets. Yet the factories produced much more than European consumers could buy and, for this reason, it became crucial to find new customers. New sources of raw material were needed too, resources which in many cases could only be found on other continents. These economic imperatives meant that the Europeans took a renewed interest in the world. The eventual result was a second wave of imperial expansion and the creation of an international system completely dominated by Europe.

This time it was the British who took the lead. It was in Britain after all that the industrial revolution started, and the trading stations and colonial outposts which remained in their hands provided them with a head start. The British also had a navy which was second to none. Moreover, throughout the nineteenth century, the British government was dominated by free-traders, by politicians, that is, who wanted to abolish customs duties and make sure that British merchants had free access to foreign markets. It was easy for the British to be in favor of free trade since they were the ones whose factories produced goods most cheaply. The strategy the British pursued was always the same. They approached the ruler of a non-European country and asked for access to its customers and its raw materials. If the country in question agreed, the British established themselves and started buying and selling. But if the country refused, the British would threaten military action. In some cases the natives eventually gave in and signed a commercial treaty, often referred to as an "unequal treaty." In other cases, when the natives stood their ground, the result was war.

This is how Britain, step by step, came to establish its worldwide preeminence. The British, that is, had no grand master plan for how to take over the world. Rather, one step led to another, and they were all guided by what were at first regarded as economic imperatives — foreign markets had to be opened up; trading posts had to be defended; British investments abroad had to be made more secure. India illustrates this rather absent-minded logic. Here the British had at first only small trading posts, but in the course of the eighteenth century they were sucked into the struggles which characterized politics in the fragmenting Mughal Empire. Read more: *The Mughal Empire* at p. 64.

Soon the East India Company made alliances with powerful Indian princes. The carrot the British dangled before them was access to international markets; the stick which they wielded was the army the British had brought with them. At the battle of Palashi — known to the English as "Plassey" — in 1757, the East India Company defeated the ruler of Bengal and his French allies. As a result, the British suddenly found itself the main power broker on the subcontinent.

At the same time it would be a mistake to exaggerate Europe's superiority — at least as far as the first half of the nineteenth century is concerned. Many locals defended themselves ferociously and often they had access to military technology which was no worse than that of the Europeans. Thus, even as their colonial empires spread, there were plenty of embarrassing reversals. The British lost wars not only in Burma and Afghanistan, but against the Asante and the people of Benin. And in 1857 they came very close to being thrown out of India.

The well of Cawnpore

In May 1857, a mutiny began among native soldiers in the army of the British East India Company. The rebels captured large parts of the northern plains of the subcontinent, including the province of Oudh and the city of Delhi, where they installed the Mughal king as their ruler. The war was characterized by great cruelty on both sides. In June 1857, the Indian rebels laid siege to the British settlement at Kanpur — "Cawnpore" to the British — but after three weeks, with little food left, the settlers accepted an offer of safe passage. As they made themselves ready to depart, however, the men were all butchered. While women and children were spared at first, they were later hacked to death and their bodies were thrown into a well — the notorious "well of Cawnpore" — which, as the story goes, "filled up to within six feet of the top."

The acts of retribution meted out by the British army were every bit as savage as the acts committed by the rebels. On the suspicion of harboring pro-rebel sympathies, the British commanders ordered entire villages to be burned. A favorite method of execution was to tie the rebels before the mouths of cannons and to blow them to pieces. As Charles Dickens's weekly, *Household Words,* assured its readers in a graphic account of this practice, this way of punishing mutineers "is one of the institutions of Hindustan." While it may seem barbarian to us, it is in fact "one of the easiest methods of passing into eternity."

As for the British public, it was largely supportive of such cruelties. Many felt betrayed by the mutineers who, according to an influential strand of opinion, had always been benevolently treated by the East India Company. In general — and as newspaper proprietors soon discovered — the British public loved reading about atrocities committed against their own countrymen. The gorier the details, the more titillating; a particular favorite were accounts of fair English maidens being raped by low-browed, brown men. Given such heinous crimes, the justice of the British retribution was never in doubt.

Read more online: https://hdl.handle.net/20.500.12434/a16b152d

The British Empire was enormous, but Britain itself was tiny. The empire was like an oak tree planted in a flower pot. Meanwhile the French began their colonial conquest of North Africa. Parts of Algeria were occupied in the 1830s and eventually incorporated into the French state. But here too the Europeans met with ferocious resistance and it took the French more than ten years to conquer Algeria. Since they were often unable to defeat their enemies outright, the French employed what they proudly described as "barbarian tactics."

Le système Bugeaud

Algeria was invaded by France in 1830. However the country soon proved difficult to govern, and the French army was harassed by Arab guerrilla fighters. In 1837, they were forced to conclude a treaty which gave Algerians control of two-thirds of their territory. The French ignored the agreement, however, and the following year the war recommenced. Looking for a more effective way to fight the Arabs, general Thomas Robert Bugeaud, the Governor-General of the colony, developed a new method of warfare — known as *le système Bugeaud* — which he argued was more suitable for African conditions. A main feature of the *système* was the *razzia* — the destruction of all resources that supported the lives and livelihoods of the Arab community, their crops, orchards, and cattle. Only by declaring war on civilians, Bugeaud argued, and by terrorizing and starving them, could the enemy be subdued. Yet, he insisted, there was nothing immoral about such methods. After all, France's aim was to civilize the Africans. "Gentlemen," as he explained to the parliament in Paris, "war is not made philanthropically; he who wills the end wills the means."

Other European powers met with similar resistance in their colonial wars. The British had to fight no fewer than five wars against the Asante, three wars in Afghanistan and Burma, and two opium wars in China. The French fought two wars in Dahomey and the Germans were fiercely resisted by the Herero of southwestern Africa. The problem in all cases was that the enemies were far away, the European forces actually quite small, and that it was difficult to administer the lands to which they laid claim. Even if one expedition was successful, the natives soon reasserted themselves, and the Europeans had to come back for a second expedition, and occasionally for several more. Colonial wars were not at all like wars in Europe, the Europeans concluded; they required tactics suitable to local conditions.

What settled these wars, in the end, was not military superiority as much as the ability to strike terror in the local population. Colonial warfare should have "pedagogical aims" — you should strike so hard and in such a devastating fashion that no one dared to resist. The *système Bugeaud* was an example of such state-sponsored terrorism, and it eventually proved effective. One by one the Algerian guerrilla fighters were killed or captured, and in 1843 their independent state collapsed.

Read more online: https://hdl.handle.net/20.500.12434/05a1d23c

In the nineteenth century this was more than anything the way the Europeans conducted colonial warfare.

Yet the big prize for European merchants was China. The country had some 350 million people — reputed to represent "a third of mankind" — and they were all, the Europeans were convinced, eager to buy their products. The only problem was that the Chinese authorities only allowed trade in the southern city of Guangzhou — known to the Europeans as "Canton" — and only for part of the year. To the British in particular this was not nearly good enough. Read more: *George Macartney at Qianlong's court* at p. 29.

They wanted access to China for their cotton fabrics and their silverware but in addition they wanted to sell opium. Opium was the solution to the perennial problem of what to sell to the Chinese. Opium was grown in India by the British East India Company, and before long the exports to China were booming. The only problem was that opium was illegal in China. When the Chinese authorities tried to stop the trade, the British embarked on two wars — the First Opium War of 1839–1842, and the Second Opium War of 1856–1860. China lost on both occasions and was eventually forced to open all its ports to foreign trade, including the trade in opium. The traditional international system of East Asia, which had had China at its center, was no more.

The European destruction of Yuanmingyuan

The Chinese emperors of the Qing dynasty did not live in the imposing buildings that tourists can still see in the center of Beijing. Rather, they lived at Yuanmingyuan. Yuanmingyuan, just northwest of Beijing, was a large pleasure garden filled with palaces, villas, temples, pagodas, lakes, flowers, and trees. It was also the location of an imperial archive and library, and the place where the emperors stored tributary gifts given to them by foreign delegations. The Yuanmingyuan was the secluded playground of the Chinese rulers; it was "the garden of gardens" and a vision of paradise.

In October 1860, a combined army of British and French troops entered Yuanmingyuan and destroyed the whole compound. Between October 6 and 9, the French looted many of the contents of the palaces. The soldiers, including many officers, ran from room to room, "decked out in the most ridiculous-looking costumes they could find," looking for loot. The ceramics were smashed, the artwork pulled down, the jewelry pilfered and rolls of the emperor's best silk were used to tie up the army's horses. "Officers and men seemed to have been seized with a temporary insanity"; "a furious thirst has taken hold of us"; it was an "orgiastic rampage of looting." Then on October 18, James Bruce, the eighth Lord Elgin, the highest-ranking diplomat, and leader of the British mission to China, decided to burn the entire compound to the ground. Since most of the buildings were made of cedar-wood, they burned quickly, but since the compound was so huge it still took the British soldiers two days to complete the task.

The Europeans committed this act of barbarism in order to "civilize" the Chinese. China had isolated itself and failed to keep up with world events, but now the Europeans were going to help them. By waging war on the Chinese, they were going to force them to open up to the world market and to influences from abroad. The destruction of Yuanmingyuan was the act of barbarism which was to decide the matter. The destruction terrorized the emperor and the court and made them realize that they were powerless against the intruders.

Read more online: https://hdl.handle.net/20.500.12434/58535007

From being the "Middle Kingdom," and the country responsible for keeping Heaven and Earth in harmony with each other, China became a peripheral player in an international system controlled by Europe.

The Japanese market was pried open in much the same fashion, although here threats were enough, and it was the Americans who took the lead. Since the early seventeenth century, Japan had had only limited interactions with the rest of the world; all official trade was restricted to only one city, Nagasaki, in the far south. Read more: *A Japanese international system?* at p. 36.

However, in the summer of 1853, the American Matthew Perry appeared in Edo harbor on board a steam-driven gunboat, demanding that Japan open up its markets. Initially at a loss for what to do, the Japanese began making concessions. Eventually, their policy of seclusion unraveled. An important force behind the change in policy was the *daimyo*, the local rulers, especially the ones in the south of the country who had already been engaging in clandestine trade with the outside world for a long time. Read more: *The Ryukyu Islands as the center of the world* at p. 38.

In 1868, the changes set in motion led to the overthrow of the Tokugawa government. Soon Japan also found itself a small player in an international system dominated by Europe.

The apotheosis of colonialism

As a result of the industrial revolution, and the relentless pace of economic development it unleashed, the Europeans gained a new sense of self-confidence. This radically changed their view of the rest of the world, and of Asia in particular. From the first faltering contacts in the Middle Ages to the end of the eighteenth century, the Europeans had admired and looked up to Asia. However, in the first part of the nineteenth century, almost overnight, Asia became an object of scorn. The problem, more than anything, was that Asia had failed to develop in the European fashion. Asia had missed out on the industrial revolution. A country like China, the Europeans now decided, was "stagnant" and "stuck in the past"; it made no progress and as a result it could not be said to have a proper history. In order to give the semblance of scientific validity to such claims, many Europeans made references to biology. Misreading Charles Darwin's *The Origin of the Species*, published in 1859, they decided that the different "races" of the world were locked in an inescapable struggle. The Europeans had proven themselves superior and thus deserved to rule over all others. The "inferior races" were to be their servants, and the least developed people of all would come to be destroyed. Such was the logic of human history. To help history along, the Europeans carried out genocides against the people of Tasmania, Tierra del Fuego, the Herero people of Namibia, and many others. Read more: *The Ryukyu Islands as the center of the world* at p. 191.

The nineteenth century had been quite peaceful, as far as European history goes. There were some wars to be sure, but nothing like the wholesale destruction that was to take place in the twentieth century. In the last couple of decades of the nineteenth century, however, the mood began to change. A more aggressive form of nationalism emerged, and one country after another began looking for ways to assert themselves. Italy was united in 1861 and Germany in 1871. Both countries — Germany in particular — were on the rise and they wanted a bigger role, and a bigger say, in world affairs. One way for a country to assert itself was to acquire colonies. Colonial possessions became a symbol of great-power status and the new European nation-states often proved themselves to be very aggressive colonizers.

It was then that Africa for the first time came into focus as a continent to explore and exploit. The Europeans had been trading with Africa since the fifteenth century, but much as in Asia, their presence had been limited to small trading ports along the coast. The only exception was the southernmost part of the continent where Dutch farmers had settled. Meanwhile the Europeans knew nothing whatsoever about the inner parts of the continent. This gradually changed in the course of the nineteenth century as European adventurers and missionaries went on voyages through the jungles, often supported by "national geographical societies" in their respective home countries. In their footsteps came agents of large trading companies, European soldiers, settlers and colonizers. The Europeans found gold and ivory, but also diamonds and copper, palm oil, cocoa, bananas and other "colonial produce." There was plenty of money to be made in getting these products back to markets in Europe. As a result, little by little,

Africa was divided up. Although the African kingdoms often defended themselves successfully, the Europeans always returned with larger and more powerful armies. It was in order to regulate this "scramble for Africa" that all countries with colonial aspirations met at a conference in Berlin in 1884.

The Berlin Conference

After 1871, European imperialism in Africa entered a new phase. Until this time only small groups of investors, explorers and missionaries had taken an interest in this part of the world. Except for the Dutch settlement in South Africa and the French in Algeria, their presence had been restricted to a few trading ports along the coast. The rest of Africa was too remote, too malaria-ridden, and simply not a sufficiently profitable proposition. After 1871, however, Europeans suddenly went on to explore and colonize the interior too. Before long the whole continent, except for Ethiopia, was divided between them. Read more: *Countries that were never colonized* at p. 196.

The reason for this burst of colonial ambition had little to do with Africa and everything to do with Europe itself. France turned to Africa as a way to compensate for the humiliating loss in the war against Germany in 1871. For the French, it was a way to prove to themselves that they still were a world power. Britain became interested in Africa mainly as a way to check French ambitions. Germany, which was united only in 1871, aimed to catch up with the other European powers. Africa was a good place to do it, since much of the land there seemed to be empty. Meanwhile, the Ottoman Empire, which up to this point had ruled much of North Africa, was too weak to defend its former possessions. Technological advances assisted the Europeans. Steamships took them up Africa's rivers, quinine helped them fight malaria, and far more lethal weapons helped them fight the natives.

In order to find an orderly way to resolve these conflicts, fourteen European countries gathered for a conference in Berlin in November 1884. On the wall of the conference hall was a large map of Africa on which the Europeans staked out their claims. Only two of the delegates had themselves set foot in Africa, and no Africans were present. The great winner was King Leopold II of Belgium who managed to acquire all of Congo as his personal possession. He presented himself to the global community as a great humanist and friend of the African people. In the subsequent conquest of the continent, millions of Africans died.

Read more online: **https://hdl.handle.net/20.500.12434/e73db31d**

The meeting, by all accounts, was a very civilized affair. The participants gathered around a large map of Africa and divided the various territories between themselves. Elsewhere in the world the French added Indochina to its growing empire and Britain occupied Burma and Malaya. Meanwhile the Russians moved into Central Asia and the United States pushed westward across the great North American plains towards the Pacific Ocean. This is how it happened that, by the time of the First World War, most parts of the world were under European control, or were controlled by European settler societies. There were some scattered exceptions to this rule, but in these ostensibly independent countries the Europeans still had a strong presence.

Countries that were never colonized

Not all non-European countries were colonized by the Europeans, not even at the height of Europe's power. Which countries were these and why did they manage to preserve their independence? First of all, we have the ancient empires of Asia — Persia, China, and Japan. They were far too big and far too far away to be colonized. This does not mean, however, that the Europeans did not meddle in their affairs. China was something of a "semi-colony," and Japan was forced to accept humiliating terms in the treaties they concluded with European powers. In addition, we have countries such as Nepal, Bhutan, and Afghanistan which are best described as "buffer states." That is, they were left as cushions between European empires — or, to be precise, between Britain and Russia. The Afghans defended themselves ferociously in no fewer than three Anglo-Afghan wars and, in the end, Britain decided it was better to leave them alone. A third group includes Ethiopia and Thailand. Both were established monarchies and the kings in question were very skillful in appealing to the international community for support. In addition, they were good at organizing their own bureaucracies. Essentially, they colonized their own countries using administrative methods which were very close to those employed by the Europeans themselves.

Then there is Liberia in West Africa which was established by the American Colonization Society, an American charity, as a place to which former slaves could be repatriated. It was not a colony, but not really an independent country either. In addition, there were states which now are independent — such as Korea, Taiwan, and Mongolia — which were colonized, but not by the Europeans. The final case is the Ottoman Empire. The Ottomans were not colonized by the Europeans; indeed they were themselves a part of the European system of states. They were also a large and ancient empire, although in the nineteenth century this was shrinking precipitously.

Read more online: https://hdl.handle.net/20.500.12434/1f204a45

When we think of the colonial era today, it is generally this second burst of colonial expansion that we have in mind. In the last decades of the nineteenth century the Europeans really did come to rule almost all of the rest of the world. Their methods were often ruthless and exploitative. There were many wars and the occasional genocide. The atrocities were backed up by ideas of European superiority based in the alleged science of race biology. At the same time we should remember that the apogee of colonialism only lasted for about fifty years. In terms of world history, this is nothing but a short parenthesis. Already in 1914, by the time of the First World War, the Europeans found themselves busy with other matters, and in 1945, by the end of the Second World War, colonial empires were an anachronism. Europe was devastated by the two world wars and colonies had become an expensive luxury. Things were once again about to change.

Decolonization

Independence and statehood are most conveniently measured in terms of membership of the United Nations. The United Nations today has well over 190 member states. This number can be contrasted with the fifty-seven independent states that joined the organization before the year 1950. Something has happened, in other words, since the time of the founding of the UN — the number of independent states in the world has increased four-fold! This is the story of decolonization, of how the former colonies made themselves independent from their European rulers.

By 1945, as we have said, colonialism had become an anachronism. Colonies were a net drain on the resources of European countries and colonialism had little public support. Although there certainly were individual business interests which gained considerably from the existing arrangements, the European countries as a whole did not. This was particularly the case where there was determined local resistance to colonial rule. As Europeans came to realize to their chagrin, when faced with a local enemy bent on fighting for its independence, the Europeans would always, sooner or later, lose. The locals were fighting on their own turf after all, and the Europeans were far from home. The Europeans had the clocks, as the saying went, but the locals had the time. Maintaining an empire under such circumstances would have required a commitment that simply did not exist.

The process of decolonization began in an unlikely place: the island of Saint-Domingue in the West Indies, a French colony and the country we today call Haiti.

Revolution in Saint-Domingue

On August 22, 1791, the slaves on the French island of Saint-Domingue in the Caribbean began a rebellion which ended with independence for the new country of Haiti in 1804. This was the first successful slave uprising in the Americas, and Haiti was the second country, after the United States, to become independent of Europe. The French had first arrived in the 1660s, and in 1697 they established a colony there. Saint-Domingue had been a quiet, provincial outpost until the first sugarcane plantations were established. When in the eighteenth century Europeans began their intense love affair with sugar, Caribbean plantations became the main source of the produce. The laborers required for the task were imported as slaves from Africa. Read more: *Dancing kings and female warriors of Dahomey* at p. 139. Soon the plantation owners in Saint-Domingue were making enormous profits, and the 40,000 Europeans on the island were the owners of some 500,000 African slaves.

The French Revolution of 1789 provided the slaves with a language in which to formulate their grievances. They too wanted *liberté*, *égalité*, and *fraternité*. In addition, the voodoo religion united the community around a shared, African, identity. The leader of the uprising, Toussaint Louverture, was a freed slave who soon proved himself to be a very talented general who, before long, had the slave masters on the run. However, once Napoleon Bonaparte had come to power in Paris, he sent a punitive expedition to the Caribbean. They captured Toussaint Louverture and dispatched him to France. Nonetheless, the revolution itself was unstoppable. New, equally talented leaders emerged, and in 1803 the French army was conclusively defeated. Independence was declared the following year. The country was renamed "Haiti," meaning "mountainous place" in the language spoken by the Taino, the people who had lived there before the Europeans arrived.

The subsequent history of Haiti is a sad one. By the nineteenth century, the sugar boom was over, and the country's new elite proved itself to be both authoritarian and corrupt. The United States invaded the island in 1915 and occupied it until 1934. Since 1945, the country has had a number of dictators and successive military coups have taken place. Today Haiti is the poorest country in the western hemisphere.

Read more online: https://hdl.handle.net/20.500.12434/744a8bb0

In 1791, inspired by news of the French Revolution, and fed up with being exploited for their labor, a vast rebellion broke out among the slaves on the plantations, and in 1804, the country declared itself independent. A similar independence struggle began in India in 1857. *Read more: The well of Cawnpore at p. 190.*

British rule in India was always fragile and depended heavily on the collaboration of local elites and on the loyalty of the indigenous army. When Muslims and Hindu soldiers joined forces, rallying behind the institution of the Mughal emperor, the British found themselves in a seemingly hopeless situation. Eventually the British reasserted their power, but it was a close call.

Starting in the late 1950s, and accelerating in the 1960s, one former colony after another made itself independent, and by 1970 there were few colonies left. Those that remain today are geographical curiosities like the Malvinas Islands in the South Atlantic, which are a British possession, and Nouvelle-Calédonie (New Caledonia) in the Pacific, which remains French. This is not to say that the struggle for independence was an easy process or that the Europeans gave up without a fight. Well into the 1950s, the French believed they could defend their possessions in Indochina. However, at the battle of Dien Bien Phu in 1954, they were decisively defeated. From this time onward, the United States gradually came to take over responsibility for what in the 1960s was known as "the Vietnam War." Yet the U.S. too was also eventually defeated by the Vietnamese and its armies were expelled from Indochina in 1975.

Another bloody conflict fought by the French took place in Algeria. Here a sizable group of European settlers, numbering well over one million people, had considered Algeria their home for generations. An armed uprising began in 1954 which ended with independence for the country in 1962. The British, meanwhile, were fighting guerrillas in both Kenya and Malaya. Here too the conflicts were bloody, but the independence movements eventually won.

This is how the European way of organizing international politics became the universal norm and the European type of state the only viable political unit. This outcome was a consequence of colonialism, yet colonialism itself was actually not the cause. After all, a colonized country is the very opposite of a sovereign state; colonized peoples have no nation-states and enjoy no self-determination. It was instead through the process of liberating themselves from the colonizers that the European models were copied. The Europeans would only grant sovereignty to states that reminded them of their own. The only way to become an independent state, that is, was to become an independent state of the European kind. The creation of such a state was consequently the project in which all non-European political leaders were engaged. All independence movements wanted their respective territories and fortified borders, their own capitals, armies, foreign ministries, flags, national anthems and all the other paraphernalia of sovereign statehood. They all wanted to become a version of what the Europeans were.

Yet, in far too many cases the newly independent states ran into difficulties. The political institutions were too weak, the economy was not developing, or not developing fast enough. Often there were highly valued commodities — gold, diamond, oil — over which men with weapons were prepared to fight. The new national leaders — in many cases educated in the schools of the colonial powers and trusted by the Europeans as "one of theirs" — often had no nations that they could lead. Instead, nations had to be "built" — constructed, assembled, imagined — but this, in many instances, turned out to be an impossible task. The outcome was a long series of "failed states," states, that is, which have failed to live up to the European standard. Whether it made sense for the newly independent states to live up to European standards in the first place was rarely discussed. Whether there were alternative, non-European ways of organizing a state and its foreign relations was never discussed either. The pre-colonial history of the non-European world was never allowed to play a role in the world of independent states which now came to be established.

G. K. Chesterton on Indian nationalism

G. K. Chesterton, 1874–1936, was a British journalist and author, still known today for the *Father Brown* series of detective stories. Chesterton was also a philosopher of sorts and a devout Catholic. On September 18, 1909, he wrote an article in the *Illustrated London News* in which he discussed Indian nationalism. He did not like it, but not for the reasons one might expect. Indian nationalists, he declared, are "not very Indian and not very national." What they want for their country are all the trappings of *our* government — they want our parliament, our judiciary, our newspapers, our science. The fact that Indian nationalists want all these things is evidence that they really want to be English. As a result, "[w]e cannot feel certain that the Indian Nationalist is national."

Mahatma Gandhi, the leader of the Indian independence movement, who was visiting London at the time, read Chesterton's article when it first appeared and, according to his biographer, "he was thunderstruck." On the boat back to South Africa two months later he wrote the first draft of a book, *Hind Swaraj*, where he addressed the problem of "home rule." Clearly, Chesterton's thoughts were still with him. In order to obtain home rule, Gandhi insisted, we must first make sure that we have a home that is truly our own. If we only copy English institutions, our country will not be "Hindustan," but instead "Englistan." For a country to be independent, it must be defined in independent terms. India must be herself, not a version of Britain. Starting from this premise, the rest of the book elaborates on what home rule really means.

Chesterton and Gandhi were romantics, and they were quick to denounce the evils of modern society. "It is machinery that has impoverished India," Gandhi argued, and in particular the factories of Manchester that had wiped out India's indigenous cotton industry. Gandhi's famous response was to learn how to spin his own yarn using a hand-loom, and to make his own clothes. This, he argued, was the way to make India self-sufficient. Only a self-sufficient India would be able to rule itself.

Read more online: https://hdl.handle.net/20.500.12434/e13224c8

This is how we all came to live in a European world.

Further reading

Chakrabarty, Dipesh. *Provincializing Europe*: *Postcolonial Thought and Historical Difference*. Princeton: Princeton University Press, 2000.

Harlow, Barbara, and Mia Carter, eds. *The Scramble for Africa*. Durham: Duke University Press, 2003.

Hillenbrand, Carole. *The Crusades*: *Islamic Perspectives*. Edinburgh: Edinburgh University Press, 1999.

Lemarchand, René, ed. *Forgotten Genocides*: *Oblivion, Denial, and Memory*. Philadelphia: University of Pennsylvania Press, 2011.

Nandy, Ashis. *The Intimate Enemy*: *Loss and Recovery of Self Under Colonialism*. Oxford: Oxford University Press, 1994.

Osterhammel, Jürgen. *The Transformation of the World*: *A Global History of the Nineteenth Century*. Princeton: Princeton University Press, 2014.

Ringmar, Erik. *Liberal Barbarism*: *The European Destruction of the Palace of the Emperor of China*. New York: Palgrave, 2013.

Ringrose, David R. *Expansion and Global Interaction, 1200–1700*. New York: Longman, 2001.

Todorov, Tzvetan. *The Conquest of America*: *The Question of the Other*. New York: Harper & Row, 1994.

Trouillot, Michel-Rolph. *Silencing the Past*: *Power and the Production of History*. Boston: Beacon Press, 1995.

Timeline

1095	First Crusade called for by Pope Urban II.
1295	Marco Polo returns to Venice after 24 years in China.
1492	Cristoforo Colombo arrives in the Caribbean and establishes a colony in Hispaniola, today's Haiti.
1498	Francisco da Gama arrives in Calicut. This was the first successful journey by sea between Europe and India.
1602	The Dutch East India Company, Vereenigde Oostindische Compagnie, known as VOC, is established in Amsterdam.
1620	*The Mayflower* carrying English settlers arrives at Plymouth Rock.
1763	The Seven Years War is concluded. France loses most positions in India and North America.
1776	European settlers in North America declare independence.
1804	Haiti declares independence from France.
1830	France invades and colonizes Algeria.
1857	The Indian Uprising comes close to expelling the British from India.
1885	The Berlin Conference is concluded. Africa divided between European powers.
1947	India and Pakistan declare independence from Britain.
1954	The Battle of Dien Bien Phu. French forces are defeated by a Vietnamese army.
1975	The United States withdraws from Vietnam.

Short dictionary

conquistador, Spanish	"Conqueror." Spanish soldier during the colonization of the Americas.
daimyo, Japanese	Literally, "big name." A title given to the rulers of Japan's semi-autonomous provinces during the Tokugawa period.
Faranj, Arabic	Literally, "Frank." "European." Name given to the waves of armies from Europe who invaded the Middle East from the eleventh to the thirteenth century. Cf. the Thai *farang* and the Malay *ferenggi.*
ketou, Mandarin Chinese	From the Cantonese *kautau.* "Kowtow." Ceremonial Chinese greeting.
Mundus novus, Latin	"New world," meaning North and South America.
Pax Mongolica, Latin	"Mongol peace." Refers to the stabilizing effect which the Mongol Empire had on commerce and travel across the Eurasian landmass in the thirteenth and fourteenth centuries.
peso de ocho, Spanish	Known as the "Spanish dollar." Silver coins minted in Potosí, Bolivia. Legal tender throughout the Spanish empire and much of the world.
razzia, borrowed via French and Italian from the Arabic *ghaziya*	"Raiding." Tactics applied by the French forces in Algeria in the 1830s. See "*système Bugeaud.*"
Reconquista, La. Spanish	Literally, "The reconquest." The attempt by Christian princes in northern Spain to occupy al-Andalus. Completed in 1492.
système Bugeaud, French	System of genocidal warfare instituted by Marshal Thomas Robert Bugeaud during the French occupation of Algeria in the 1830s and 40s.
terra nullius, Latin	'Nobody's land." Principle of international law used to justify the occupation of foreign lands.
Vinland, Swedish	Literally, "wine land." The Viking name for North America.

Think about

A sea route to India
- Who were the Vikings?
- What were the Crusaders trying to achieve?
- Why did the Europeans started looking for a sea route to Asia?

Europeans in the "New World"
- What explains the genocide of indigenous people in the Americas?
- What is the "Columbian exchange"?
- Who were the Puritans?

A commercial world economy
- What political roles did the East India companies play?
- Give an account of the trans-Atlantic slave trade.
- Why and how did the settler societies of the Americas achieve independence?

An industrial world economy
- How did the industrial revolution change Europe's relations to the rest of the world?
- What were the characteristic battlefield tactics of Europe's colonial wars?
- How was the Chinese market eventually opened up to foreign trade?

The apotheosis of colonialism
- How were the kingdoms of Asia turned into objects of ridicule?
- What happened at the Berlin Conference in 1884-85?
- Why did European states start searching for colonies in the latter part of the nineteenth century?

Decolonization
- Why did most colonies achieve independence in the decades after the Second World War?
- Give an account of Algeria's independence struggle. And Vietnam's.
- What were some of the challenges faced by the newly independent states?

Contemporary political map of the world from OpenStreetMap, https://www.openstreetmap.org/#map=3/27.92/16.79

Afterthoughts: Walls and Bridges

The question is how to go on from here. The question is how the story will continue. During decolonization, the Europeans were convinced that their way of organizing international politics was the only alternative. They were also convinced that their international system constituted a great improvement on the international systems which previously had existed elsewhere in the world. The European version of an international system allows for sovereignty and self-determination, and thereby for democracy and liberal rights. These, no doubt, are good values and unique achievements. However, learning about non-European alternatives to the European international system, we might nevertheless decide to question that conclusion. Or, if nothing else, we can compare what we have today with what existed before the European international system took over the world.

The fundamental problem of the European system is the mass deaths it causes. The idea of sovereign states who determine their own fates, and look after their own interests without regard for others, has had disastrous consequences. There are few years in Europe's history of the last four centuries when there has not been a war in one place or another. In the twentieth century alone almost 100 million people perished in wars between sovereign states, and tens of millions more died in genocides which the principles of sovereignty and non-interference made possible. By contrast, several of the non-European international systems we have learned about in this book were less war-prone — although certainly none was peaceful. Moreover, although sovereignty has not been an official principle of an international system anywhere except in Europe, there has in practice been a lot of scope for self-determination. The various political entities of East Asia were independent although, at the same time, they were dependent on the Chinese; the emirs of Central Asia ruled themselves although they all ostensibly were a part of the Abbasid Caliphate; the kings of Southeast Asia were heavily influenced by Indian culture, but India played no role in running their countries. There is no contradiction here, although it might seem that way from a European perspective.

However, perhaps the problems caused by sovereignty are about to go away. Today we are living in a world that is becoming increasingly global. Borders seem to matter less and less; walls are coming down all around us and bridges are being built even between far-away cultures and societies. We are trading and exchanging with each other at an unprecedented rate — swapping goods and services but also ideas and lifestyles. We are all becoming more and more civilized, we could say, while our respective cultures are becoming increasingly alike. As always, and never more so than now, the spread of civilization goes together with widespread cultural destruction.

There are many who worry about such a world — a fully globalized world without walls and cultures, where sovereignty is a thing of the past. How can we make a life for ourselves, they wonder, if we belong to no place in particular and have no unique identity? People who worry about such things often argue that we must rebuild our walls, close our borders, and protect ourselves from what is coming towards us from the outside. Yet the question is what political, economic and social consequences will flow from such a reaction. Will higher walls not lead to more misunderstandings, less trade and more wars? Will we not save our culture, and defend our sovereignty, while losing our civilization?

However, if this book has taught us anything, it is surely that this is a false choice. The choice is not between perfect sovereignty and no sovereignty at all. It is not a choice between walls everywhere and no walls whatsoever, or between being a member of a distinct culture or of a global, uniform civilization. That only appears to be the choice as long as we look at the world from a European point of view. Yet, and as we also have learned, the European international system is actually quite extreme; many other international systems have made compromises that are more appealing. There are all kinds of international institutional arrangements that allow both independence and coordination, a strong sense of self and a strong sense of international community. By learning about these alternatives, we can learn more about which options are available to us. So what is your favorite international system? Was there ever one part of the world, and one time, where the walls were just the right height and the bridges were sufficiently many? Where human beings had a strong sense of a home and yet were perfectly open to the challenges that contacts with foreign cultures allow? A time when people were secure in their identities yet also prepared to question themselves and to change? Was there ever a time when self-determination could be combined with prosperity and peace? By thinking about such questions perhaps we can come up with new ways to imagine our future.

Lightning Source UK Ltd.
Milton Keynes UK
UKHW051819240719
346742UK00001B/4/P

History of International Relations

A Non-European Perspective

Erik Ringmar

Existing textbooks on international relations treat history in a cursory fashion and perpetuate a Euro-centric perspective. This textbook pioneers a new approach by historicizing the material traditionally taught in International Relations courses, and by explicitly focusing on non-European cases, debates and issues.

The volume is divided into three parts. The first part focuses on the international systems that traditionally existed in Europe, East Asia, pre-Columbian Central and South America, Africa and Polynesia. The second part discusses the ways in which these international systems were brought into contact with each other through the agency of Mongols in Central Asia, Arabs in the Mediterranean and the Indian Ocean, Indic and Sinic societies in South East Asia, and the Europeans through their travels and colonial expansion. The concluding section concerns contemporary issues: the processes of decolonization, neo-colonialism and globalization — and their consequences on contemporary society.

History of International Relations provides a unique textbook for undergraduate and graduate students of international relations; and anybody interested in international relations theory, history, and contemporary politics.

As with all Open Book publications, this entire book is available to read for free on the publisher's website. Printed and digital editions, together with supplementary digital material, can also be found at www.openbookpublishers.com

Cover image: Al-Idrisi, *Tabula Rogeriana* (1154), Bibliotheque nationale de France (MSO Arabe 2221). Cover design: Anna Gatti.

ISBN 978-1-78374-022-2